# Foundations of National Identity

# New Directions in Anthropology

General Editor: **Jacqueline Waldren**, *Institute of Social Anthropology, University of Oxford*

# FOUNDATIONS OF NATIONAL IDENTITY

## From Catalonia to Europe

Josep R. Llobera

**Berghahn Books**
New York • Oxford

First published in 2004 by

## *Berghahn Books*

www.berghahnbooks.com

Copyright © 2004 Josep R. Llobera

**Library of Congress Cataloging-in-Publication Data**

Llobera, Josep R.
    Foundations of national identity / Josep R. Llobera.
        p. cm.
    Includes bibliographical references and index.
    ISBN 1-57181-612-7 (alk. paper)
        1. Nationalism. 2. Nationalism--Spain--Catalonia--History.
    3. Nationalism--Europe--History. I. Title.

JC311.L724 2003
320.54'094--dc21                                           2003052319

**British Library Cataloguing in Publication Data**

A catalogue record for this book is available from the British Library.


Printed in the United States on acid-free paper.

ISBN 1-57181-612-7 hardback

# CONTENTS

# PREFACE

In this book I propose to examine the nature of national identity with special emphasis on Catalanism in the context of a comprehensive theoretical framework, as well as a European historical and contemporary reality. In this sense, this book is neither exclusively theoretical nor conclusively descriptive; it hopefully aims to achieve a compromise between these two different perspectives. This book presents a theoretical discussion and a comparative dimension of nationalism in Europe, as well as a historical and contemporary description of Catalan identity. It should be noted that an important emphasis is put, even in Europe, on primordialism, that is, on the importance of old allegiances such as race, kinship, territory, religion, language, culture, history, way of life, etc.

The project is essentially the undertaking of the 1990s, although some of the research began in the late 1980s and spills into the new century. Some chapters have been published as complete essays in journals in a variety of languages. This preface presents an outline of the book structure and a brief personal and intellectual history. The structure of the book is comprehensive, presenting a variety of dimensions that are characteristic of the nation, at least in Europe. The approach emphasises realities that are not always perceived as central; in practice they are often rejected because, as I mentioned before, they are primordial.

The first chapter analyses a general framework that is essential to characterise nationhood. It is presented theoretically at a rather sophisticated level, but there is also a comprehensive characterisation of the Catalan case. It is here that the influential contribution of the Catalan historian in the 1950s, J. Vicens-Vives, is emphasised. Chapter two tackles subject-matter that is relatively untouched by the majority of social scientists: the idea of national sentiment. It is a comprehensive chapter, looking at a variety of perspectives that have to be kept to a minimum. There is a brief reference to the emotional Catalan material, which is complemented with French and Polish sophisticated references. Chapter three examines some very basic primordialist perspectives of Catalonia: kinship, religion and territory. Native anthropologists and geographers have studied them; the contributions of Terrades, Bestard, Comas and Nogué are quite original. Chapter four is concerned with the topic of national character. It focuses on how the Catalan ideologists of the late nineteenth century (Almirall, Prat de la Riba and Gener) differentiated between Catalans and Castilians/Spaniards.

Chapter five deals with a national element that is essential to many countries: language. To say that the force of language is typical of both ethnic and civic nationalism is an often-ignored reality. Language has undoubtedly an emotional role in national identity, but as the case studies of French and English languages clearly show, there has been a historical association of language and national identity. Chapter six deals with a concept that is central to anthropology: culture. The objective here is to investigate the concept of culture in the context of a complex and changing reality. In many respects, the local, the regional, the national, the European and the global are presented as theoretical discussions in which anthropologists (Friedman) and other social scientists (especially Anthony Smith, Wallerstein and Giner) participate. Chapter seven considers historical memory as a key element of nation-building. A reference is made to the theoretical framework (with special reference to the works of Halbwachs and Nora), but this chapter is also dedicated to studying the role of historical memory in the remaking of Catalan national identity in recent times.

Chapter eight deals with the problem of whether nationalism leads inevitably to conflict and violence. The Janus character of nationalism, as expressed by Tom Nairn, is a well-known reality, that is, it has a good side and a dark side. The chapter is essentially theoretical (centred in the work of Van Evera, Brown, Brubaker and Laitin), but it also covers a wide range of empirical examples. More specifically, it presents the case study of Catalonia, and some references to the Basque Country, in great detail. It tackles the topic of contemporary politics in the context of society, and emphasises the confrontation between nationalists and socialists, as well as other political groups, in Catalonia. In chapter nine I deal with the nationalist implications of the economic, political and cultural process of the unification of Europe; this is a process of integration which has taken place since the early 1950s. A specific comparison between Spain and the U.K. is offered to exemplify the complex realities. Chapter ten addresses the issue of the theories of nationalism: in spite of a massive growth of interest since the 1980s, nationalist theory is far from explanatory. The problem is that most studies are either purely normative or too non-comparative.

We are now dealing with the second and final element. Given the political and moral delicacy of approaching the subject-matter of nationalism, it may be useful to make public both my personal and academic background. My national identity is rather complex. Born in Cuba (with a moderate paternal Cuban inclination), I grew up happily and freely, and was taught by a thoughtful teacher in a small Catalan village (Rocafort de Queralt) in the Spanish postwar period (1940s). Attending a Jesuit school in Barcelona as a boarder meant suffering a compulsory training in Spanish and Catholicism. I was reluctant to accept these

# INTRODUCTION

This book has much to do with Catalonia. The example of Catalan nationalism is interesting in that it presents a social reality that is often considered in terms of a submerged nation, particularly on a wider European level. Paraphrasing Montesquieu one could start by asking: *Comment peut-on être Catalan?* The question is not purely rhetorical. Indeed, how can one be a Catalan (or a Scot, or a Breton, or a Basque) in the new century? In other words, what sense does it make to opt for a small-nation identity? We all have available much wider identities, and yet some people stubbornly persist in clinging to their ethnonational roots. In democratic countries this patriotic sentiment may be tolerated, but it is not well understood how people can apparently go against the march of history. At a time when, we are told, the nation-state is in the process of being at least partly superseded by supranational institutions like the European Union, what is the rationale behind the insistence on sticking to parochial loyalties? What's wrong in being simply British, French, Spanish or Belgian – or, even better, European? Why the insistence on being provincial and chauvinistic? Is that what it is?

Nationalism is a dirty word, particularly the nationalism of others. There has been a tendency to equate ethnonational identity with 'tribalism', with all the negative overtones of this term. In the past few years, and particularly since the disintegration of the Soviet Union and Yugoslavia, we have been served a steady diet of prejudices and half-truths concerning the causes of the malaise that has overtaken the old communist world. Prior to 1989 social scientists were still praising the communist world for having solved the national question. Now, no less a luminary than Professor Eric Hobsbawm sees the root of all ills East and West in the unfurling of nationalism, with its twin demons of xenophobia and separatism running alongside each other. No doubt the much heralded death of the national problem in Eastern Europe was somewhat exaggerated, but that seems to matter little to the old communist sympathisers. As Tom Nairn rightly remarked years ago, nationalism is neither good nor evil – it all depends on the use that social groups make of it.

Catalonia, Scotland and Flanders, to mention a few, are neither provinces nor regions, but nations – small, perhaps, but nonetheless quietly proud of being what they are, and not what others depict them to be. More than anything else they strive to be civilised nations, and hence abhor political shouting and screaming, although they firmly state what for them is the obvious difference – peculiarity, particularism.

Names matter. In most European languages Catalan exists as a sort of reality; it is *Katalonien* for the Germans, *Catalogne* for the French and *Katalonja* for the Poles. If I say 'Catalonia is a nation', how many people will understand my utterance? Do they know what this thing 'Catalonia' is? And, if they can surmise that this is a land in the north-eastern corner of the Iberian peninsula, will they agree that it is nation, or will they rather think that it is a province or a region within Spain? Perhaps only the Basques, who have a fondness for things Catalan and are in love with the Catalan language and culture (*Katalantzaletasun*), are in a position to understand. Insofar as Catalonia is concerned, it has been a land of economic progress for many coming from poor areas of Spain (and now from Latin America and North and West Africa). It has not required its newcomers to become culturally or linguistically Catalan, although it has asked for a degree of respect for its language and culture. Castilian still has a powerful presence in Catalonia, and its power of appeal as a prestige language is unlikely to disappear. Although most people who now live in Catalonia understand Catalan, perhaps only two thirds speak it and one third writes it. However, the limited social use of Catalan worries sociolinguists and politicians alike.

At the time of the 1992 Olympic Games, the autonomous government of Catalonia ran an advertisement in the international press with the slogan: Where is Catalonia? This is a relevant question, which captures, in a peculiar way, the essence of the geographical conundrum of Catalonia: its invisibility. Many foreign visitors to the Costa Brava or Barcelona do not recognise Catalonia as the reality they see; for them it is just a part of Spain. It is an index of the success of centuries of obfuscation by the Spanish state, attempting to submerge the multinational reality of Spain into a uniform one. If the unity of early modern Spain was cemented with the expulsion of Jews and Moriscos, the century of the Enlightenment saw the suppression of Catalan political institutions and the first official onslaught against its language and culture.

Catalonia is a small country (30,000 sq. km), the size of Belgium, but with 6 million people it is more populous than Scotland. In modern times it has expressed its national identity quietly, but with perseverance, and has often (as under Franco) paid a heavy price for its idiosyncrasy. It is a miracle that Catalan identity has survived against the odds of Mammon and Leviathan. But it has, and here to prove it are its romance language that thrives at the spoken level, in the media and in literature, a true explosion of popular activities and festivals of all sorts, a strong sense of a common past, a sharing of identity symbols and last, but certainly not least, a determined consciousness and will to be Catalan. If that annoys some travellers and visitors who are probably nostalgic for the good old days when Catalan language and culture were invisible to the foreign eye, *tant pis*.

At no other time in the history of modern Catalonia has a higher level of 'nationalisation of the masses' been achieved, in spite of the fact that perhaps as much as 50 per cent of the population is of recent (post-civil-war) immigrant origin. This is not to minimise the conflictive aspects of bilingualism and of culture clashes. But, with regional autonomy, post-Francoist Catalonia has been a land of consensus, where the different political groups have put their country first, and their partisan options second. The overwhelming majority of the population has accepted a basic platform of nationalist demands. The fact that the nationalist coalition led by Jordi Pujol has won six successive elections to the Catalan Parliament is ample proof that his right-of-centre economic policies and his moderate nationalism are the favourite recipe for both the Catalan stomach and the Catalan soul.

Catalonia has long been an outward-looking country, open to Europe both economically and culturally, and it has thrived in both areas. Industrialisation started there earlier than anywhere else in the Iberian peninsula and there is nothing comparable to *art modernista* in the whole of Europe. Was it a coincidence that the first modern patriotic ode to be written in Catalan coincided with the introduction of the steam engine into Catalan industry in the 1830s? In the twentieth century Catalonia has produced renowned cultural figures of world fame: people like the architect Antoni Gaudí, the painters Joan Miró and Salvador Dalí, the musician Pau Casals and the opera singers Victoria de los Angeles, Montserrat Caballé and Josep Carreras. As for the Barça football club, it is undoubtedly a famous and universal phenomenon!

History has taught the Catalans to restrain their political demands; neither Spain nor France would have tolerated a Pyrenean state. The European Union was the miracle the Catalans had been praying would happen for centuries. It allowed them to imagine a solution to an insoluble problem: how to be part of the Spanish state without being absorbed by it. Catalans tend to see Spain in political, not cultural terms. Spain may be a nation, but it is not *their* nation – only insofar as the expression 'nation of nations' makes sense (and in chapter nine I will show that it does not) can Spain be a cultural reality for Catalans. Furthermore, only a decentralised Spanish state (which is federal in some aspects and confederal in others) can satisfy the Catalan conception of the political pact. And, if separatism is not yet seriously on the agenda, it is essentially a question of pragmatism. Catalans believe that a deepening of the Spanish state of the autonomies and the development of the 'Europe of the regions' can bring about the same results as independence, without the painfulness of formal separation.

When, in the run-up to the 1992 Olympic Games in Barcelona, the Catalan Autonomous Government ran a series of advertisements in the international press telling the where and what of Catalonia, the point was to get across to the Western world the idea that Catalonia was a 'country' (in French *pays* and in German *Heimat*), albeit lost in the immensity of the Hispanic landscape. The Spanish Constitution implicitly recognises Catalonia as a 'historical nationality', whatever the meaning of the euphemism, which does not dare to call a nation by its name. Some enlightened Spanish ideologues (and God knows they are few and far between) are even willing to accept that Catalonia is a nation, only to qualify it by saying that Spain is also a nation, that is, a 'nation of nations'. But, then, France is also a 'nation of nations', albeit the latter are, so to speak, 'deactivated'. Unlike Catalonia, the nations of France are part of a 'tamed memory' (although Corsica is perhaps an exception). The Catalans have not forgotten their long history, and more specifically they remember well their misadventures within the Spanish state. Even in the new century the history of the brutal repression of Catalan language and culture by Franco has been deflated or totally ignored by the Spaniards. As demonstrated in public pronouncements in the spring of 2001, this is a conviction shared by the King and the Prime Minister, by the Minister of Education and the President of the Royal Academy of History and by the bourgeoisie and rank and file of the population of Spain. However, as a witness and victim of the period between 1940s and the 1960s, I am well aware of the pervasive repression of Catalan identity during Francoism.

The Olympic Games were thunder and lightning, but Catalonia remained. The Catalans were enthusiastic about them because they gave Barcelona the chance to move, at least in terms of infrastructure, into the twenty-first century. They were divided, however, about the effects of the Olympic Games on the international projection of Catalonia. Optimists believed that they helped to spread to the world the symbols of Catalan identity (language, flag, etc.); pessimists held the view that the Olympic Games were a ceremony of confusion. Still the agreement reached by the Town Hall of Barcelona, the Autonomous Government of Catalonia, the Spanish state and the International Olympic Committee concerning the display of Catalan symbols and the use of Catalan as one of the official languages, along with English, French and Spanish, suggests perhaps that the optimists were right.

Today Catalonia is at a critical point, as is perceptively shown in *La societat catalana* edited by Salvador Giner. What is happening at the beginning of the millennium affects all levels of society. Profound social changes are under way, from the demographic and economic scales to the linguistic and ideological shades. Geographically situated in the north-west Mediterranean sphere, the country projects itself at a world level and it is extremely prosperous as an economic unit. The question remains if, in the long run, Catalonia will be thriving in the context of progressive integration in the European Union.

The social structure of Catalonia has noticeably changed. Class struggle is already a feature of the past; the bourgeoisie and the working class have entered into a new world regulated by negotiations and agreements. In terms of the distribution of wealth, the country has progressively moved, through redistribution, like the rest of Spain, to become essentially a welfare state. However, the increasing number of South American and African workers in the economy is perceived, to a certain extent, as a threat – particularly in relation to the North African Muslims. On the other hand, many of these immigrants are helots, that is, poor, with limited access to welfare and illegal.

An important problem has appeared at the political level, in the sense that there is a growing tension between Catalonia and the Spanish government in relation to the issue of sovereignty. Catalonia's powers are often scaled down by state intervention. Will the future bring more Catalan autonomy or centralisation? Finally, it must be remembered that in Catalonia demography and language are closely related. Half the population are of non-Catalan, Spanish-speaking origin. A certain anxiety has developed, even if compromise has hitherto successfully prevailed. What will the future bring? A bilingual and bicultural society, or a more integrated and homogeneous one?

A Catalan identity in Europe, like a Scottish or a Welsh one, is not a chimera, but a necessity. The peoples of Europe, whether small or large, are willing to unite, even to renounce part of their sovereignty, to achieve essentially two objectives: prosperity and peace. They do not believe that this requires the emasculation of what history and will have made of them. In language that some may find idealist (but which I believe expresses historical realities), I would say that the spirit of the nation is what gives people their sense of being, their authenticity; it is changeable, but it also shows continuity. In a world in which so many national species are in danger of disappearing, the Catalans, like many other small European peoples, affirm their will to survive as a nation and to fight, by democratic means, against the rampant process of homogenisation that afflicts our planet. If that makes them 'provincial', so be it.

This book also deals with nationalism in Europe, especially on its western side. It is hardly a novelty to state that, in spite of some voices who claim to the contrary, that is, people who live in the land of wishful thinking, ethnic and national identities continue to be present and in some cases dominate the political scene in a variety of countries, East and West and South and North. The reasons for the persistence, and at times recrudescence, of ethnic and national identities vary from case to case. An obvious cause is that most existing states are not proper nation-states (one state, one nation) and, of those, only very few have made fair arrangements to satisfy the demands of the their constituent *ethnies* and nations. The process of cultural globalisation, which threatens to melt into thin air the perceived solidity of local cultures, is another factor often invoked to account for the reinvigoration of ethnicities and nationalism. No nation, no matter how secure its cultural foundations might appear to be, is immune to the real or imaginary fears of cultural erosion, hybridity or disintegration.

France is a case in point: a country struggling on various fronts to defend its essential *valeurs identitaires*. At a general level, American culture and the English language are seen both as a worldwide threat and desirable commodities. Immigrants, tourists and diasporas are anathematised in various degrees, particularly when, as part of the politics of multiculturalism, the alien character is forced upon essentialist communities. The degree of suspicion with which large percentages of the public opinion of some countries look at the supposedly centralising aims of the European Union betrays a defence mechanism that can only be explained if it is assumed that national identities are perceived as undermined in favour of a vague and unspecified European identity.

These signs of our time point out that the emotional attachment to ethnicity and nationhood is still paramount to most people. The cosmopolitan discourses emanating from nationally displaced but influential intellectuals give the impression that the contemporary condition of most people is made up of a multiplicity of ethnic and national identities. Being Kurdish, Muslim, Scottish, British and European all in one go is part of this conception of national identity as a series of concentric or criss-cross circles. Although sceptical, I am not denying the possibility of multiple identity, especially when the other component is complementary or rarely clashes. As a general rule, full national identities of the cultural type tend to exclude each other; a multiple identity needs to be further explored and clarified.

A good example is that you are neither allowed nor can you properly be, say, French and Portuguese. Today, the condition of migration, although hardly modern, seems to be more than ever an object of existential concern and scholarly interest. To a Portuguese person who migrates to France there are a number of available possibilities, some of which depend on the French and Portuguese politico-legal framework, others being in the realm of more or less conscious decisions made by individuals in the realm of culture. In other words, all the cultural-level immigrants have the choice, at least in theory, of placing themselves in a continuum: from preserving a maximum of Portuguese culture and accepting a minimum of the French, to embracing a maximum of French and retaining a minimum of the Portuguese. There is an additional element that often complicates things even for those who wish to fully assimilate into French culture: it is the degree of native acceptability of the second-generation immigrants.

It is also important and interesting to look at the issue of national identity and self-determination. Let me start with what appears, at first sight, as an incontrovertible fact: the existence of contradictory political trends in the area of nationalism. In Eastern Europe, using this expression in the widest possible geographical sense, one of the effects of the Revolutions of 1989 was to unfreeze sentiments of national identity, which had been hidden from the public eye for decades. With the collapse of the communist system a nationalist agenda made its appearance with the avowed objective of asserting the sovereignty of nations which had hitherto languished under the Soviet umbrella (this would be the case of countries such as Poland, Hungary, Bulgaria, etc.) or had been shrouded in the myths of presumed federal arrangements (exemplified in the cases of the ex-Soviet Union and the ex-Yugoslavia).

When the chips were down no attempt was made to democratise the admittedly deficient federal structures; what prevailed was a mood of despondency and distrust towards the existent multinational states. As is well-known, what followed was a period, not totally closed, in which there was a proliferation of new nation-states, only numerically comparable in the European scenario to the developments that resulted following the implementation of the Wilson Doctrine after the First World War. The breaking down or the extreme weakening of state structures is a factor common to both historical processes, but recent events have, on the whole, been self-generated (within the area), while after the First World War the decisive factor came from a military victory. In both cases, as Ernest Gellner has rightly remarked, the emergence of a host of new nation-states created as many national problems as it had solved, given the ethnic mix of the region.

To conclude on this issue it is important to emphasise that the situation in Western Europe appears in a rather different light. While ethnonationalist demands have kept the momentum and have even increased numerically (with the emergence, for example, of the Northern League in Italy) and in terms of intensity (particularly among the Scots, Welsh and Irish, the Basques and Catalans, the Flemings, Corsicans, etc.) the drive towards the constitution of independent states seems to have been deflected (with exceptions). This apparent contradiction is resolved if we take into account the fact that what is renounced is formal or *de jure* independence; in practice, however, most ethnonations aspire to high levels of self-government, but they hope to achieve it in the framework of a European Union or, to be more precise, as a result of a double motion that involves the transfer of sovereignty from the existing states downwards (to the ethnonations) and upwards (to the European Union).

In the ethnonationalist calculations there is indeed a pragmatic rationale, which considers a number of the traditional attributes of the nation-state as irremediably dated. Why, for example, create a new currency when the Euro will progressively substitute the existing ones? In this respect, it is important to emphasise the forward-looking, modernising character of most ethnonationalisms, and their acceptance of the European Union as their future economic, political and cultural horizon for the foreseeable future. It is, of course, a particular vision of the European Union that they embrace: one in which the principle of subsidiarity is interpreted to mean that the region or ethnonation is the natural and appropriate level to which devolution of powers should accrue.

# 1
# THE BUILDING-BLOCKS OF NATIONHOOD. A THEORETICAL APPROACH TO CATALONIA

## Theoretical Introduction

National ideologies are often said to reflect the French cliché 'Plus ça change, plus ça reste la même chose'. The point is worth generalising to the history of nationalism in Western Europe. The idea of an 'eternal nation' is quite a powerful one. However, in this chapter I shall maintain that if we want to understand nationalism we should reverse the cliché to obtain 'Plus ça reste la même chose, plus ça change'. In this sense national ideologies are a dialectical precipitate of the old and the new. Though they project an image of continuity, they are pierced by discontinuities; though they conjure up the idea of an immutable ideological core and an adaptable periphery, in fact both core and periphery are constantly redefined.

The history of nationalism in Western Europe offers a good number of examples in which the nation is conceived as a quasi-eternal, motionless reality. The idea of *la France éternelle* is not only a metaphor of romantic French historiography, it has also been a first-class ideological weapon of all Republican regimes in France. The echoes of such an idea reverberate even in Braudel's (1985–86) posthumous work on French identity.

Why this pretence of continuity? A physicist might say that the explanation must reside in some sort of irrational fear that peoples have of the historical void. It is true that, in its origins and fundamentals, national identity is an attempt to preserve the 'ways of our forebears', but reality is constantly changing and nationalist ideologies tend to limit our perceptions to the same image where there are in

8

fact different realities. Even modernising or future-oriented nationalisms must pay lip service to this idea of continuity. Expressed in positive terms nationalism emphasises the need for roots, the need for tradition in the life of any community; it evokes 'the possession in common of a rich heritage of memories' (Renan 1947: 903). The organic analogy is here an inevitable point of reference. And yet the organic conception of the nation is hardly an adequate theoretical tool to handle the complexities of the would-be modern nation-state. The reason is that for the ideologists of the nation-state the cultural definition of the nation (Herder) is always subordinated to political objectives or implicitly abandoned because of recalcitrant internal national heterogeneity.

The sociological myth of the nation-state, that is, the belief that because the nation-state happens to be the paramount ideology of the modern state it must correspond to a sociological reality, is a serious epistemological obstacle for the explanation of nationalism. For how can we account for the survival of ethnonational identities in harsh political environments, particularly in cases where the modern state engages all its bureaucratic machinery in policies of cultural, if not physical, genocide? It is my contention that contemporary ethnonationalist ideologies, if they have managed to establish themselves on a sound cultural and political basis, are extremely resilient and can endure, at times in a hibernated form, all sorts of repressive policies.

In the long run the history of Western Europe is the history of the qualified failure of the so-called nation-state. The celebration of the national state, however, continues unabated by both social scientists and politicians. The question to ask is how much of a success story was state-generated nationalism in Western Europe? There is, of course, no easy answer to the question. The fact of the matter is that the nation-state is far from being hegemonic; in other words, most Western European states are, to a varying degree of consciousness, multinational. The history of Europe after 1789 shows that ethnonations are not anomalous entities or mere vestiges from the past, but rather dynamic configurations with a life of their own. Whether they form an independent state or not is often the result of a variety of factors including the international conjuncture. In any case, there is every good reason to see ethnonations as one of the typical paths to modernity, though this point may be in opposition to all those authors (Wallerstein 1974; Tilly 1975; Gellner 1983; and Giddens 1985) who see European history in terms of the rise and practical monopoly of the nation-state in modern times. What is the case is that old national identities die hard, even if in practice they have to survive in revamped form. Historical nationalities or ethnonations are not self-propelling entities, although they may, of course, survive for a long time as cultural and linguistic fossils; the question is surely: under which conditions can they have a new lease of life? A variety of theories have been put forward in the past few years to account for the persistence or revival of ethnonationalism. In some cases they are only revamped theories from the past.

There are at least four different ways of conceiving the nation that form the basis of four major explanatory frameworks: essentialism, economism, culturalism and eclecticism (Llobera 1987).

The essentialist conception, originating in Herder and Romanticism in general, assumes that nations are natural, organic, quasi-eternal entities created by God since time immemorial. Each nation is characterised by the existence of a peculiar language, a culture, and a specific contribution to make to the design that divinity has installed for mankind. The idea that every nation has been chosen by God to perform a specific role in history can easily be secularised, and hence the appearance of ideas such as 'manifest destiny' and 'common historical destiny'. Furthermore, the essentialist vision of the nation emphasises the ideational and emotive aspects of *communitas*, but tends to exclude economic, social and political dimensions, and fails to perceive the intrinsic historicity of the nation. Today this particular conception of the nation is limited, at least in its extreme form, to naive or radical advocates of nationalism.

An extremely popular form of explanation has been economism. It comes under different guises and it is favoured both by Marxists and non-Marxists alike. In the final analysis, however, the common denominator of classical Marxism, internal colonialism, world-systems theory, and some modernisation theories is the assumption that economic interests lie underneath the idea of nation. The fact that by its own ambiguity the nationalist discourse can be used to justify, hide or combat economic inequality or exploitation, as well as political power and cultural supremacy, is not a sufficient reason to reduce nationalism to the ideology of a class, and in so doing deny the specificity of the national phenomena.

Culturalism seems to stand as the polar opposite of economism. In fact, both are variants of a conception of society which assumes that the part can explain the whole. By focusing on culture as the key to nationalism, an array of historians and sociologists of modernity have undoubtedly located a crucial factor in the development of nationalism in the last two centuries: the need for some sort of cultural identity and adaptation at a time of rapid social and economic change, with its concomitant effects of alienation and anomie. Whether the nation also satisfies the psychological need for belonging or whether it embodies a sacred character borrowed from religion is a matter for discussion. In any case, culturalism envisages nationalism as a ready-made response to the requirements of modernisation. By ignoring the long-term genesis of nationalism and its multifarious phenomenal appearances, culturalism privileges just one particular moment, no matter how important, of its existence.

Eclectic explanatory frameworks are the result of the disenchantment with unidimensional, factor theories of nationalism. They follow, on the whole, the palaeofunctionalist argument that a social precipitate originates as the result of a combination of interacting elements. The candidates for such combinations, as well as the specific weight attributed to each of them, will vary from author to author, but we can be certain of encountering geographic, economic, cultural, religious, historical and linguistic factors. Eclectic approaches are as unobjectionable as they are uninteresting. The idea that society consists of interrelated parts was a revolutionary invention, but it belongs in the annals of the contributions made by the *philosophes* of the Enlightenment to the social sciences. Today the minimum programme of functionalism is a pure sociological truism, and it should not be metamorphosed into a theoretical framework.

The point of view adopted in this book, that of the concrete totality, keeps clear of both economism and culturalism, while at the same time transcending eclectic empiricism by conceiving of society 'as a structural, evolving, self-forming whole' (Kosik 1976: 18). The social totality is not constituted by facts; rather the latter can only be comprehended from the standpoint of the whole. History is the result of a complex dialectical process in which no a priori primacy is given to any factor. However, once ideas and institutions have appeared in history they acquire a life of their own and under certain conditions, to be investigated empirically, have a perdurable effect on society. Structural history cannot explain all that happened and why it happened. Many areas of social life, particularly in the sphere of nationalism, are the result of historical events that are difficult to predict (wars, invasions, annexations, etc.) and may always remain impervious to our enquiries.

## Catalonia: Its Modern Historians

In 1954 a slender volume entitled *Noticia de Catalunya* was published in Barcelona. Its author, Professor Jaume Vicens-Vives, was one of the leading historians of Catalonia, having published extensively on a variety of topics. The book, however, was not strictly speaking a standard history text. It belonged to a rather old-fashioned genre: studies of national character. The fact that it was published at all was a victory at a time when Franco's Spain was just slowly moving away from the quasi-totalitarian mentality that had presided over the post-civil-war years. The rigid censors who determined the intellectual destinies of the country considered books that could in any way be construed as exalting a sentiment of Catalan identity anathema.

As is common with countries without a state of their own, in the past century and a half Catalonia has often felt the need to reassure itself that it has a national identity separate from that of the entity – the Spanish state – into which its historical existence has been fully incorporated since the beginning of the eighteenth century. This need was particularly obvious after a period in which a policy of cultural genocide had tried to raze Catalan national consciousness to the ground. In fact, concern for the fate of Catalan identity in the aftermath of the catastrophe of 1939 led a number of Catalans in exile to meditate about what constituted the historical identity of Catalonia. The philosopher Josep Ferrater Mora opened the series with his *Formes de vida catalana* (1944), followed by Josep Trueta's *L'esperit de Catalunya* (1953) and *Meditació catalana* (1953) by Carles Cardó among others (Trueta was a traumatologist and Cardó a priest).

That there was an essentialist leaning in most of these writings, a search for the 'eternal' Catalonia, is hardly surprising at a time of acute crisis. There was an awareness that the defeat of the Catalan nation at the hand of Franco was just another episode in the long history of a nation which, though successful in the Middle Ages, had suffered many defeats in the modern period. Through these texts there also runs *nolens volens* an implicit sense of astonishment at the fact that Catalonia, a civilised and mature society, could have found itself entangled in the web of savagery that characterised the Spanish Civil War. How could Catalonia have found herself involved in the politics of extremism? Was it the result of being part of the Spanish state? Or perhaps it was because the national character oscillated between common sense (*sentit comú*) and emotional outbursts (*rauxa*), as Vicens-Vives pointed out. By the 1960s, this reflective concern had spread to other Catalan-speaking areas as the titles of other books by Joan Fuster and Josep Melià, respectively, *Nosaltres els valencians* (1962) and *Els mallorquins* (1967), clearly indicate. Even the contemporary reality of Catalonia, with an increasing immigrant population from other parts of Spain, began to receive attention, as F. Candel's *Els altres catalans* (1964) proves.

Many of these were popular books and, although dismissed by the purists as essayistic adventurism lacking the appropriate scholarly apparatus, they nonetheless had a notable impact, reviving the dormant Catalan consciousness. In addition, these attempts, thinly disguised as historical disquisitions, and aimed at generating a discourse on the Catalan question, had the merit of establishing some of the parameters for the intellectual discussions on Catalonia in the late 1950s and the 1960s. There was nothing morbid in this national self-reflection; it was just a quasi-automatic survival mechanism, which paid off in the long run.

It would be unfair, however, to assume that the main merit of Jaume Vicens-Vives' work was the publication of *Noticia de Cataluña*. By the time of his premature death in 1960, he had radically changed the panorama of postwar Catalan history, paving the way for the pleiad of scholars who flourished in the 1960s and 1970s. Vicens-Vives' influence transcended the boundaries of his country and of his discipline. By introducing the methodology of the *Annales* school, he renewed the historiography of Catalonia by anchoring it in a totalising project in which demography and economic history, particularly that of the modern and contemporary periods, played essential roles. On the other hand, his firm rejection of the kind of romantic history associated with nationalist movements was of the utmost importance in obtaining the scientific credibility that he considered crucial for a lasting effect in the local and international community of historians. For Vicens-Vives, the Catalan nation was not for ever given, but had to be reinterpreted in each historical period in accordance with a variety of interacting factors, from demographic pressures to the will of the people, and including, obviously, the economic conjuncture and the struggle between different groups for domination.

His *Industrials i politics del segle XIX* (1958), a study of the ethos and achievements of the Catalan bourgeoisie written with M. Llorens, was a brilliant synthesis that became an exemplar for future scholars.

It is idle to speculate about the direction that Catalan historiography might have taken had Vicens-Vives lived for another twenty or more years. In any case the publication in 1962 of *La Catalogne dans l'Espagne moderne. Recherches sur les fondements économiques des structures nationals* (3 vols.), a thesis by Pierre Vilar which had been long in the making, had made an impact on the way of writing the history of Catalonia in general, and on the 'Catalan national fact' (*fet nacional català*) in particular, to the extent that thirty years later his original work is still considered exemplary, along with a number of seminal papers that he has since published. Perhaps one of the reasons for his influence among scholars writing on Catalonia was that he continued in many ways the trajectory indicated by Vicens-Vives, also embracing the *Annales* idea of total history, albeit with more of a Marxist bias.

Although presented as an attempt to capture modern Catalonia in totality, Vilar's monograph emphasises, as the title of the book suggests, the economic foundations of the country: what made possible the development of the productive forces of Catalonia in the eighteenth century. Perhaps the awesomeness of the task led Vilar to concentrate exclusively on the economic aspects and on the period up to the eighteenth century, without, however, abandoning the aim of seizing the totality. Many of the articles that followed have explored political and ideological issues concerning Catalan nationalism, which he envisages as the highest manifestation of the Catalan historical totality. It has been repeatedly said, after *Industrials i Politics* and *La Catalogne dans l'Espagne moderne*, that no history of the Catalans can be written that ignores the role of demographic and socio-economic factors, in particular the class structure. Unfortunately, in the simplistic minds of some, this has been used as an excuse to indulge in a vision of history in which the ascending Catalan bourgeoisie was the exclusive originator and *Träger* (carrier) of nationalism. This is not to suggest, however, that Vilar, who in many respects has over the years followed a narrow Marxist-cum-Stalinist interpretation of the national question, has been totally immune to criticism; in fact, he has been willing to modify his conception along voluntaristic lines.

It is hardly surprising that the current hegemonic discourse on Catalonia should be historical. In addition to the simple fact that history is likely to dominate in any endeavour dealing with the national question, if only because the issues of origins and development are often paramount, neither sociology nor anthropology has until fairly recently played other than a marginal role in Catalan universities. As to why foreign anthropological scientists have chosen to study Andalusia, Castile or the Basque Country in preference to Catalonia, it is difficult to explain, except perhaps to say that the last failed the test of 'exoticism'. There is no Catalan equivalent to, for example, Pitt-Rivers' *People of the Sierra*, in terms either of its early date of publication in the early 1950s or of its influence.

E. Hansen's *Rural Catalonia under Franco* (1977), which has never been translated into Spanish or Catalan, is but a pale reflection, unable by its many weaknesses to galvanise any intellectual followers. Foreign historians, however, have found the Catalan anomaly within the Spanish state, or even Europe, interesting enough to elicit theoretical attention. John Elliot's *The Revolt of the Catalans* (1963) is only the first of a series of monographs and books of synthesis published by Anglo-Saxon and French authors, among others, on different periods of Catalan history in the aftermath of Vicens-Vives' death, and acknowledging, and following to diverse degrees, his mastery.

But what are the sociological characteristics that stem from the history of Catalonia? Salvador Giner has referred, in his *Social Structure of Catalonia* (1980), to a number of features that strongly differentiate Catalonia from the rest of the Iberian peninsula, bringing it closer to the patterns of historical development that are typical of France and England. First and foremost Catalonia was a feudal society. In the Middle Ages, Castile was essentially a warring society organised around the militarised crusading principle of the reconquest of the Moorish lands, with a nobility subordinated to the monarchy and with a very 'imperfect' feudalism; Catalonia by the year 1000 had started to develop a process of feudalisation which pervaded the whole society. What is important to emphasise in the present context is the contractual aspect of the feudal relationship of vassalage. From early on, Catalan society can be characterised by the existence of the idea of the pact as central to social relationships. The compilation of Catalan customs and practices known as the *Usatges* (dating from 1150) reflects the pactist nature of Catalan medieval society.

Historical sociologists have noted the strong continuity existing between feudalism and capitalism; in other words, capitalism tended to develop in those countries that had first passed through a feudal stage. It has been suggested that the strong implantation of feudalism in Catalonia may also account for the fact that Catalonia was the first and only area within the Iberian peninsula to develop an early bourgeoisie and to have effected the transition to capitalism at approximately the same time as other Western European countries. While in the words of Jordi Nadal the industrial revolution failed in the Spain of the nineteenth century, for Catalonia the century was extremely successful from an industrial point of view. The textile industry in particular was spread all over the country, and was the quasi-provider for the Spanish and colonial markets. In *Industrials i politics*, Vicens-Vives and Llorens have shown how this was the period of bourgeois plenitude, and others, like Pierre Vilar, saw nineteenth-century industrialisation as the most significant of the facts that differentiate Catalonia from the rest of Spain, and perhaps one of the most important foundations for the development of the national question in Catalonia.

The fact that in Catalonia modernity made its appearance at the same time as in the rest of Europe should not blind us to the fact that Catalonia had entered into the orbit of the Castilian monarchy in the late fifteenth century (through a union of unequal crowns), and that from the beginning of the eighteenth century it had been part of a centralised Spanish state. The progressive loss of the political autonomy of Catalonia in the modern period is an important *factum* that can only be overlooked at a high intellectual cost; but the political subordination of Catalonia also had important cultural consequences because political domination went along, at least to a certain extent, with cultural domination. The diffusion of European ideas in Catalonia, if not stopped, was certainly restrained by the obscurantist regime that characterised traditional Spain. Even the nineteenth century with its ups and downs was not more progressive, with alternating Spanish liberalism and absolutism.

A society like Catalonia, in which industrial development had radically changed the socio-economic fabric, was more likely than the rest of Spain to be affected by the appearance of scientific ideologies such as positivism, evolutionism and social Darwinism in the second half of the nineteenth century. The impact was felt in a broad spectrum of intellectual and artistic activities, from science to literature and music, from social theory to the visual arts and philosophy. But since many of the European social thinkers who peddled these ideas, especially Comte and Spencer, challenged the status quo represented by the Spanish state and the Catholic Church, as well as the rigid social structures and hierarchies of the country, not surprisingly, these thinkers were seen as threats which had to be tackled at all costs. Even in Catalonia, modernity only managed to penetrate in a limited way; the existence of constraining institutional settings common to the whole of Spain produced a world that was only partly receptive to these ideas.

The awareness of Catalan identity, established on the basis of a distinctive culture, history and language, among other features, was not an unknown phenomenon prior to the second half of the nineteenth century, but it manifested itself with vigour, first culturally and then politically, only in this period. However, Pierre Vilar has maintained that medieval Catalonia is perhaps the polity to which the label 'nation-state' can be applied least anachronistically amongst European countries. By the mid-thirteenth century, the first solid manifestations of national consciousness can be observed.

By the turn of the twentieth century, the emergence of a fully-fledged Catalan nationalist movement, aware nonetheless of its numerical and structural limitations in the face of the Spanish state, had shaped and coloured the perception of Catalonia in the twentieth century, to the extent that researchers, both insiders and outsiders, have had to come to terms with it in one way or another, positively or negatively. Needless to say, the specific study of Catalan nationalism has flourished particularly in the period after Franco's death. It has been a task in which historians, but also anthropologists and sociologists, as well as political scientists and literary critics among others, have participated.

## Catalonia: A Historical Case Study

The history of Catalonia provides an excellent laboratory for the study of the vicissitudes of the national question in the nineteenth and twentieth centuries. In its modern form, Catalan national identity was recreated in the second half of the nineteenth century (see chapter 4). Nationalist ideologies against the state are, on the whole, recreated, while state-generated national identities can be, if not created *ex nihilo*, at least based on thin ice. In Western Europe most states have existed for a long time and have managed with varying success to metamorphose themselves into nations. In Catalonia, the development and consolidation of such an identity were made possible by the existence of the five following conditions: a strong ethnonational potential, the appeal of the model of romantic nationalism, a thriving bourgeois civil society, a weak and inefficient Spanish state and a strong Catalan national Church.

### *1. A Strong Ethnonational Potential*

The standard raw materials on which national identity is built were definitely present in Catalonia, beginning with the existence of a long-lasting and original medieval Catalan polity with a clearly differentiated political autonomy within the Crown of Aragon (Bisson 1986). When the dynastic union of the Crowns of Castile and Aragon was effected in the second half of the fifteenth century, the sovereignty of the Catalan parliament (*Corts*) was preserved (Reglá 1973). The Catalan revolts of 1640 and 1701 against the monarchy reflected, no matter how ambiguously, a reaction against the real or potential loss of autonomy (Elliot 1963). Second, there is the differential fact of a written and literary language in existence since the Middle Ages (Nadal and Prats 1982). Although after the end of the fifteenth century Catalan declined as a language of culture and after 1714 it suffered state persecution, by the nineteenth century it was still the language spoken by the majority of the population (Carbonell 1979). Third, there is the existence of a common body of ideas, beliefs, practices, norms etc. that may be referred to as culture in the widest sense of the term (Vicens-Vives 1954). Fourth, a certain sense of historical identity had been preserved (García-Cárcel 1985). However, such elements are no doubt problematic in that they are not clear-cut objective factors, but represent rather ideological constructs and hence malleable and open to manipulation.

### *2. The Appeal of the Model of Romantic Nationalism*

The development of romantic historiography in different parts of Europe in the early nineteenth century had a profound effect on Catalonia. While the

Napoleonic invasions had generated feelings of both Catalan and Spanish patriotism (Vilar 1973; Fontana et al. 1980), by the 1940s romantic historians started to glorify the Catalan past. There followed between 1833 and 1866 an intellectual attempt to revitalise Catalan culture and language known as the *Renaixença* (Pi de Cabanyes 1979).

## 3. A Thriving Bourgeois Civil Society

Catalonia was the first area within the Spanish state to experience the Industrial Revolution. While the rest of the country exhibited a pre-industrial social structure characterised by the existence of a traditional land-owning oligarchy and a subjected peasantry, in Catalonia a modern capitalist system developed with the appearance of two major antagonistic classes: the bourgeoisie and the proletariat (Vicens-Vives and Llorens 1958; Izard 1978). These developments were far from sudden: there had been a dynamic bourgeois civil society for a good part of the eighteenth century (Vilar 1962). The existence of such a more or less enlightened bourgeoisie was the precondition for the intellectual take-off of Catalan cultural nationalism in the nineteenth century (Moreu-Rey 1966; Lluch 1973). This is not to deny the existence of a popular though diffuse consciousness of Catalan identity during the same period which manifested itself first through Carlism and then through Republican Federalism (Termes 1976; Camps i Giró 1978).

## 4. A Weak and Inefficient Spanish State

This statement has to be understood in relative terms. The centralising and homogenising tendencies of the Spanish state in the nineteenth and twentieth centuries were as pronounced as they were elsewhere. The model adopted by Spanish politicians often mirrored the Jacobin French state (Linz 1973). Two caveats, however, should be noted. First, the Spanish state had neither the financial nor the administrative machinery to enforce the cultural and linguistic homogenisation of the country as the French did between 1870 and 1914 (Weber 1979). Second, from the moment that Catalan nationalism became a political force at the turn of the century, an additional and formidable obstacle to homogenisation was erected (Rossinyol 1974; De Riquer 1994).

## 5. A Strong Catalan 'National' Church

In the modern period the Catholic Church in Catalonia has exhibited a firm commitment to defend the Catalan language and culture against the impositions and encroachments of the Spanish state. In this sense, it has often been, because of its relative autonomy from the state, the only collective entity that could articulate and propagate Catalan identity to vast masses of the population. There is a clear historical continuity in this attitude of both the hierarchy and the rank and file of the parish priests, which justifies the expression Catalan 'national' Church (Bonet 1984; Gomis 1995).

The special way in which these five factors combined explains how between 1886 and 1906 the Catalan people gave themselves a nationalist ideology (Solé-Tura 1974; Riquer 1977) and later managed to obtain, through political struggle, a representation of their interests in the Spanish parliament (Gonzalez-Casanova 1974). This process culminated in the concession of limited autonomy in 1913 (*Mancomunitat*) (Camps i Arboix 1963) and the establishment of a form of self-government (*Generalitat*) during the Second Republic in the 1930s (Gerpe 1977). The nationalist movement in Catalonia was never the monopoly of a single class, though its leadership might have been at certain moments in time. In any case, by the 1930s it was a popular-based movement led by a centre-left party (Sallés 1986; Poblet 1975).

The Spanish Civil War (1936–1939) was fought on both sides not only as a class war, but also as a war in which different conceptions of the nation and of the state were at stake. The Republicans were defending a moderately autonomist vision of the Spanish state, the Francoists a highly centralised and uniform one based on the fascist model (Ramirez 1978). Not surprisingly both Basques and Catalans sided firmly with the Republican faction, even if their political philosophy was much more radically federalist or separatist than the Republican consensus allowed for. It should be made absolutely clear that the centralist vision of the state was not a monopoly of the extreme Spanish right, but was typical of the whole political spectrum (Gerpe 1977). The main difference was, of course, that, while the democratic parties were prepared to compromise and accept part of the demands for autonomy from the Catalans and the Basques, the fascists were not.

With Franco's victory there began a systematic cultural genocide of the Catalan nation. Except for the upper echelons of the bourgeoisie, which had a volte-face after July 1936 and decided to support Franco by sacrificing their Catalan identity at the altar of their class interests, the Catalan population had been steadfastly Republican and had backed the autonomous government (*Generalitat*) (Cruells 1978). Francoist repression was from the very start conceived as a surgical operation aimed at extirpating the cancer of Catalan nationalism; there was an organised attempt to wipe out all the symptoms of the political disease referred to as 'separatism'. This expression was understood not only in the strictly political dimension of self-government, but was also used as a rather blanket term to include the spoken or written use of the Catalan language in most spheres of life, the display of symbols of Catalan identity (flags, monuments, music, etc.), the existence of Catalan civic institutions (of professional, literary, cultural, recreational character), etc. (Benet 1973). It should also be made absolutely clear that the Francoist state, modelled as it was on the fascist paragons, was no longer a weak and inefficient state in that it used all of its modern machinery (education, media, etc.) to consciously generate a Spanish national ideology. For the first time in the modern period there was a serious attempt on the part of the Spanish state at nation-building (Arbós and Puigsec 1980).

The history of the forty years of Francoism in Catalonia is first and foremost the history of the survival of a diffused and contracted Catalan identity and then, in the 1950s, of the progressive consolidation of such identity, fundamentally at the cultural and linguistic levels, but also with a political dimension. After 1959, the political element became more apparent, only to explode after Franco's death. To many observers of Catalan political reality, including many social scientists, the sudden nationalist effervescence of the late 1970s came as a complete surprise insofar as they had wrongly assumed that nationalism, at least in Catalonia, was a crepuscular ideology. The poet Salvador Espriu's statement that 'we have lived to save the words for you' conjures up the right kind of image of the Catalan intelligentsia during Franco's dictatorship.

It is the more surprising that anthropologists, who should know better than to focus on surface structures, also believed that Catalan identity was disappearing and that it was not a political force with which to be reckoned. A case in point of early dismissal of Catalan nationalism was, of course, Hansen's *Rural Catalonia under Franco*, which was published in 1977 at the time when more than a million Catalans were demonstrating for political autonomy in the streets of Barcelona (see chapter 7 for details). *Sic transit gloria mundi.* Hansen's book is just one of many examples of the dangers of generalising about an ethnonation on the basis of traditional fieldwork and poorly digested history. Furthermore, it illustrates the incapacity of modernisation theories to account for the survival of ethnonationalism.

The attitude of the majority of the Catalan population towards cultural genocide was that of passive resistance. Research on this topic is fraught with ideological and methodological problems and not surprisingly is rather rare. In the early period public manifestations of Catalan identity were limited and ambiguous. In the private sphere of the family, things were different, and it was here that Catalan was spoken and a certain amount of cultural identity preserved. In any case the task of upholding, continuing and transmitting Catalan national identity, particularly at the height of the repression (1939–59), was the work of a small but devoted intelligentsia who had survived the common fate of the vanquished (execution, exile, prison, ostracism) and who, contrary to all odds, went against the current of history (Fabre et al. 1978; Colomer 1984). This attitude is best exemplified in a lyric composition which became a popular song of the late 1960s and 1970s and which had been written in 1965 by Salvador Espriu (1975: 113), one of the leading Catalan poets of the postwar period.

But we have lived to save the words for you,
To return to you the name of everything,
That you may travel along the straight road
That leads to the mastery of the earth.

............................................

Now ye say: 'We shall be faithful and true
For ever more to our people's service'

The long period of fascist repression generated a predictable defence mechanism among the custodians of Catalan identity: an essentialist vision of the nation, that is, the idea that ultimately the Catalan nation, if not altogether eternal and immutable, was a multisecular reality based on quasi-biological, environmental and psychological facts. Even the most scholarly of philosophico-historical works of the period – J. Ferrater-Mora's *Les formes de la vida catalana* ([1944] 1955), J. Vicens-Vives' *Noticia de Catalunya* (1954) and J. Fuster's *Nosaltres els valencians* (1962) – did not escape an essentialist tint, though as S. Giner (1980) has remarked, these three books constitute serious attempts to tackle in a structural way the history of Catalonia.

## Catalonia: An Excursus on Essentialism

Nationalist ideologies may well partly be responses to the processes of industrialisation and modernisation, but they also encapsulate the traditional values of society. Catalonia is no exception. As I have mentioned above, nineteenth-century *Catalanism* incorporated, from its very inception, a belief in an idealised, romanticised past. This vision did not only refer to military or literary glories, but also assumed the existence, in some unidentified but foregone time, of an idyllic, conflict-free peasant society (Giner 1980). This conservative ideology, often referred to as *pairalisme* (see chapter 3), was usually allied with a Catholic conception of the history of Catalonia (Ramisa 1985) and with the belief that the political wisdom of the Catalans resides in compromise (*pactisme*) (Sobrequés 1982).

It is arguable how important this traditional component was, but nationalisms against the state – and Catalonia is a typical example – are particularly vulnerable to essentialist conceptions of the nation. In fact, because of their precariousness these nationalisms need to mythologise the past in order to take off as viable ideologies. It is true that at a later stage, as confirmed by evidence from Catalonia between 1900 and 1936 (Galí 1978), they become more involved in forward-looking communal projects in which people can participate in a rational-instrumental way, although the integrative aspects of the mythologico-ritual are also preserved. The force of nationalism as a symbolic system lies in the fact that it mediates between the past and the future, while providing an affective dimension for the present. To establish itself on a solid basis, Catalan nationalism, as with many other nationalisms against the state, had to be 'looking back with relish' and finding an anchor point in the past. Only then could it be hoped in the Catalan mind to uncover a sense of identity. The presence of a weak state was no doubt a great help. The importance of cultural nationalism is here crucial: if it has managed to develop before the state has come to exist in its modern democratic form, the chances of recreating a clear national identity are much higher.

Modernity, in its post-French revolutionary mode, equates state with nation and the latter with the participation of the people (whichever way this participation is defined) in the state. What we have here is, of course, a political nationalism in which the identification is with the state, albeit a special kind of state since the demise of the absolute, personalised monarchy. On the other hand, fascism represents the apogee of state nationalism. The existence of cultural nationalism complicates the picture by focusing on the so-called natural factors of *convivència* (living together), and allows us to see the state in terms of artificiality, uniformity and compulsion. The following table of opposites could be suggested:

| **Nation** | **State** |
| --- | --- |
| Culture | Politics |
| Variety | Uniformity |
| Freedom | Compulsion |
| Organic | Artificial |
| Romantic | Rational |
| Religious | Secular |
| Individualism | Collectivism |
| (individualising collectivity) | (collectivising individuality) |
| Affective | Instrumental |

The process of industrialisation that took place in Catalonia in the nineteenth century was accompanied by major social changes along patterns similar to those that were happening in other industrialising Western European countries (Vicens-Vives and Llorens 1958). Barcelona, from being a city-emporium with its ups and downs since the Middle Ages, suddenly became the most important industrial centre of Spain. At first modernisation affected only the Catalan hinterland: the late nineteenth century and early twentieth century saw a massive migration from countryside to town, especially in the direction of Barcelona, which soon became a megalopolis. By the 1930s migration from other parts of Spain was already visible, though it only became numerically significant during Franco's era.

By the 1980s figures suggest that 60 per cent of the people living in Catalonia were of non-Catalan origin: the result of different waves of migrations from different regions of Spain, but particularly from the south (Andalusia) (Termes

1984). While prior to the war a significant percentage of the migrant population was assimilated culturally and linguistically, this was not the case with the large influx of people during the Franco period (Candel 1964). It was a question not only of numbers, but of the existence of a political regime that did not acknowledge Catalan national identity, but even until its very end stifled its multifarious manifestations. Not surprisingly most of the immigrants did not learn the language and culture of Catalonia, nor did they develop a Catalan national consciousness (Strubell 1981; Esteva 1984; Prats et al. 1990; Branchadell 1997).

The presence in Catalonia of a large, newly arrived working-class population that was culturally and linguistically non-Catalan was potentially conflictive. At the bottom of the system of social stratification, the immigrants were the carriers of the official language of the state and hence were perceived as linguistic oppressors. But dictatorships blur differences; and in any case the magnitude of the problem was not realised until the 1970s, at the height of nationalist fervour. It was at this time that the two-communities theory began to appear, no matter how reluctantly and indirectly in the language of the politicians. Some intellectuals voiced the right of the immigrant community to defend their language, culture and identity of origin now potentially threatened by Catalan essentialism (De Miguel 1980). What had happened is that for a long period of time the two communities had not only lived apart, but under Franco had had no chance to articulate and express their ideological positions. In fact, the underground political parties had reached a sort of implicit ideological truce concerning the national question: they all acknowledged, at least in principle, the right of Catalonia to self-government (Colomer et al. 1976). It is a reflection of the isolationism of the Catalan ideologists during Franco's period that they decided to stick to an essentialist vision of Catalonia in which the immigrant population was not considered an important variable. In their idealist conception it was assumed that the immigrants would miraculously be assimilated (Pujol 1976).

Another idea that was partly the consequence of the intense Catalan essentialism of Franco's era was a pancatalanism of sorts. Having focused on a traditional definition of the nation (common language, common culture, common past), it followed that, territorially, the area that fitted the definition and which can be designated as the Catalan Countries (*Països Catalans*) was larger than the area in which a modern Catalan national consciousness had developed. The starting point of the notion of Catalan Countries was of course the idealised medieval Kingdom of Aragon in which Catalonia *sensu stricto* played the leading economic, political, military and cultural role. The Kingdom of Aragon was created by the dynastic union of Catalonia and Aragon in the mid-thirteenth century. Conceived as a confederation in which its constituent parts preserved their identity and autonomy, it expanded southwards and eastwards. Some of the conquered territories (Balearic Islands) were colonised by Catalans, others (like Valencia) jointly by Catalans and Aragonese. Within the Crown of Aragon the different territories had their own self-governing institutions, which were preserved with the union of the Crowns of Castile and Aragon in the second half of the fifteenth century (Bisson 1986).

The slow emergence of the Spanish state no doubt had negative effects on the Catalan identity of the different territories (Castilian becoming the only prestige language in Spain). Furthermore, a portion of the north-east of Catalonia was forcefully incorporated into the French state by the mid-seventeenth century. But it was not until the beginning of the eighteenth century that the autonomous institutions were scrapped and a policy of linguistic Castilianisation was implanted (Ferrer 1985). By the late nineteenth century, when Catalan nationalism developed, all the territories that in the Middle Ages could have been defined as 'Catalan' had taken different economic, social and political paths, even if they still preserved a certain linguistic and cultural unity. Though the ideologists of Catalanism maintained the fiction of a Greater Catalonia, in practice the notion was never on the political agenda. The Francoist period contributed only to exacerbate the differences and even rivalries between the different areas of the supposed Catalan Countries (Balcells et al. 1980). Rightly or wrongly, the Principality (*Principat*) of Catalonia was often seen as exerting a kind of cultural domination, which was presented at times as oppressive by certain sectors in the Balearic Islands and Valencia.

In the re-creation of the nineteenth-century Catalan identity, the emphasis should be on the territorial selectivity of the features that were chosen to constitute the nation. The exclusion of Valencia, the Balearic Islands and northern Catalonia from the nationalist definition has to be carefully scrutinised, particularly when the romantic vision of a Medieval Catalonia would have them included. Was the decision to exclude them the result of political realism or were the different entities already different in the Middle Ages (in spite of all belonging to the Crown of Aragon)? After all, the attempt was not to recreate the medieval Crown of Aragon (a sort of confederation presided over by a monarch). Because the definition that was used of the nation was a cultural and linguistic one, Aragon could hardly be included.

The period between 1969 and 1976 is noticeable for a remarkable flourishing of free ideological discussions on Catalan nationalism: free because the arguments were basically unencumbered with the consideration of *realpolitik* which was characteristic of the post-1977 political positioning. In this period there developed the idea of a utopian Greater Catalonia in which cultural and linguistic diversity was minimised, if not altogether ignored. This was the work of a relatively small group of intellectuals, writers, professionals and politicians belonging to all shades of the political spectrum of Catalonia, but with some participation also from the other Catalan-speaking areas (Cahner et al. 1977).

The party politics of the late 1970s and 1980s shattered the utopian vision of a Greater Catalonia, particularly after the new Spanish Constitution (1978), while accepting the right of the nationalities and regions of Spain to autonomy, consecrated what was already a *fait accompli*: the separate existence as political entities of Catalonia, Valencia and the Balearic Islands (Solé-Tura 1985). More importantly, it also confronted many politicians with the bitter reality of a Catalonia that was splitting into two different communities: the division was along linguistic and cultural lines, but coincided roughly with class and status lines. The nationalist coalition occupies the centre of the political semicircle and attracts mainly the Catalan-speaking middle and lower-middle classes (Marcet 1984; Lorés 1985; Giner et al. 1996). Although their Catalanism is moderate, they are often perceived by Castilian-speakers as extreme. The fact that the parties of the left, while representing on the whole the non-Catalan-speaking working-class constituencies, are in fact controlled by leaders and cadres who in the main belong to the Catalan-speaking intelligentsia and hence endorse Catalanism in its basics explains why the politics of confrontation between the two communities has been kept, for the time being, to a minimum (Lorés 1985; Giner et al. 1996).

## Conclusion: The Eternal Recurrence?

In Catalonia the time of illusions is now over. For the time being, the great effervescence of nationalism that flourished in the aftermath of Franco's death is a thing of the past. It is obvious that the two communities are there to stay and that they exhibit real differences. What is at stake is whether they can live together: in other words, whether a common project of the future is feasible. It will no doubt require concessions on both sides, particularly at the linguistic level. Language is a key marker of Catalan identity, but Catalan is far from being the language of the majority of the population of Catalonia. Most sociolinguistic studies on the future of Catalan as both a popular language and a language of high culture are pessimistic in tone (Argente 1981). But the history of the Catalan language shows that these Cassandra-type predictions have been disproved by the sheer determination of an often small but extremely committed and active group of people who fought against the 'current of history' and managed to change its direction (Woolard 1989; Vallverdú 1990; Flaquer 1996). Whether such 'heroics' are still possible in a mass-media society dominated by alien cultures is another matter.

The present linguistic policies of the Autonomous Government (*Generalitat*) aim at creating, in the course of a generation, a perfectly bilingual population, though insisting, in accordance with the Statute of Autonomy, that in fact Catalan is the 'natural' (*propi*) language of Catalonia, while Castilian is the official language of the Spanish state (Argelaguet 1998). Because class confrontations can easily manifest themselves as ethnic confrontations, Catalan society will have to make provisions for a system of economic rewards and mobility which is seen to operate freely and equitably by the Spanish-speaking working classes. However, if there were to be a serious economic crisis this would not be easy to implement.

But the viability of Catalonia as a nation will depend, in the final instance, on its ability to develop a cultural and political identity which, while appearing to preserve the essence of the past, will allow the possibility of a common future for all those who live in Catalonia. In this context there have been a number of attempts at redefining Catalan culture with the aim of forging a weapon with which to face the challenge of the postmodern era (Castellet 1983; Vilar et al. 1983; Gifreu et al. 1987; Giner et al. 1996). A cultural model should provide not only a way of mediating between the contradictions of Catalan society *sensu stricto*, but also a means of relating to the Catalan Countries, the Spanish state, the EU and the world at large. It is plain that an exclusively inward-looking culture will not be viable, while an exclusively outward-looking culture could mean a total loss of the traditional identity.

Cultures have indeed a life of their own, independent of individual human wills. Cultural models propounded by an otiose intelligentsia from its intellectual ivory tower may be construed as mere *flatus vocis*, but organic intellectuals may be rooted in the life of the community and hence they may be in a better position to articulate projects that respond to the cultural requirements needed for the survival of a given society. In any case, the living forces of the community will decide which particular project (or combination of projects) is to become cultural reality. Paraphrasing Marx we could say that, although history sets constraints on human behaviour, conscious human beings make their own history.

# 2
# NATIONAL SENTIMENTS AS AN ULTIMATE REALITY. A COMPARISON BETWEEN CATALONIA AND POLAND

## Introduction

I would like to begin by emphasising the important but ignored concept of national sentiment. As I have said elsewhere, I believe that a theory of nationalism cannot be comprehensive without 'an understanding of the subjective feelings or sentiments of ethnic and national identity, along with the concomitant elements of consciousness' (Llobera 1987: 21). The difficulty in writing this was captured by René Descartes when he wrote at the beginning of his treatise on the *Passions de l'âme* in 1649:

> There is nothing in which the defective nature of the sciences we have received from the ancients appears more clearly than in what they have written on the passions; for, although this is a matter which has at all times been the object of much investigation, and though it would not appear to be one of the most difficult, in as much as since every one has experience of the passions within himself, there is no necessity to borrow one's observations from elsewhere in order to discover their nature; yet that which the ancients have taught regarding them is both so slight, and for the most part so far from credible, that I am unable to entertain my hope of approximating to the truth except by shunning the paths which they have followed. This is why I shall be here obliged to write as though I were treating of a matter which no one ever touched before me (Descartes 1968: 331).

To start at the beginning, we are not even clear about the meaning of the expression 'national sentiments'. For sure, we all use the expression repeatedly, but any attempt to go beyond the obvious produces utterances in which the term 'ineffable' (or similar words) figures prominently. Or else we think in terms of supposed synonyms such as 'feelings', 'emotions', 'affections', 'passions', etc., which do not help much. Are, for example, national emotions the same as national sentiments, or are the former a debased type of the latter?

If we consult dictionaries the definitions are not very illuminating. For example, in defining nationalist sentiment the recent *International Encyclopaedia of Ethics* offers the following : 'It is the feeling of anger aroused by the violation of the nationalist principle or the feeling of satisfaction aroused by its fulfilment' (Akomolafe 1995: 592). This definition is very poor and basic, and, if anything, it raises more questions than it answers. We are still navigating in a sea of banalities. Do not misunderstand me, with banalities one can write a book on nationalism, and an interesting one at that (Billig 1995); after all, the reproduction of national sentiments is effected through the routinised, unconscious daily flagging of symbols and of linguistic habits which are often banal.

Philosophers have established that sentiments are phenomena of the moral sensibility, that they are the products of an idea and that they only connect with the external world in a mediated and distant way. In the area of sentiments it is perhaps useful to distinguish different types of dispositions:

1. Attitudes towards particular objects: admiration, contempt, gratitude, resentment, jealousy, hate, sympathy, etc.
2. Dispositions to act and feel in certain ways towards objects of a certain kind under certain circumstances: generosity, benevolence, humility, etc.
3. Tendencies towards emotional states: irritability, excitability, fearfulness, etc.

National sentiments consist of a mixture of elements: cognitive and emotional, collective and individual, as well as formal and informal roles and expectations (François et al. 1992: 15). As we shall see, two important emotions that existed in pre-modern and pre-national times – love and hatred – will figure pre-eminently in our analysis of national sentiments. Some of the key issues are: how are national sentiments carried and transmitted, and which objects and mechanisms are used to inculcate and perpetuate national sentiments.

## Theoretical Approaches

It is my contention in this chapter that, while nationalism is a language that may convey economic and political realities, when stripped of these shells it contains a spiritual core that essentially consists of sentiments. It is not my intention, however, to enter into a theoretical discussion about the strengths and weaknesses of the different theories of nationalism. I have to take issue, however, with those who cannot see beyond their economistic lenses. Most Marxists are viscerally incapable of understanding nationalism. They may no longer hoist the flag of historical materialism up their academic masts, but, nonetheless, behind their postmodernist veneer there often hides the old-fashioned economic or class determinism of yesteryear. On the whole, Marxists are culturally incapable of perceiving the complexities of nationalism; they are condemned to see only one aspect of reality. Max Weber was much more accurate when he referred to the nation, since he insisted that 'the fervour of this emotional influence does not, in the main, have an economic origin. It is based upon sentiments of prestige' (Weber 1978, II: 921). For Weber 'the idea of the nation (…) stands in very intimate relation to prestige interests (…) The significance of the nation is usually anchored in the superiority, or at least the irreplaceability, of the culture values that are to be preserved and developed through the cultivation of the peculiarity of the group' (Weber 1978, II: 925).

Most social scientists, anthropologists included, have been uninterested in explaining national sentiments. Benedict Anderson rightly said that Ernst Gellner, for example, has not thought it interesting or relevant to explain the 'emotional appeal [of nationalism] or its attachment to a seemingly fabricated antiquity' (Anderson 1993: 615). Even those who, like Anthony Smith (1981; 1986), John Armstrong (1982) and Benedict Anderson himself who have looked more carefully at the antecedents of modern nationalism and have explored the medieval or early modern memories, territorial attachments, myths and identities, have not seriously delved into the issue of national sentiments. Walter Connor, in a little known article published for the first time in 1987 (Connor 1994), made two important, related points: first, that social scientists tend to underrate the emotional power of nationalism and, second, that they tend to assume that nationalist demands can be satisfied in economic terms.

What is the bond that unites those who form a nation? One can list a number of objective factors, namely common language, common culture, common history, common religion, etc.; yet this type of answer is not completely satisfactory. What is missing, and anthropologists have consciously or unconsciously avoided this factor in recent years, is kinship, that is, the putative belief that a nation is a kinship group writ large. Anthropologists may prefer to ignore this, but, historically, nationalist leaders have frequently referred to the idea of common descent, often expressed in terms of shared blood and the like. One has only to examine the speeches of the nationalist leaders, left and right, east and west, past and present, to probe the emotional dimension of nationalism. That there is a belief in a shared sense of consanguinity among those who belong to a nation is well attested by the variety of quotes provided by Connor.

Catalonia, again, provides us with an interesting example on this point. In 1938, in the middle of a civil war that Catalonia was doubly losing, as a nation and as a progressive democracy, the then President of the Autonomous Government of Catalonia (*Generalitat*) Lluis Companys – the man who three years later was delivered by the German authorities of France to Franco and was shot in the Castle of Montjuïc after a farce of a trial – said to the Catalan Parliament:

> Catalonia and freedom are one and the same thing; where there is freedom, there is my country (…) Those who were born in this dearly loved country, in this land of peace, well-being, culture and law, and do not defend it, are not racially Catalan and do not deserve to be free.

Of course, in this context the word 'race' refers to common ancestry, common stock, which is not incompatible with people being aware that a nation may well be the result of the mixture of a number of *ethnies*, and that the picture may become complicated by successive layers of immigrants. But the fact that the nation, or at least its ancestry, lives in the *longue durée* helps to create this sense of distant origins. In the Catalan case the roots of the nation can be conceptualised as Frankish – insofar as Catalonia was born politically as an offshoot of the Carolingian Empire.

It is not so easy to describe the non-rational feelings that bond nationals, and it comes in different guises: psychic structure, internal identity, blood-ties, social 'chemistry', etc. Connor believes that 'the national bond is subconscious and emotional, rather than conscious and rational in inspiration' (Connor 1994: 203). The only way of finding out about this sentiment is indirectly: by 'examining the type of catalysts to which it responds' (Connor 1994: 203). And this we shall do later.

In spite of all the reservations of anthropologists, one should mention the primordialist and the sociobiological perspectives. Primordialism assumes that group identity is a given, that there exist in all societies certain primordial, irrational attachments based on blood, race, language, religion, region, etc. They are, in the words of Clifford Geertz (1963), ineffable and yet coercive ties, which are the result of a long process of crystallisation. Modern states, particularly but not exclusively in the Third World, are superimposed on the primordial realities made up of ethnic groups or communities.

The sociobiological approach starts with the assumption that nationalism is the result of the extension of kin selection to a wider sphere of individuals who are defined in terms of putative common descent. Sociobiological explanations are not necessarily articulated in terms of genetic determinism, although it may be heuristically useful to make such an assumption. Most sociobiologists do not suggest that nationalism can be explained solely in terms of genetic mechanisms, that is, without linking them with the results of the human and social sciences. The sociobiological approach insists that nationalism combines both rational and irrational elements; it is a 'primitive mind' with modern techniques. The word nationalism expresses different realities: a love of country, the assertion of national identity and national dignity, but also the xenophobic obsession to obtain these things through violence and sacrificing other nations. Nationalism builds on ethnocentrism towards the in-group and xenophobia towards the out-group.

For Shaw and Wong, nationalism 'fosters pride, dignity and related sentiments among members of the in-group, thereby constituting a moral and philosophical basis on which to demand political sovereignty' (1989: 137). Nationalism has its roots in the past, but it is a contemporary vehicle through which to vent human propensities to war. It is important in this context to emphasise the psychological dimensions of nationalism; a bond is established between the individual and the nation based on the idea that the latter is a family writ large. The individual identifies with the nation and hence tends to prefer it to other nations. The extensive use of kin terms to refer to the nation reflects this psycho-affective reality that Edgar Morin has called 'matri-patriotic', with an associated fraternal/sororal component (Morin 1994: 167). I shall return to Edgar Morin's ideas later.

Sociobiologists often fail to account for the formation, evolution and eventual disappearance of nations; in this respect the historical and social sciences have an essential role to play. However, sociobiologists, by identifying certain human propensities for conflict and warfare that have served *homo sapiens sapiens* well as successful inclusive fitness maximisers, point out that these mechanisms, useful at an early stage of development, today risk the global annihilation of the human species. Recognising these propensities could be the first step towards their neutralisation.

It is not my task in this chapter to either defend or attack primordialism and sociobiological approaches to nationalism. It is a well-known fact, though, that most anthropologists are extremely uncomfortable with such universalistic theories. Gellner, for example, does not deny that there are 'dark instinctual drives in human beings (…) which make them wish to be close to others of the same "blood" or culture (or both) (…) and lead them to detest those they consider alien, resent their proximity, and resent even more strongly the rule of foreigners' (Gellner 1993: 410). What he objects to is the idea that this 'atavistic' theory of nationalism can account for modern nationalism. But surely the point is not whether primordialism can provide a comprehensive explanation of nationalism, which it cannot, but whether it can at least contribute to clarify one aspect of nationalism, namely national sentiments.

The idea of nationalism makes its appearance in modern times in a world consisting of states of different sizes and ethnic compositions. It stands to historical reason that, where there is ethnic homogeneity and there exists an independent state, the making of a modern nation-state will be easier than if we have to deal with a new multinational state. Modernity, then, sees the unholy alliance of state and nation. As we know, the slogan is: no nation without state, no state which is not a nation. One can argue as to whether nations are invented or recreated. What is important, though, is how successful they are, how appealing is the imagined community that they intend to project on a given population. Here the role played by what Gramsci called organic intellectuals is noteworthy; whether these intellectuals are at the service of state nationalism or of a nationalism against the state is irrelevant (Hroch 1985).

## National Sentiments: A Working Scheme

In examining national sentiments I propose to look at two major dimensions: which sentiments are being instilled and what are the carriers of national sentiments. I shall also refer briefly to the following issues: how are national sentiments implanted in the human mind, which mechanisms are used to instil national sentiments, what triggers national sentiments to be remembered or recalled, how are national sentiments reinforced and how are national sentiments intensified.

### *Which Sentiments are Being Instilled?*

Love of country is perhaps the most important national sentiment to be learnt; in any case, it is a general expression that refers to one of the most powerful human impulses, present in the Western tradition since the Græco-Roman and Judaeo-Christian traditions took root. The concept of love of country draws its strength, its character and its imagery from the familial and religious spheres.

Love of country is extremely possessive and requires absolute loyalty. One cannot serve two lords. In modernity, loyalty to the state and loyalty to the nation have often been at variance, and painful choices have had to be made. Class loyalties were shown to be inoperative when French and German socialist workers sided with their country rather than with internationalist values in 1914. The concept also refers to the idea of beauty, which has a religious connotation because in the final instance the divinity contemplates the world that he has created as something beautiful. Extended to the nation it reads as follows: to feel the beauty of one's country is to love it. A concomitant sentiment is that of pride in one's own country, accompanied by indifference or disdain for other countries. Pride is not an easy sentiment to convey when the country has been repeatedly defeated at war or if it is in a state of prostration or decline.

Love of country is not a new sentiment but rather builds upon the legacy of the ancient world. In a recent book, Viroli (1995) has explored the formation of a powerful sentiment that extols the virtue of both religious and political patriotism. By the end of the eighteenth century, however, political patriotism, that is the love of one's country and its institutions, had to compete with a powerful contender that emphasised the love of one's language and culture: nationalism. Viroli insists on radically separating patriotism and nationalism, the second being an indefensible modern virtue. In this he echoes some of the ideas of Habermas, MacIntyre and Walzer. He insists that patriotism as such does not require cultural homogeneity. However, my contention is that cultural issues will not go away so easily and that the powerful sentiments that animate both patriotism and nationalism are often indistinguishable.

In my book *The God of Modernity* I have tried to show that patriotism is a sentiment that was already present in the medieval period, albeit not as a generalised sentiment. It is true, however, that, when in the early Middle Ages 'personal bonds between lord and vassal determined political life and prevailed over most other political ties, the ancient idea of patria [understood as an "aggregate of all the political, religious and moral values for which a man might care to live and die"] had all but completely faded away or disintegrated' (Kantorowicz 1957: 233). By the middle of the thirteenth century the idea of the *regnum* as a *patria*, that is, 'as an object of political devotion and semi-religious emotion' (Kantorowicz 1957: 232), made its appearance both in France and England, as can be seen in both legal and literary terminology. The French language of the time pointed for example at things such as the idea of a 'holy soil of our sweet France', often conceived as the 'land of the free' (*franci*) (Kantorowicz 1957: 237). It was repeatedly said that God embraces France with a special love. To defend France was a religious duty. What might be called patriotic propaganda made its appearance in the fourteenth century. When Philip IV was calling for '*amor patriae* of all his subjects' he was doing so in the name of the fatherland, and not in defence of the native village or province; he was referring to 'the whole kingdom of France'. An important legal councillor of the time, William of Nogaret, stated that he was ready to defend and willing to die for 'his king and his fatherland, the realm of France'. In the expression used, the highest value was *patriam meam regnum Franciae*; in this context 'it was a merit rather than a crime if a man killed his own father' (Kantorowitz 1957: 250).

What had happened is that the idea of *corpus mysticus*, which had originally been predicated on the Church, had been extended, by the thirteenth and fourteenth centuries, to the body politic. The language used to refer to this new reality was the classical word *patria*, with all the emotional overtones that were attached to it in the Roman world.

That love of country is paramount, and overrides love of family, has been a leitmotiv of the nationalist literature of all times. In a famous nineteenth-century Catalan patriotic poem entitled 'In the Mulberry Graveyard' (*Al Fossar de les Moreres*), which refers to the eighteenth-century War of Succession, a man and his grandson refuse burial to the body of a traitor (that is, a person who had taken the Franco-Castilian side in the war) in whom they recognise their son and father, respectively. The final lines of the poem read:

> In the mulberrry graveyard
> We don't bury traitors;
> Even if we lose our flags,
> It will be our tomb of honour.

In theory, love of country and love of mankind are not incompatible; the latter could be envisaged as the culmination of an evolutionary process in which each stage would incorporate the previous one: an *ethnie* would subsume families, a nation would subsume *ethnies*, humanity would subsume nations. Herder's love of the German language and culture, for example, did not prevent him from loving, admiring and enjoying the languages and literatures of other countries; furthermore, the axis of his political philosophy is what we could call 'human mutuality'.

In the past two centuries we have lived in a world consisting of political entities named states and of cultural entities named nations. Congruence between state and nation has only obtained in a limited number of cases. States, as Norbert Elias has forcefully remarked, have been predatory and expansionist. Nationalisms have aimed either at homogenising states culturally and linguistically, or at securing self-determination for subjected nations. In either case the ensuing processes have often been accompanied by conflict, violence and war.

It is therefore understandable that love of country has gone hand in hand with hatred of enemies. The school textbooks of the French Third Republic aim not only at generating a love of things French, but also at instilling an anti-German feeling justified in terms of the military defeat of 1870 and the territorial losses of Alsace and Lorraine. In the past few years the popular media and important sectors of the English establishment cannot express their English identity unless it is by means of a crass Germanophobia, and more general xenophobia.

It may well be that love of country and hatred of enemies subsumes a great deal of what occurs under the label of national sentiments. As we have seen, in its extreme form this sentiment may require the sacrifice of one's own life, and then the Horatian line *Dulce et decorum est pro patria mori* (it is sweet and becoming to die for one's own country) summarises it well. The obverse is that you are required to kill your enemies if the case arises, that is, in defence of the interests of your country (where the term 'interests' should be understood in the widest possible sense). In modern times at least, it is the doctrine of national interest that will induce people to kill or to be killed in the name of their country. George Santayana, the American philosopher of Spanish origin, neatly captured the difference between self-interest and national interest. As he put it:

> Patriotism does not consist in considering the private and sordid interests of others as well as one's own, by a kind of sympathy which is merely vicarious or epidemic selfishness; patriotism consists rather in being sensitive to a set of interests which no one could have had if he had lived in isolation, but which accrue to men conscious of living in society, and in a society having the scope and history of a nation (Santayana [1905] 1980: 181–82).

The Spanish Civil War is an excellent case study for the consideration of how different types of collective interests may clash in an irreconcilable way. Very different from the romantic, naive and generally misleading stereotypes conveyed by movies like Ken Loach's *Land and Freedom* (or the even more grotesque *Libertarias* by the Spanish film maker Vicente Aranda), the Catalan dimension of the Spanish conflict presents a series of collective actors confronted with conflictive interests and the need to make extremely difficult choices. Without wanting to be exhaustive, different political groups had to decide along four major axes: (1) Spanish national interests versus Catalan national interests; (2) religious interests versus anti-religious interests; (3) bourgeois interests versus workers' interest and (4) democratic interests versus dictatorial interests.

The Francoist upheaval of 18 July 1936 failed in Catalonia essentially because the working-class parties defeated the rebel army in street fights. There followed a period of a few months which can be described as a revolutionary interlude, in which power was shared by three collective actors: the Catalan Autonomous Government (*Generalitat*), the central Spanish government and the revolutionary (particularly anarchist) working-class organisations.

In this context, the *Lliga Catalana* (Catalan League), which was a reasonably democratic, Catalan nationalist party, with strong bourgeois and religious interests, found itself in an extremely difficult position. The Popular Revolution had unfurled anti-bourgeois and anti-religious sentiments which led to the mostly wild killing of many thousands of people (approximately 8,000 – of whom 2,500 were priests and nuns – during the whole civil war period, though most were killed in the first few months) and the fleeing abroad of many more thousands (approximately 16,000). The way out for the Catalan League was to side reluctantly with Franco, with whom their lives and properties would be safeguarded; they also knew very well that Catalan national identity and democracy would be in jeopardy.

One could argue ad infinitum as to where Catalan national interests lay. A case in point would be that of the members of UDC (the Catalan Christian Democrats). It was a nationalist, right-of-centre, bourgeois, religious party which sided with the Catalan Autonomous Government and the Spanish Republic. Due to the so-called popular repression, many Christian Democrats had to flee abroad, some were killed. Symptomatic of the fate of the party was what happened to its leader Carrasco i Formiguera. The *Generalitat* had sent him as ambassador to the Basque Country as a way of escaping the 'anarchist' death squads in Barcelona; on his way to the Basque Country by sea, his boat was captured by the Francoist navy. He was sentenced to death and executed.

Even the party in power at the *Generalitat* at the time of the upheaval, that is *Esquerra Republicana de Catalunya*, which was nationalist, left-of-centre, and with a wide social basis, was not exempt from problems. In spite of their rhetoric, their agenda was not revolutionary, but rather reformist. Although far from being a clerical party, many members were religious. Siding with Franco was not an option, but the uncontrolled terror of the summer of 1936 was not their choice either.

34

Another dimension is the cult of the hero. The patriot who has taken his commitment to his country usually to the final consequences is also part of the configuration that characterises love of country. The virtues of the hero are well known, but it is courage and sacrifice that have been highlighted since antiquity. The exemplary value of the hero was not lost to nineteenth-century schoolbook writers, who everywhere in Europe put him or her at the centre of national histories. Joan of Arc is a good case in point. It could be said that the telling of her story in many schoolbooks is hardly more than a heroic genealogy.

Even in the most essentialist visions of the nation, room needs to be made for the vagaries of history. To use the organic metaphor so much loved by romantics, nations may grow and decay, and they may even eventually die, but how can they come to terms with decadence and phagocytosis (that is, being absorbed by another country)? It is not uncommon that sentiments of despair occur in these circumstances, particularly among the intelligentsia. Whether these sentiments can be channelled in a redeeming direction is another matter. In 'Pan Tadeusz', the Polish national poet par excellence Adam Mickiewicz (to whom I shall refer later) expresses Poland's predicament under Czarist rule in this way:

O mother Poland, thou that in this hour
Art laid within the grave – what man hath power
To speak of thee today? Whose lips would dare
To boast that they will find that word so rare
That it shall melt marmoreal despair,
And lift the gravestone from the hearts of men,
And unlock eyes that brim with tears again,
And should release the frozen tide of tears?
Those lips shall not be found in many years.

Because nations seem to have a profound fear of a historical vacuum, a sentiment of love for the past seems to be an essential part of national identity. In some cases biological continuity is emphasised, in others cultural persistence. No doubt the early association of nationalism with romanticism helped perhaps in intensifying the sense of nostalgia for the past that nationalism had inherited from the classical tradition.

Finally, even if love of country functions at a rather abstract level, and the object of love is an imagined collective construct, an important dimension of the inculcated sentiments is that they are meant to affect everyday behaviour towards our countrymen. Two sentiments related to love of country are apposite in this context: sympathy and altruism. In the words of G. Bruno, who wrote *Le Tour de la France par deux enfants* (the most successful of nineteenth-century French school reading textbooks): 'the children of the same country must love and help each other as if they were children of the same mother' (Bruno [1905] 1983: 13). National consciousness is a specific form of group solidarity that binds together a group of people who have certain objectives to achieve (Hertz 1944). Insofar as national identity cuts across and dominates other identities, it is perhaps not an anachronism to say that it generates a form of mechanical solidarity that totalitarian regimes, to Marcel Mauss's despair, have been particularly good at manipulating.

## What are the Carriers of National Sentiments?

What are the catalysts that trigger off national sentiments? Without wanting to be exhaustive one would have to mention symbols, music, poetry, language (including familial metaphors) and geography and history. Anthony Cohen has succinctly defined symbols as 'things standing for other things' (Cohen 1985: 18). The interpretation of symbols is not straightforward and their meaning is open to changing individual or collective circumstances. In the context of this section I use symbol in the sense of sign, that is, 'a visual or physical expression' (Cohen 1985: 18). Flags are particularly relevant as carriers of national sentiments, although maps have also played, and continue to play, an important role in anchoring the nation in a given territorial reality that can be the object of love.

When considering the symbolic significance of national flags one can always start with Durkheim's dictum that 'the soldier who falls defending his flag certainly does not believe he has sacrificed himself to a piece of cloth' (Durkheim [1912] 1995: 229). What he is telling us is that in the mind of the soldier there is a close association between flag and country, and that, in fact, the soldier dies for his country. Firth has, however, suggested that the soldier may well not always be conscious of this association and that the flag may be treated as a reality in itself (Firth 1973: 339). According to Firth, Durkheim's treatment of the topic emphasises three points: 'First, the flag, a specific material object, is taken as the representative of a very general object, a country, of abstract as well as of material character. Secondly, the material symbol becomes in itself an object of sentiment which is transferred from the object represented (…) Thirdly, attitudes to the symbol are not merely intellectual and emotional; they also tend to take shape in action' (Firth 1973: 339–40). An interesting point is the extent to which indoctrination is required to effect the transference. Durkheim tended to believe that the process was to a great extent spontaneous, but not everybody agrees with this rather optimistic statement. A final point worth making is that national flags tend to be considered sacred, and that is why their 'desecration' is punishable by law in many countries.

National flags play on limited colour variations and patterning. To the uneducated eye the Catalan flag and the Spanish flag may appear to be very similar: they both have a yellow background and red stripes. However, the Catalan flag is characterised by four vertical red stripes on a yellow background, while the Spanish one is formed by three broad horizontal stripes, red, yellow, red, with the yellow stripe double the width of the red ones. In fact, the Spanish flag, which was adopted in 1785, derives from the medieval arms of Catalonia and Aragon. When in the nineteenth century the four-striped flag was taken up as a symbol of Catalan identity and displayed in demonstrations and publicised by civic entities, it proved to be a tremendous rallying point. Within the Spanish state, the Catalan flag had an ambiguous status that was not resolved until 1931, when, with the coming of the Second Republic and Catalan autonomy, the Catalan flag was officially endorsed. Under Franco, that is, between 1939 and 1975, the public display of the Catalan flag was strictly forbidden. It was not until 1976 that such display was decriminalised. The Statute of Autonomy of 1979 enshrined the traditional four red stripes on a yellow background as the official flag of Catalonia.

Maps are the graphic representation of the territory of a state or of a nation. Territorial boundaries are essential and also tend to be 'sacralised'. 'Without territory and without tradition', Edward Shils has said, 'there can be no nation' (Shils 1995: 118). Maps relate something abstract to something concrete, and this allows a quicker and more effective identification of the individual with an abstract concept. Maps are extremely successful icons for the transmission of national identity and consciousness. As we shall explore in more detail in the next chapter, they are also great instruments for national or state manipulation, because they can convey specific irredentist or revanchist messages (Nogué 1991). According to Nogué, generally speaking maps perform three basic obvious functions: (1) 'they solve the problem of perception of the boundaries of the national territory; (2) they help to perceive, and hence visualise, the totality of the territory and (3) they have an emblematic value' (Nogué 1991: 75). Maps have been extremely useful for conveying the idea of what constitutes the core territory of a country. In the case of the Israelis and the Palestinians the war of historical maps has been an important feature of their confrontation (Cohen and Maier 1983).

The extent to which music, particularly in the form of songs, is a powerful source of patriotic sentiment is something schoolteachers know extremely well. The national anthem, in particular, is a potent stimulus for national identification; on the appropriate occasions it generates strong feelings of patriotism. Music also plays an important role in national rituals, including major sporting events. During wars popular songs may take a patriotic meaning, a well-recorded fact of both world wars in this century (Smart 1995).

That there are so-called national composers is a well-established fact of the nineteenth and twentieth centuries. Whether a single name can be picked up to represent a country is of course arguable: Elgar for England? Wagner for Germany? Sibelius for Finland? Borodin for Russia? What is important, however, is that these composers have produced music with a characteristic national flavour, often inspired by the folk music of their respective countries.

In a recent paper, Mach (1994) has insisted that in the case of Poland, although Chopin became the undisputed national composer and even a 'national hero' who was the object of a cult (Mach 1994: 92), when it came to choosing a national anthem in 1918 it was the Dabrowski Mazurka of Josef Wybicki that was selected. This was a folk tune for the Polish military fighting in Italy for Napoleon. Whatever the reasons for this choice, Mach suggests that the Polish national anthem 'expresses the idea of the nation alive, even if deprived of its own state'. 'Chopin's works', as Norman Davies, has remarked, 'were built on his experiences in the formative years in Warsaw, distilled from the Polish melodies, harmonies and rhythms that he heard in his youth, and inspired by a bitter sweet nostalgia for the land of his birth; they represent the quintessence of Polishness' (Davies 1981: 27). Mach states that that the Polonaise in A major, Opus 40, No.1 is 'for a Pole the proof and expression of this patriotic feeling, and one of the greatest masterpieces of Polish national culture' (Mach 1994: 64). However, the same could be said of the Polonaise in F sharp minor, Opus 44, which some Poles think is more accomplished. This, of course, raises the issue of what happens when a national composer achieves international recognition, a topic that I do not propose to tackle here.

In the case of Catalonia the national anthem is a popular seventeenth-century song celebrating the Revolt of the Catalans against Castilian rule between 1640 and 1652. A nineteenth-century Catalan folklorist (Manuel Milà i Fontanals) incorporated this song into his *Catalan Little Ballads* (1883). By the end of the century, the song, known as *Els segadors* (The Reapers) was regularly sung at Catalan demonstrations, with new music inspired by a popular tune arranged in 1892. '*Els segadors*' thus became the de facto national anthem of Catalonia. In 1899 its words were somewhat shortened to be adapted to the needs of public acts. During the dictatorships of Primo de Rivera (1923–1930) and of Franco (1939–1975) the Catalan national anthem was banned, though alternative songs, less politically overt, played a similar role. In 1931 there were some attempts within the Catalanist movement to have a less controversial and less combative (anti-Castilian) song as the national anthem, but the proposal was defeated by popular pressure. Between 1975, the date of Franco's death, and 1979, the date of the Statute of Autonomy, '*Els segadors*' became once again a collective song that figured in all mass demonstrations and political acts of the period. On 11 September 1976, thousands of Catalans gathered just outside Barcelona (in Sant Boi) to commemorate the National Day of Catalonia. They sung '*Els segadors*' with tremendous heart and it resonated all over Catalonia through the radio. Only in 1993 did the song legally become the National Anthem of Catalonia, and its official position was such that in 1994 it was played at the very beginning of the opening ceremonies of the Olympic Games in Barcelona.

The next carrier of national sentiments that I intend to look into is poetry. To make things simple I shall continue with the Polish example. In the same way that we have national composers, we have also national poets. In the case of Poland one of the most powerful candidates for that role is the romantic nineteenth-century writer Adam Mickiewicz, who lived between 1798 and 1855. Mickiewicz embodies the poet and the fighter, the pilgrim and the leader. He is Poland's national poet not only because his life was dedicated to the Polish nation, but also because his poetry was the spiritual food of generations to come. *Pan Tadeusz*, published in 1832–34, is a long poem in which Mickiewicz tells about growing up in Lithuania. The metamorphosis of the main character, Robak, from a rebellious gentleman into an anonymous servant, exemplifies the fate of the Poles. The poem had a major impact on Polish national consciousness, implanting the image of the Polish *Volksgeist* and landscape. As I said above, *Pan Tadeusz* deals with the everyday, country life of Lithuania at the beginning of the nineteenth century. It is a description of a way of life that had vanished. But 'to successive generations of Poles this poem will embody the ideals, the sentiments, and the way of life of the whole nation' (Mackenzie 1964: xiii).

In his other major national work, *Dziady*, translated as *Forefathers*, a cycle of poetic drama in four parts (written in the 1820s and 1830s), Mickiewicz presents a vision of the resurrection of Poland in the apocalyptic language of the Gospel according to John. The book dramatises the conflict of conscience of the Polish patriot in front of the defeat of his country, but also his belief in its future redemption. Poland is the Messiah of nations and, though crucified, it will rise from the dead. Not surprisingly, *Forefathers* (particularly Part III) has been seen as a perennial statement of Polish patriotism and a testimony of the nation's love of freedom. At every moment in history, when Poland's existence has been threatened, Mickiewicz's poems have been a rallying point for patriotism. It is also interesting to note that, although Part III of *Forefathers* is centrally concerned with an intense national feeling, it is never jingoistic. The oppressive Russian figures do not mean a condemnation of the Russian nation as a whole.

I will only discuss language briefly because it is dealt with in more detail in chapter 5. From Herder and Fichte through the nationalist literature of the nineteenth century, language has often been seen as a carrier of what is distinctive and creative about a nation. In this respect language expresses the soul or spirit of the nation. The Portuguese poet Fernando Pessoa stated that 'language is the foundation of the nation because language is thought in action and (…) action is the essence of life' (Pessoa 1979: 121).

Nowhere demonstrates the importance of national language better than Wales. As Khleif has remarked: 'for the Welsh person, it unlocks centuries of Welsh experience, of a unique way of symbolising the world and expressing human emotions and social relations. Language is both the social history of a people and its *Anschauung*; it structures both the social perception of a people's past and the interpretation of its future. Language creates consciousness (…) A native language ties a people more closely to its landscape and breeds definable loyalties to it' (Khleif 1979: 34).

In the words of Joshua Fishman 'language is part of the message of nationalism' (Fishman 1972: 44). Language, along with people and land, has often had a sacred character in the nationalist pantheon. Language allows people to relate to a heroic and glorious past. Perhaps more importantly language is the tool that allows the expression of the authentic essence of a country. Language individualises countries, emphasises uniqueness.

It is true that language is far from being a clear criterion of nationality in all cases, as any work on nationalism will emphatically indicate. However, this is not incompatible with two facts: firstly, language has often been a criterion, if not the major criterion, for contrasting one nation with another; in the case of Welsh it is advanced as the 'supreme mark' (Khleif 1979: 347) of nationhood; secondly, each language, particularly at the poetic level, conveys a unique way of expressing the inner and the outer worlds of the linguistic community (Fishman 1972: 44–55).

Finally, what can be said about geography and history that is not perhaps already known? Both subjects began to be taught in the primary and secondary schools of most Western European states in the second half of the nineteenth century. Geography and history were considered key disciplines, and were in fact always seen as complementary. Even in countries like France, as Eugen Weber (1979) has amply shown, not only was the percentage of illiterate people very high, but also they were 'nationally' and linguistically bereft from the viewpoint of the French nation-state.

The role played by the *Petit Lavisse*, that is, the *Histoire de France* for primary schools, is well-known. Millions of French children were brought up, from 1884 until 1950, with a vision of France that was patriotic and moralising in the extreme. It is also a profoundly mythological history, which refers to an 'eternal' France, a land of freedom and justice. It is a history which 'forgets', in the best tradition of Renan, the unpalatable episodes of the past, be it the wars of religion, the *ethnies* of the hexagon, or the colonial massacres. Pierre Nora has called Ernest Lavisse the *instituteur national*, the national teacher *par excellence*. Lavisse's impact has been so overwhelming that even recent French school textbooks are prisoners of his historical schemes. In 1987 Suzanne Citron published *Le Mythe national. L'historie de la France en question*; it is a deconstructionist text that aims at dismantling the old Lavissean history, putting forward a more plural, existential and critical approach.

### How are National Sentiments Implanted in the Human Mind?

National sentiments are learnt through the process of socialisation. In modern times, family and school are the essential tools of indoctrination; where universal conscription exists, the army reinforces the messages that are implanted in the individual at an early age. In the recent past the conscript armies also played a remedial role in nationalist indoctrination in those societies where either family or school proved to be unsatisfactory in their roles. As far as the family is concerned, it often transmits the national sentiments of a subordinate nation and not that of the dominant one. As for the school, unless it was compulsory and attendance strictly policed, an important percentage of the population could escape from the net of nationalist indoctrination. In Pierre Nora's *Les Lieux de la mémoire* (1986–1992) there are some good case studies of the role of the French school system and of the French Army in the transmission of national sentiments.

The role of the family in the inducement of national sentiments is also well documented. A good case in point, continuing with our Polish ethnography, is that of the active insurrectionary Aleksandra Pilsudska. In her memoirs she describes how she was initiated into love of her country at the tender age of seven:

> My grandmother was a woman of great intelligence and strength of character. Patriotism was the main motor of her life and in the conspiratorial work of the January Rising she had played a prominent part. The Rising's failure caused the greatest trauma of her life. Henceforth she always wore the same black dress, and on her finger a ring decorated with a white cross in pearls on black enamel.
>
> – It is a ring of mourning for those who died, she said.
> But when I asked to put it on my finger, she shook her head.
> – You can only wear it when you are a real patriot.
> – And what does that mean Grandma, 'being a patriot'?
> – A patriot is someone who loves Poland above everything else in the world and will abandon everything, even life itself, for her Freedom.
> – I want to fight for Poland Grandma, I said, only half comprehending.
> After a while my grandmother's eyes flashed.
> – Yes … Do you promise to fight for Poland my child?
> – I promise Grandma. I repeated enthralled by the ominous feeling.
> Then she caressed me, and placing the ring on my finger, held it there tightly.
> – Now there run along … But don't forget, and don't tell a soul.

This was 1889 and the young Ola Szczerbinska (1882–1963) began a revolutionary career like that of her grandmother and that of her husband, Józef Pilsudski, first president of Poland (quoted in Davies 1984: 137).

That national sentiments are a family affair can also be expressed in the harsh language of the poet. In a poem by W.B. Yeats entitled 'Remorse for Intemperate Speech' we can read:

> Nothing said or done can reach
> My fanatic heart.
> Out of Ireland have we come.
> Great hatred, little room,
> Maimed us at the start.
> I carry from my mother's womb
> A fanatic heart.

There are two dimensions worth mentioning in this context. On the one hand there is the sheer art of implanting in the child's mind the words and images that are conducive to the generation of national sentiments. Usually this is done through repetition or mnemonics, or a combination of both. The idea of repetition may be out of fashion in many educational quarters, but I have heard Jacques Chirac declare recently (28.6.96): '*la pédagogie, c'est la répétition*'.

All the institutions involved in national indoctrination (family, school, army) must use a system of rewards and punishments. Modern schools have used different types of rewards (prizes, distinctions, extra holidays, scholarships, etc.) to encourage pupils to conform to the national ideology. Alternatively, they have also penalised (through physical punishment, isolation, sense of ridicule, etc.) those pupils who were recalcitrant in accepting the national values. A good case in point would be the punishment inflicted on pupils who persisted in using their mother tongue, and not the official state language, in class or during breaks. The French *instituteurs*, through a cunning use of rewards and punishments, made possible the process of *francisation* of many areas of geographical France in the late nineteenth century. National and linguistic indoctrination are closely associated processes.

## What Triggers National Sentiments to be Remembered or Recalled?

The first point that arises is: why is it necessary to bring back national sentiments to the mind? The simple answer is that societies have realised that national sentiments are volatile and that they have to compete with other types of sentiments. It is not always the case that nationalist sentiments are exclusivistic and it is well known that religious sentiments often reinforce national ones. James Joyce, in 'Gas for the Burner', expressed this fusion of nationalism and religion with this ironic doublet:

Ireland my first and only love
Where Christ and Caesar go hand in glove.

National sentiments have to compete with class and gender allegiances. They are, perhaps more importantly, undermined by more egotistic sentiments. And, finally, they have also to contend with the general routinisation of all things sacred.

In the 1980s the literature on history and memory has grown exponentially. Following on from the developments of the leading Durkheimian Maurice Halbwachs, an array of scholars have delved into the issue of the social mechanisms that allow societies to remember. Halbwachs' starting point was that 'individual recollections only exist and are localised in the past by linking with the memory of others: one only remembers as a member of a social group' (Wachtel 1986: 211).

A major contribution to the issue of how nations remember is found in the collective work edited by Pierre Nora under the title of *Les Lieux de la mémoire*, which I have mentioned before. It deals with the representation of the French national memory. What I want to emphasise here is that these sites or places of memory are vital in bringing back the past into the present. This array of sites of memory has been invested with an enduring and emotive symbolic significance. What are these sites of memory? Nora distinguishes four types: symbolic sites (commemorations, pilgrimages, anniversaries, etc.), monumental sites (buildings, cemeteries, etc.), topographic sites (museums, archives, libraries, etc.) and functional sites (manuals, autobiographies, associations, etc.) Many of these *lieux de mémoire* have a double function: that of nation-building and that of nation-recalling. In the area of nation-recalling there is little doubt that symbolic sites play a paramount role; anniversaries, commemorations, celebrations, etc. are a regular reminder of national identity, and of the sentiments associated with it.

I am well aware that the issues of national memory are much more complex and controversial than I have had the opportunity to discuss here. I have dealt with the topic of national memory through a case study of Catalonia in chapter 7.

## How are National Sentiments Reinforced?

This is an issue closely related to the previous one, but it aims at uncovering the more everyday and banal elements that reinforce national identity, and hence national sentiments. This is often a sphere that lies at a non-conscious level, and it tends to operate in a haphazard and piecemeal way. Until recently (Billig 1995) it had not received much attention. Billig refers to the daily flagging of the homeland as it occurs through the mass media. What I want to emphasise here are not the areas we are all familiar with, and which function essentially at the conscious level – whether they are politicians' speeches or sports news. In fact there are more subtle and insidious ways of reinforcing the dichotomy between the 'us' and 'them', between what is 'ours' and what is 'alien'. The manner in which information is presented, with a clear division between home and abroad and with an overwhelming domination of home news, are powerful ways of structuring people's minds nationally.

## How are National Sentiments Intensified?

In the conclusion to the *Elementary Forms of Religious Life*, Durkheim remarks that all societies, if they want to survive, must maintain their unity and specific characteristics, and that the way to do that is by periodic gatherings in which individuals come together, and through ceremonies and rituals which strongly reassert their common sentiments. It is irrelevant whether the assembly celebrates a strictly religious belief or an important event in the life of the nation (Durkheim 1960: 610).

The problem is what happens when the country lacks moral fibre, when it goes through a period of malaise and mediocrity. Durkheim was confident that such a situation could be solved by the resurgence of creative effervescence which would renew ideals and create new formulae that could serve as a guidance to the nation. Durkheim is nowhere explicit as to which institutional forms will effect the salvation, and a commentator like Ranulf could ask rhetorically in the late nineteen thirties: 'is not the rise of fascism an event which, in due logic, Durkheim ought to have welcomed as that salvation from individualism for which he had been trying rather gropingly to prepare the way?' (Ranulf 1939: 31).

This comment could be easily dismissed as the musings of a disgruntled, unemployed Scandinavian sociologist. However, what is fascinating is that in the article Ranulf refers to, and quotes from, two letters that Marcel Mauss had sent him. In the first letter (November 1936) Mauss writes as follows:

Durkheim and I were the founders of the theory of the authority of the *représentation collective*. That great modern societies, which had more or less emerged from the Middle Ages, could be subject to suggestion as Australians are by their dances, and made to turn around like children in a ring, is something that we had not really foreseen. We did not put our minds to this return to primitivism. We were satisfied with a few allusions to the state of the crowds, when something quite different was at stake (Gane 1992: 214).

And in another letter (May 1939), Mauss concludes:

I think that all this is a real tragedy for us, an unwelcome verification of the things we had been suggesting and the proof that we should perhaps have expected this verification in the bad case rather than a verification in the good (Gane 1992: 214–15).

What Mauss seems to have discovered, or rather unpleasantly stumbled upon, is the amazing ability of modern totalitarian states to intensify national sentiments to a degree of paroxysm never anticipated. We know now, especially through the studies on Nazi Germany by George Mosse, the mechanisms and the scope of such mass manipulation. In this respect, the Durkheimian School was ill prepared to understand such practices because of their reluctance to come to terms with crowd psychology.

family and at home' (Loewenberg 1992: 94). Modern theories of nationalism downplay this factor, and tend to agree with Gellner that 'nationalism does not have very deep roots in the human psyche' (Gellner 1983: 34). Deutsch, in a book somewhat forgotten today, recognised as early as 1953 that nationalism was based on a common social culture that stemmed from the family and the home; it was the actual feeling of familiarity, comfort and safety that made nationalism possible.

The sentiments generated during an early age towards parents and siblings create what Morin has called a 'psycho-affective component which can be labelled matri-patriotic' (Morin 1987: 225); these are later extended to the nation. Latin languages, for example, play with the bisexuality of the nation. The nation is envisaged as a mother who is protective and loving and hence must be cherished, but also as a father who is virile and represents authority, and must be obeyed even to the point of sacrificing one's life. The French word *patrie* (a feminine name for a masculine concept) expresses this fusion of the maternal and the paternal. Morin insists that in the expression *mère-patrie* there exists a kind of sacramentalisation of the nation. The sentiments required are those of effusion (towards the mother) and of obedience (towards the father). In this sense, one can also speak of national language in terms of a kinship language. The expression 'blood and soil' (*Blut und Boden*) exemplifies well traditional types of national identity. As Morin puts it:

> The matri-patriotic component implies a fraternal/sororal component (that is, among the children of the same fatherland) and a very strong sentiment of the fatherland as homeland (*Heimat*), that is, the fatherland as a roof, as a house (peoples might be wanderers, but fatherlands are not). It is easy to understand that from this conception should emerge the idea of common blood, and that this affective or emotional metaphor, when taken literally, may become national racism (Morin 1987: 225).

Connor has provided a long list of 'familial' metaphors used in English to indicate this state of things. In addition to 'fatherland' and 'motherland', we have 'ancestral land', 'land of our fathers', 'sacred soil', 'land where our fathers died', 'native land', 'cradle of the nation', 'homeland', etc. (Connor 1994: 205). These expressions, and other similar ones, occur in many other European languages, and certainly in those of Latin roots. Furthermore, in Italian and Portuguese the word *matria* signifies the land that feeds you and rears you; it is culture at the affective/emotive level.

I would like to make a final point to close these introductory remarks. In an article entitled 'Kinship, Nationality and Religion in American Culture', David Schneider (1977) has said that in America – and it is probably safe to generalise it to most Western cultures – one becomes a national by birth or through a process of what is rightly called naturalisation. And this, adds Schneider, is not unlike kinship: there is kin by birth and there is kin by law. In fact, kinship and nationality are structured in a similar, if not identical way. 'What is the role of a national or of a kin? To love his country, that is his fatherland/motherland. It is also to support and to be loyal to his nation and to all those who belong to the big family that is the nation. Loyalty to own's country is the most generalised expression of the diffuse, enduring solidarity that starts with the family' (Schneider 1977: 61). Schneider concludes by saying that kinship and nationality (and he adds religion as well) are all the same thing, culturally speaking. A case in point is that of Judaism, where family, nation and religion form an inseparable totality.

In relation to our second issue it is useful to introduce N. Poulantzas' expression 'the history of a territory and the territorialisation of a history' (Poulantzas 1978: 114). The importance of territory is not emphasised by most social scientists, unless they are geographers. There is little doubt however that a territory is perhaps one of the most concrete and important phenomena that exist for human beings, as it also reflects their psychological characteristics. In this respect, it is possible to assert that identifying with a given territory is an important feature of a given human group. At the level of territoriality, groups exercise control over a geographical area and they do that by reifying their power. In this way, they can exert the control over other people who, for a variety of reasons, do not really belong to the territory. This tends to be a phenomenon that belongs to the *longue durée*, but they can be manipulated favourably in the context of modern society.

An important characteristic of the modern development of nationalism is to realise that state nationalism is not always successful precisely because of the importance of nationalisms against the state. In Western Europe the case of France is often presented as an exception, but then we must be aware that the French state had a long existence and was powerful. Consequently, when the state required a cultural and a linguistic process of unity in the second half of the nineteenth century, it was endowed with the appropriate structure to achieve its end. Of course, the problem for most Western European states, excepting perhaps Portugal, is that they were not nation-states, but rather multinations. As for countries like Italy and Germany, they are projecting a different reality: the unification of a number of territories, either independent or belonging to an alien state, which are assumed to be part of the same nation (culturally and linguistically, at least as a national belief). If nation-states are not a very common historical reality of Western Europe, in other parts of the world, the states are rarely nationally homogeneous (perhaps only 5 per cent are truly homogeneous) (Johnston et al. 1988).

Territory is an ambiguous concept and this can clearly be seen in a situation where there are two competing ideologies: state nationalism and nationalism against the state. The definitions provided by the Basques and the Catalans of their respective geographies are incompatible with the definitions that Spaniards (mainly Castilians) offer of the whole unified country. For example, the Spaniards maintain that the Pyrenees is a clearly dividing 'reality' between France and Spain, while the Catalans and the Basques consider the mountains as unifying their countries. It is not surprising that the sophisticated Spanish sociologist Juan Linz would affirm that the modern nation-states would found their basis on territoriality and not allow primordialist elements such as race, common descent, language, culture, etc. to dominate the discourse because of their diversifying tendency.

The fact that the state is powerful, and has the right of monopoly to legitimate violence, is a reality that goes back a few thousand years (Van den Berghe 1990). In this respect it would be naive to assume that *ethnies* or nations have become massively independent in the past two hundred years. As Gellner remarked there may be 6,000 *ethnies* but only 200 states. There is little doubt that the state is often powerful and able to suppress the independence or autonomy of a variety of *ethnies* or nations that are within their territories. However, the collapse of the Soviet Union in 1989–92 was the beginning of many new states. Yugoslavia, outside the Russian influence, began a process of disintegration in 1991. Which social science or history foresaw these developments? The answer is: practically none.

After kinship and territory, the third point to be considered is religion. It is a well-known fact that nationalism does not only command great aspects of the sacred, but it is in fact a kind of religion. According to Ninian Smart (1995), nationalism displays a number of dimensions of religion, but I will be dealing specifically with the following ones: material, mythical, ritualistic, ethical and doctrinal. Perhaps the only thing that is missing from nationalism is the idea of a transcendental god, though it often relies on a notion of god and has an essence of it, what the Japanese refer to as *kokutai*.

If we start with the first dimension of sacred nationalism we would mention the material. Land is a crucial factor here, but also monuments (both ancient and modern) and sacred spaces (birthplaces and cemeteries of heroes). As to national religious sites, they are common to all European countries. The second element, the mythic, corresponds to what could be called the narrative of the nation, that is, the learning that stems from education and that generates identity and pride. National histories are always idealised and censored, and it is often possible to observe that history and religion often go together. In this sense, states adopt saints as patrons; Saint George, for example, is the patron saint of England and Catalonia. Most remembrances of victories and revolutions, representations of political independence, inaugurations of presidents, etc. are conducted with great solemnity and subjected to high ritualism in which a religious dimension is emphasised. As to the next dimension we know that the ethical values of nationalism are often embedded in society. Often the love of the family is quite central, giving a strong sense of origin to the inhabitants. In some cases, for example those of Irish and Polish Catholicism, religion is superimposed on nationalism. At the doctrinal level metaphysics is often presented as an excuse for nationalism and even imperialism; it is a well-established fact that self-aggrandising nations become empires with the argument of spreading Christianity. In other case, patriotism is reinforced with revolutionary religion.

In conclusion, Smart emphasises that nationalism and religion are a typical syncretism or blending. That is why it is important to study both realities, though sometimes there are important phenomenological distinctions between these two realities, particularly when nationalism defines itself by non-religious factors (like language, history, etc.). However, it is important to remember that the blending of nationalism and religion might be a thing of the past or of recent times. The case of the blending of Irish nationalism and Catholicism is a good point insofar as it is, essentially, a twentieth-century phenomenon (Ben-Israel 1986).

## A Catalan Case Study

Catalonia has generally elicited rather limited attention in the specialised literature. It is only in the past few years that anthropologists working in Catalonia have paid some albeit passing attention to the issue of kinship, identity and nationality. This has, inevitably, taken the form of 'rediscovering' the work of some late nineteenth-century or early twentieth-century Catalan legal scholars, historians or folklorists who had highlighted the idiosyncrasies of Catalan kinship *vis-à-vis* the Castilian one. However, as ethnic markers go, kinship and the family perhaps never figured prominently in the definition of Catalan national identity. Prat de la Riba, who published his seminal *Catalan Nationality* in 1906, did not refer, specifically, to anything distinctively Catalan, although he mentioned a long list of particularising Catalan features; it is true, however, that kinship and the family could be, and traditionally were, subsumed under the label of 'law'. Let me highlight the points that I am trying to make in this context:

First, national identity is about difference. If we think of the world as divided into nations, each nation combines in a peculiar way a number of ethnic features or markers. It is often the case that, in neighbouring, culturally similar nations, the efforts to mark the fewer differences are always bigger than elsewhere. This is very much the case of Catalonia and Castile/Spain, and it is related to both kinship and territory.

Second, in the case of Catalonia kinship is an ethnic marker with a limited though not unimportant presence. Although much more emphasis is given to the existence of a distinctive language, a specific history, etc., kinship, particularly at the turn of the century, played a distinctive role in the generalised attempt to differentiate things Catalan. Surprisingly enough, the Francoist period, as I have demonstrated elsewhere (1994), reinforced Catalan essentialism, and specifically a certain petrified vision of the past (including family and kinship), at a time when many of the institutions referred to were long gone under the impact of the accelerated process of industrialisation. As for the territory there is a difference between Catalonia and Castile.

Third, the survival to recent times of the concept of *pairalisme* – an ideology which emphasised the idiosyncrasy of Catalan kinship – is something which has to be emphasised. A term coined by jurists, historians and politicians, *pairalisme* functions at a number of levels of the social register. The word derives from the Occitan *paire* (meaning, of course, father) and indicates, in the first instance, a positive attitude towards the father, and generally speaking towards the ancestors. *Pairalisme*, which could be called rural familism, conjures up a number of institutions, including the centrality of the ancestral house and of primogeniture, which were meant to be typical of the Catalan countryside. It implies also a certain rural paternalism in which class relations were substituted by kinship ones. At the most general level, it projects an image of the countryside in which the dominant element was a 'non-conflictive, homogeneous Catalan peasantry', that was the basis of the Catalan nation. I shall come back to the concept of *pairalisme*. A final point is a clear connection between the Catalan countryside (a part of the Catalan territory) and *pairalisme*.

Fourth, a final point on *pairalisme*. This concept still has presence today, although it was more frequent at the turn of the past century. As a term it can be found in the speech of politicians and in literature, as well as other non-Catalan specific kinship and family metaphors.

## The Origins of Catalan Kinship

Perhaps the only anthropologist who has looked into the origins of Catalan kinship is Ignasi Terradas (1984). He maintains that any research on origins is bound to be somewhat conjectural given the scarcity of materials. The period that he considers is the early Middle Ages. However, it does not make much sense to talk about kinship in isolation; in other words 'the existence of institutionalised kinship is a political and economic phenomenon linked to the social totality' (Terradas 1984: 19). Nonetheless, there has been some speculation concerning the existence of pre-Roman kinship features as a way to assert the specificity of the future Catalan national identity, features that would have been preserved in the isolated Pyrenean valleys. In this sense the origins of the Catalan stem family (*familia pairal*) would be found in the pre-Roman peoples (Iberian and others). What seems to be the case, leaving aside other considerations, is that the *familia pairal* or stem family, which would appear as typically Catalan by the thirteenth and fourteenth centuries, did not come to exist earlier than the ninth and tenth centuries. This is a type of family that is essentially bilateral and patrifocal. Traditional Roman kinship distinguished between agnatic and cognatic relationships. *Patria potestas* was only exerted over the agnatic group; the cognatic group was formed by relatives, both by affinity and consanguinity, who did not form part of the agnatic group. By the early Middle Ages it is no longer clear who are the agnatic and cognatic relatives, because the terms have changed meaning.

Terradas maintains that the development of the *familia pairal* reflects the agrarian crisis of the Carolingian period and its resolution. And here is where the institution of unigeniture, usually male primogeniture or the *hereu* (heir) system, is relevant. In no way should these early *families pairals* be seen as similar to the Roman agnatic groups, although they are patrilocal, patrifocal and tend to enforce male primogeniture. The mistake is to bring into the early feudal period categories like lineage, which is typical of tribal societies where there is no political superstructure. The institution of the *hereu* (heir), that is, usually male primogeniture with indivisible inheritance, appeared as an attempt to attach peasants to the land; 'these people received land on the liberal tenure of *aprisio*, which created a quasi-proprietary right under comital protection' (Bisson 1986: 21). This type of colonisation was encouraged from the late ninth century onwards, when the east Pyrenean counties that later would constitute the nucleus of Catalonia started to detach themselves from the Carolingian Empire and become autonomous under Count Guifré and his successors. Why was the institution of the *hereu* appropriate to the circumstances? First, because in this system a family was fixed or fastened to a piece of land, while at the same time the non-heirs were forced to look for land elsewhere. Second, it established a principle of authority within the *familia pairal*. At a wider political level, expansion also favoured the interests of the Church and the nobility, which in this way could increase their income.

In the mid-eleventh century the process of conquest and colonisation of Muslim-held lands came to a standstill, at least for a time. This was the result of the establishment of a rather severe process of servitude in the countryside. 'The representatives of the Counts and the local, small nobility, seized public property, usurped Church property and confiscated land under the control of the peasants and constituted themselves as hereditary lords. Peasants were left with the usufruct of the property, which was subjected to a series of limitations. In addition part of the peasants were prohibited from leaving the manor without paying a ransom or *remença*. Hence the expression *pagesos de remença* or ransom peasants' (Balcells 1996: 3–4). After the demographic devastation cause by the plague (Black Death as it is called) in the fourteenth century, the Catalan countryside was depopulated and many properties were left fallow. The existing feudalism started to crumble under these conditions. There followed a protracted struggle between feudal lords and the feudalised peasants (*pagesos de remença*). After a century of confrontations, in the late fifteenth century (1468) King Ferdinand decided to free the *pagesos de remença* of their most onerous servile duties and allow them to buy their freedom and have rights to the lands that they had cultivated as servile tenant farmers. This was the beginning of a solid class of free peasants, unheard of in other parts of the Iberian peninsula, which in the centuries to come would become proprietors of the lands they cultivated.

Ultimately, Terradas, in his research, sees the meaning of Catalan kinship changing; it is not something perennial, but evolves with the general conditions of the country, and more specifically with the transition from feudalism to capitalism.

### The Making of Pairalisme: Religion, Patriotism and Traditionalism

I have already said that the importance of the family as a defining feature of Catalan national identity was perceived and emphasised for the first time in the late nineteenth century. Originally, it came from the more traditional, religious, conservative and ruralist perspective, which was competing with a more progressive, democratic, popular and urban viewpoint. The group defending the *pairalist* vision of Catalonia was centred in the northern town of Vic and published a magazine called the *Voice of Montserrat* (The Virgin of Montserrat being the female patron saint of Catalonia). Their leading figure was Torras i Bages. The terminology used by Torras and his colleagues is not always clearly nationalist. They refer to Catalonia indistinctively as region, country, nationality and fatherland (*patria*) and to Spain as state and nation – they called their doctrine regionalism, not nationalism.

Bishop Josep Torras i Bages, whose see was in Vic, was one of the most important public figures of his time in Catalonia. In his book *The Catalan Tradition* (1892) he clearly relates family and country; here follows a representative quote:

> The family is the substance and base of social organisation. Social decadence supposes decay in the family. Social regeneration, social reconstruction, must begin with the reconstruction of the family. We turn our eyes to Spain, and we will see that the spirit is strongest in those nationalities that have the strongest regional spirit. Love for the homestead, the desire to preserve the patrimony, the order of the family hierarchy ... all is superior where regional life has been maintained, even in the decayed form, as opposed to those areas which are confused with the great mass, the nation (Torras i Bages 1966: 67).

Generally speaking his book presents a romantic, conservative and Catholic vision of Catalonia. His well-known statement 'If Catalonia is to exist, it must be Christian' perfectly exemplifies his state of mind. A well-known source of his inspiration was Herder's doctrine of the *Volksgeist*. In this context Catalonia is envisaged as a God-created moral person, with a clear place in the history of Europe, a thriving medieval nation which went underground and has been reawakened by the Romantic movement. Torras i Bages insisted that the foundation of Catalan regionalism can only be found in the Catalan tradition, and specifically in the past thinkers who clearly show the existence of a Catalan national character.

As I have said above, his thought is not always clearly nationalist in the modern sense of the term. Catalonia is referred to both as a region and as a nationality, and the movement he favours is called regionalism. The modern centralising, unitary state – Spain in this case – is envisaged as an artificial entity that cannot generate patriotic sentiments: only the region or nationality can. The unitary state (a term not used by Torras) does not bring human harmony and its interventionism leads to the collapse of the natural, social bonds. Only the small units (regions) generate sentiments that give strength to the social body.

For Torras i Bages patriotic love develops only at the level of the small unit (region); the state can generate a similar, but never such a powerful and beautiful sentiment. He insists that patriotic sentiments resemble filial love. For him our country is like our mother; it is the cause of our being, and we are what we are, because she is what she is. The children of the country reflect the qualities of the mother. For Torras i Bages it is only at the level of the region that human beings can become truly patriotic. It is like an instinctive sentiment, but it is also a civilising principle. It attaches a people to a territory, it encourages the flourishing of the spirit of the family and it creates a tradition that transmits ancient wisdom. As he puts it quite radically:

> Love of country is like a preservation instinct; solidarity and identification with the fatherland is so absolute that it is not surprising to see it expressed in the following Horatian line: *Dulce et decorum est pro patria mori* (it is sweet and becoming to die for one's own country). To believe that human beings will be willing to sacrifice their lives for a distant and abstract unitary state would be to ignore human nature ( [1892] 1966: 64).

It is in this context that Torras i Bages brings out again the family imagery. The state is not a *patria* (fatherland); it is a distant and unknown mother, and hence it can hardly elicit any sentiments of love or just superficial ones. Only the region is a truly *mare patria* (a fatherland as a mother). There are other sentiments (the sentiment of humanity and that of the state), but it is only the patriotic sentiment that is crucial, and also the most natural and lasting one.

Another important dimension for Torras i Bages, following the ideas of Le Play, is that one must put an end to the disorder existing in modern society. Three basic institutions that had been allowed to decay and had been attacked by modern revolutionaries were religion, family and property. These institutions could not be imposed by force, though society had the duty to protect them from dangerous influences. How did he justify the primacy of these institutions? He argued that they corresponded to basic instincts of human nature and insisted that religion, family and property were best protected and flourished more freely in the context of regionalism, while centralism weakened them and ended up by destroying them.

It may seem surprising to see Torras i Bages defending the thesis that regionalism has beneficial effects on religion. Admittedly, Christianity is universal, but each people has its specific and peculiar way of expressing its religiosity: what is natural, i.e. religious, and vice versa. Religion helps to preserve the existing social order. There is a strong attack on cosmopolitanism as a false god – in that he is a faithful follower of Herder. Man's nature is religious, but it manifests itself in a specific place: in other words, in a specific culture and in a specific language.

It is then fair to conclude that there is a clear connection between family and country in the mind of Torras i Bages. The family is the foundation of social organisation; social decadence implies the decline of the family. A morally vigorous and united family is a source of societal strength. There is a clear correlation between a thriving fatherland and the love of the homestead and family, and vice versa. Regionalism favours the family spirit, while statism (centralism) endangers it by enhancing individualistic and egotistical values. In addition, regionalism is more natural since it follows the divine law. Torras i Bages closes his argument by saying that the homestead or ancestral home *(casa pairal)* is the pillar of Catalonia.

A final brief reference to kinship and national identity in Catalan poetry: during the nineteenth and twentieth centuries Catalan patriotic poetry has often used kinship and family imagery to convey the sentiments which are deemed appropriate to the fatherland. In one of the most popular nineteenth-century poets (Pitarra) we find different registers of the word *patria*. One of his poems connects fatherland with the ordinary things of life: a hearth with a fire, wife and children, the home. In another, loyalty to the fatherland takes precedence over family duties.

A recurrent theme is that of one's country as mother earth. For example, a poem entitled 'The day of the clay men' brings together earth, mother, blood and country. The country is envisaged as a mother who is defended, against her enemies, by her children to the point of offering their blood (Didac Ruiz), which fertilises the earth (Angel Guimerà). Sometimes Catalonia is compared to both an oak tree and a mother. As earth, the mother country appears also as a nourishing and generous mother, as a sweet and quiet mother looking after her children (Josep M. Lopez-Picó). The continuity of the fatherland is also emphasised; the children may die, but the mother country is eternal (Apelles Mestres). Finally, when reference is made to Catalonia and Spain, the point is made that you cannot have two mothers; you are born only in one country that is your true mother (F. Arnau).

## *Anthropologists and Historians Come to Terms with* Pairalisme

In a recent article J. Bestard (1995) has perceptively summarised the contribution made by jurists to the issue of *pairalisme*. He says:

> The Catalan legal scholars and folklorists of the turn of the century created a new image of the Catalan family as they imagined a new nation. They announced the

modernity of the nation on the basis of tradition; family is the metaphor linking customary local practices with homogeneous law. The family has its law (Maspons i Anglesell dixit) and that law can be generalised to the nation. The idea of a homogeneous family type characteristic of Catalonia, with an old domestic organisation which is central to the social reproduction of Catalonia as a nation is due to these scholars (Bestard 1995: 250–51).

According to Bestard, one of the most powerful symbols of Catalan kinship is the house (*casa*). 'An individual receives his/her identity as a member of a house, from it depends his name and position in the community' (Bestard 1995: 257). With the term house (*casa*) two ideas converge: ideas of kinship and ideas of territory. So, in the Catalan mind the house becomes a symbol of the nation. The centrality of the house for Catalonia was perceived by a number of turn-of-the-century Catalan legal scholars: Josep Duran i Bas, Josep Faus i Condomines, Victorino Santamaria i Tous, Francesc Maspons i Anglesell and others. They related it, via Le Play, to the originality of the Catalan stem family. On the other hand, political ideologists and politicians used the institution of the house as an emblem of the Catalan nation in opposition to the centralised state.

I have already insinuated that the stem family and the house were perceived as the foundation of a homogeneous social order that was related to the national identity. However, this was happening at a time when the process of industrialisation was taking place and the nation was changing along with it. The house was a symbolic reservoir that allowed individuals to remain rooted in the past as well as active in the present and to imagine the Catalan community as nothing better than the ancestral home (*casa pairal*); the house was seen as the first circle of belonging upon which the nation was built; the house maintained the language and culture, a particularly important thing in a country were the state was alien. That is why somebody like Josep Faus, in 1907, saw 'the house as the refuge of national continuity' (Bestard 1995: 258). Another early twentieth-century legal scholar, Victorino Santamarina, insisted that the perpetuation of the family via the idea of house was the cornerstone of the Catalan family, in opposition to the Castilian one, which had no continuity and was dissolved after one generation. How was this continuity affected in the case of the Catalan family? People live in the same house and have the same house name, and this is a reason for pride and social prestige.

As I mentioned earlier, the Francoist period had the surprising effect of solidifying a kind of Catalan essentialism. *Pairalisme* was enthroned as a Catalan virtue at a time when the society had changed beyond recognition to a modern industrial one. As we have seen in chapter 1, one of the leading historians of the period, Jaume Vicens-Vives, in a book published in 1954 entitled *Notícia de Catalunya* (A panorama of Catalonia), emphasised many of the specific characteristics of Catalan kinship, while rejecting *pairalist* ideology. *Notícia de Catalunya* was an extremely influential book, and it shaped the residual and hidden Catalan nationalism in one of the darkest periods of the history of Catalonia.

It is interesting to note, as Bestard and others do, that in the industrial context of today *pairalisme* has not lost all its power. Urban people, namely people from Barcelona, often refer to their ancestral home: a rural house were the ancestors originated. More commonly, a second house in the countryside may become the *casa pairal*, with family name and Catalan flag included. *Pairalisme* has become a cultural ideal that forms part of the Catalan tradition, in which even immigrant families can participate.

## Becoming a National: The Issue of Immigration and Catalan Kinship Today

According to Comas (1993) belonging and non-belonging are essential categories of the life of individuals in modern nations and states. To be a national means to belong to the nation; to be an alien, a foreigner, denies this quality. The alien may live in our society but he/she does not belong to its core, to what we could designate as the 'community'. Different countries define this belonging to the community with different metaphors. The racial analogy was common in the past (*Reinrassiger Deutscher, italiano di razza*); in other cases blood was emphasised (full-blooded Englishman). The idea of deep roots also appears frequently. In Catalan the expression is to be '*a Català de soca-rel*', that is, a stump and root Catalan. In Spanish the expression would be '*español de pura cepa*' (Spaniard of pure stock).

An extremely interesting issue in relation to Catalonia is how it has managed to maintain and preserve its sense of national identity in spite of two extremely powerful forces working against it. First, in approximately one century the population of Catalonia has grown from two to six million inhabitants in spite of having the lowest birth rate in the whole of Europe, absorbing over three million immigrants. In the 1920s and 1930s they came from neighbouring areas, in the 1950s and 1960s mainly from Andalusia and other parts of Spain and at present they originate from North and West Africa as well as Latin America. Second, for most of this period, and particularly under Franco (1939–1975), Catalonia was subjected to the most intense 'denationalising' process ever known, with the clear and avowed aim of totally uprooting Catalan national identity.

The success story of Catalonia is that it has not only managed to preserve the identity of the original Catalans, but that it has largely managed to integrate the majority of immigrants into the larger Catalan imagined community. This has been largely done essentially through language and culture. This is a pattern, that of immigration, which had occurred in previous centuries. From afar, Catalonia may appear as a homogeneous country, while close by the situation contains important cleavages that have nonetheless generated little conflict. Who is a Catalan? For those Spanish citizens not born but living in Catalonia there are some legal requirements in terms of residence (ten years) to qualify as a Catalan. It has been a policy of the overall majority of Catalan parties (even before Franco's death) that Catalans are those who live and work in Catalonia and express the wish to be Catalans. However, unlike in other definitions of nationhood, no requirements in terms of blood or descent are needed. The requirements are at the level of residence and at the level of consciousness. Although some references may be found to a difference between the new and the old Catalans, these are rather superficial distinctions. Indeed, it would be very easy to distinguish between Catalans and non-Catalans at a non-cultural and non-linguistic level simply by reference to patronymics. It is true that today only one quarter of the Catalans can boast of four grandparents with Catalan surnames.

Renan insisted that the nation was a spiritual family and more recently Schneider (in *American Kinship*) that a kin is somebody who occupies a genealogical position or somebody who behaves like a kin. A similar thing happens at the level of the nation: a national is somebody who is born in a certain country or is somebody who behaves like the people of this country (i.e. who has adopted the culture of this country).

The nation is a metaphor of the family. Those born in the nation are like consanguineous kin, those who are incorporated into the nation (i.e. naturalised) are like in-laws. It should be theoretically possible to represent the nation as a huge genealogy showing that there is a degree of kinship among its members. These blood ties are what cements the nation as a homogeneous social reality. If we provisionally leave aside naturalisation, we can see that the nation is a natural entity (ascription by birth), unavoidable (there is no choice) and trans-historic (related to past ancestors and future descendants). Recent Catalan ideologists have emphasised the process of inclusiveness, that is, the conscious policy of integrating immigrants into the Catalan national project; in this context, language, culture and historical memory are things to be shared between the old and the new Catalans.

Concerning Catalan kinship and family the first thing to emphasise is their distinctiveness; the Catalan system of inheritance has no parallel in the rest of Spain (Puig-Salellas 1988). It is important to remember, though, that the *hereu* system was only operative in the rural areas of what is traditionally called Old Catalonia (that is, the northern half of Catalonia); the southern part of Catalonia (which corresponds to the province of Tarragona) and the urban, industrial areas did not know this system. It has been suggested that the fact that the *hereu* system was not introduced in the industrial world, tends to create a situation of indecision due to the presence, after two or three generations, of too many relatives (Puig-Salellas 1988: 15–20) at the managerial level.

In the Catalan traditional system, the heir inherits three quarters of the capital. This is a system of unigeniture, usually male primogeniture, although, if there are no male heirs, a female (*pubilla*) heir is instituted. The rest of the siblings divide among themselves a quarter of the capital: the daughters in the form of a dowry, the sons in the form of a capital stake. The paterfamilias has freedom in the designation of the *hereu*, although male primogeniture is the rule. At some stage in his life, when his children are of age, the paterfamilias decides who the *hereu* will be and he organises the marriage contract.

The *familia pairal* is strong only in some rural areas, and these are fewer and fewer. The couple, husband and wife, have become much more central than ever before. The idea of a familial patrimony is no longer relevant; children tend to marry and leave, and if they stay they are economically independent. The importance of liquid property places agricultural property in a rather secondary position. In any case, only 6 per cent of the population are employed in agriculture today, as against 50 per cent in 1900, and many more before that. Furthermore, Catalonia is a macrocephalic society, with 70 per cent of the population living around Barcelona.

## Geography and National Identity

In this section I will try to show the close relationship between geography and nationalism in the Catalan identity (Nogué 1991; Garcia-Ramon and Nogué 1994). It is a well-known fact that the majority of social scientists who are national theoreticians ignore the territorial dimension; only the geographers interested in nationalism consider the territorial element as an important factor of modern nationalism. It would be fair to say that many strictly Marxist theoreticians consider territory as an essential part of the nation. In this context, the Marxist historian Pierre Vilar is clear in emphasising the presence of a number of factors (climate, landscape, weather, etc.) which define Catalan basic identity.

An important issue which affects Catalan and Basque nationalism's relationship with territory is that the majority of Basque nationalist parties assume that Navarre is part of their territory, while the most radical also include the French Basques (North Euskadi). The radicals talk about a single unit that is made by the three Basque provinces, Navarre and the French provinces. They express this idea with the formula 4+3=1 or, in another way, Seven in One (*Zazpiak Bat*). Why the Basques are irredentists and the Catalans are not is a good question that will be considered in chapter 8. However, the conception of the territory partly explains the radicalism of the former and the moderation of the latter. One should add that this is a relatively recent phenomenon, which first emerged in the late 1960s.

In Catalonia, the attitude of most parties, particularly after 1978, is more limited and accepts a geographic conception which excludes Valencia, Balearic Islands, Andorra and French Catalonia. However, Catalans do not forget the fact that culturally and linguistically they are part of a sort of 'Greater Catalonia' (or 'Catalan Countries' as a better term, which conceives of Catalonia as the *Principat*). It is important to remember that a group or a state which practises irredentism does not necessarily require violence or war. For example, it is a well-known fact that the Spanish government has 'peacefully' revindicated Gibraltar for a long period of time.

The fact that there are different levels of territorial identity (house, village, region/province and state/nation) is well known. Human beings are sensible of these different realities, particularly in modern times. It would be fair, however, to realise that the provinces created by the Spanish state in the 1840s are denied any relevance by Catalan nationalism. However, as Nogué (1991) remarks, the fact that provinces are at least 150 years old means that they are carriers of a national reality which is very difficult to remove. The reason for the importance of territory is not only geographical but also mainly political.

Physical anthropologists have maintained that human beings tend to develop, from early times, a sentiment of territorial identity and security. One could say that each group of human beings has a profound attachment to a given territory. On the other hand, some geographers and social scientists have denied the existence of an aggressive instinct among human beings in order to account for human territoriality. The main proposition is to suggest that territoriality is not always chosen by human groups. The main factor that accounts for this variation has to do with power. In modern terms, it is the state that decides which territorial strategy it will use in order to achieve its political objectives.

It is a well-known fact that territorial divisions are problematic in states like Spain. The Basques and Catalans have been against the creation of provinces since 1833. It is perceived as a state intervention aimed at destroying the Basque and Catalan realities. In Catalonia the perception that this model was a political criterion to destroy the nation appeared in the late nineteenth century in the context of the first important political framework (*Bases de Manresa*, 1892). The insistence of Catalan nationalism, in all historical periods, has always been to defend the idea of Catalonia as a territorial division. As Nogué (1991) reminds us, a well-known geographer has expressed this reality in an appropriate manner: 'The territorial division of Catalonia in provinces was decreed by the central government in 1833. This division does neither reflect a Catalan historical tradition nor its physical, human and economic features' (Vila 1980: 7).

I have already mentioned that the connection between geography and nationalism appeared in the nineteenth century. In 1876 hiking (*excursionisme*) became an activity that was not purely a sporting or scientific activity. It acquired a political dimension that was essentially associated with one of the national dimensions of Catalonia. In 1891 there appeared the *Centre Excursioniste de Catalunya* (Hiking Centre of Catalonia), which became extremely powerful, and which still exists today. For many people (scientists, novelists, industrialists, poets, etc.) an interest in the Catalan landscape was a love and an obligation. Those who were interested in the movement had a strong commitment to find out about the nature of Catalonia. The poet Joan Maragall, writing at the beginning of the twentieth century, was clearly aware that the hikers were deeply in love with Catalonia, which was the centre, and hence the most lovable part, of the world. Many geographers were active in transmitting the geographic reality of Catalonia. This process peaked during the Second Spanish Republic, with a growing literature on the topic.

Under the Francoist regime, the hiking movement, and especially the publications supporting it, became rarer, particularly where many geographers either left the country or were not allowed to write. The recovery was slow, but it happened faster than at other levels, particularly the political. By the late 1940s, the Boy Scouts were already active in creating a Catalanist environment.

The Spanish attempts to perpetuate the provincial structure also created a malaise among Catalan geographers. It is interesting to observe that the periods during which this movement was most active were those where the level of freedom was at its highest: the Second Spanish Republic (1931–39) and the post-Francoist period (1978 onwards). However, although the territorial division was very similar in 1936 and 1987 (around forty units), the four provinces are still the most relevant division at a variety of levels (economic, political, etc.).

The Catalan Geographic Society, which was created in 1906, was very active, particularly during the Second Republic. It was kept alive and active relatively soon after the Civil War, that is, late in the 1940s, because of its more 'scientific' dimension. During the fifties and early sixties the role of the geographers, though limited, 'played a significant role in the survival of Catalan geography and its nationalistic bias during those difficult years' (Garcia-Ramon and Nogué 1994: 206). In recent years, that is, after 1978, 'nationalism, geography and pedagogical renewal has been a feature of what the professional geographers have dedicated themselves to' (García-Ramón and Nogué 1994: 206).

The political importance of the map is a factor that was made obvious as early as the end of the nineteenth century. The fact that it appears in the school system as a powerful instrument does not hide its ideological characteristics covering economic, political and military dimensions. It would be naive to believe that only the maps of Nazis and Communists are devious, although items (including the press and the TV) produced in democratic countries are rarely so extremist.

In the Catalan case it is obvious that the concept and representation of the Catalan Countries (*Països Catalans*) are a result that ceased to be a political idea among the leading political parties of Catalonia (namely socialist and nationalist) approximately in 1978. Only certain political and small groups, with the ERC (Republican Left of Catalonia) as the sole exception, are still active in maintaining a unified vision of the Catalan Countries. The leader of the ERC, Josep-Lluis Carod-Rovira, defends a perspective of Catalonia in which the geographic vision of the nation is emphasised, a comprehensive view in which Catalonia has a special place in Europe and the Mediterranean. It has a specific physical landscape that involves mountains, rivers and lakes. For example, Montserrat, Canigó, Pirineu and Montseny are quasi-sacred or at least important mountains which have been mentioned since the nineteenth century.

It would be appropriate to conclude this section of geography and nationalism by referring to the author Joan Nogué, who is a specialist on the topic. His insistence that Catalan nationalism is a territorial ideology is a powerful hypothesis that he illustrated with a survey of a continuity of authors and movements which have existed since the late nineteenth century. Perhaps an important conclusion from this research is to be aware that 'the territory is (…) a key element when one tries to understand and explain the nationalist phenomenon' (Nogué 1991: 114).

## Catalan Nationalism and Religion

To say that religion is a historically important element of Catalan society (and the Catalan Countries generally speaking) is an obvious fact. It would not be exaggerating to say that for many centuries Catholicism was the dominant ideology. In this respect, one can say that Catalan culture has also been seriously influenced by religion. In the twentieth century religion has progressively lost its hegemony, although the Francoist regime represented a certain recovery. A general framework used for this section is the one published in the Congrés de Cultural Catalana (1978) on the religious facts.

The Francoist period has been accurately described as 'national-catholicism'. In this expression there is a clear and designated reference to an alliance between Francoism and Spanish Catholicism. In Catalonia the strong anti-religious attitude adopted by the anarchists and Marxists in the 1930s led to an attempt to massacre the majority of priests, nuns and fervent Catholics during the Civil War (Massot 1987). It is obvious that the Church would see Franco's victory as a recovery of their survival and status. What was problematic, however, was the issue of language. It is a well-known fact that Catalonia was subjected to an extremely severe anti-linguistic policy with the clear objective of imposing Spanish as the only public language. But it would be fair to say that a great part of the Catalan priests contributed to the recovery of the language. In fact, in the immediate postwar period the only public dimension of Catalan was found in the Church and in some religious publications, and it was precisely the popular rooting of the Catholic Church that allowed the maintenance of the Catalan language, particularly at the popular level. It would be fair to say that the religious panorama varies in the different Catalan Countries. In fact, Valencia and Majorca showed a more developed Spanish Catholicism, although this phenomenon also existed in Catalonia.

It is possible to assert with certainty that prior to the Spanish Civil War the Catalan language held a position of centrality for the Catholic Church. Most aspects of the religious church were affected by the introduction of Catalan from preaching to catechism and from teaching to piety. It is possible to assert that the development of Catalan national identity, which started in the late nineteenth century, was correlated with the blossoming of Catalan Catholicism. However, it is fair to say that in the pre-war period the attitude of the Catholic Church in Catalonia was somewhat politically anti-Catalan.

With the triumph of Franco, the leading hierarchy of the Church in Catalonia (often of Castilian origin) was extremely reactionary and was quite happy to accept a process of Castilianisation (Bada 1987). The national-catholic ideology was destined to present a vision of Catalonia that was partly incorrect. According to it, all those parties that had supported the Republic were anti-Catholic, specifically those who were linguistically and culturally Catalan. This statement condemned the Catalan language to damnation like a shock. The autonomous language was, nonetheless, preserved and developed in large part by the rural clergy and some religious orders (Benedictines and Capuchins). On the other hand, the religious hierarchy and some orders (Jesuits and Dominicans) were against language and culture. The fact that religious texts were printed in Catalan is a sign of the linguistic recovery. By 1978 the situation had changed quite radically; it would be fair to say that most religious groups used Catalan. It is important to emphasise that the Catalan Catholic Church has shown a strong commitment to Catalan nationalism (Masnou 1986; Gomis 1995), as is obvious in their collective statement (Els Bisbes de Catalunya 1986).

## Conclusion

*Pairalisme* as an ideology is not dead; it is preserved in some form at the level of the Catalan national character. In other words, it is one of the stereotypes that are believed at some level of the Catalan psyche by a significant number of people. These values, along with many others, like the idea that the Catalans believe in compromise (*pactisme*), or that they oscillate between conservative judiciousness (*seny*) and extremist rashness (*rauxa*), are still bandied about in the political language and in everyday life. They have to be taken into account because they shape, to a certain extent, people's behaviour. On the other hand, recent ethnographic research by Andrés Barrera (1986; 1990) shows that the peasants of the north-eastern part of Catalonia still hold fast to the practices of the Catalan system of family and kinship, and they believe it to be something that differentiates them from the rest of the Spaniards.

As for geography the most appropriate attitude to mention is that of the President of Catalonia. Jordi Pujol, who was the best-known and most powerful Catalan politician for the quarter of a century after Franco's death, showed a love of mountains which were characterised by a purifying and patriotic feature. It could be argued that the love for mountains was characteristic of many conservatives and right-wing Catalan persons, but not exclusive to them. The fact that the belief in the geography of Catalonia creates a quasi-eternal image is an argument for defending its originality and assuring its difference from Spain.

As I have emphasised, religion no longer represents an active force in Catalonia. However, some of its politicians, including Pujol and people from his party, are religious, but mostly privately. On the other hand, many of the Catalan Catholic bishops are quite nationalistic, and in that sense their importance is quite notable.

# 4
# NATIONAL CHARACTER: MYTH
# AND REALITY

## Introduction

National consciousness, in the modern sense of the term (Kibre 1948; Hillgarth 1976), has existed in Catalonia for about a century. It is conventionally accepted that, as a more or less coherent body of doctrine, Catalan nationalist ideology was formulated in the period between the publication of Almirall's *Lo Catalanisme* (1886) and that of Prat de la Riba's *La nacionalitat catalana* (1906). Both works represent, in different ways, the key landmarks of a period in which Catalan national identity was recreated on the basis of the idea of *Volksgeist*. Almirall's work was the first to articulate a number of literary, historiographical and philosophical intimations of the uniqueness of Catalonia (that had existed since the 1830s) into a well-formulated scheme based on the existence of a distinct Catalan character, as opposed to a Castilian one. If Almirall's book signalled the beginning of an era of ideological and political struggles to constitute Catalanism as a force to be reckoned with within the Spanish state, Prat de la Riba's book represented the culmination, synthesis and quintessence of this whole period. The work of Prat de la Riba signified not only that had the idea of a Catalan nation as a spiritual principle been intellectually established, but, more importantly, that this idea had become, if one is allowed to paraphrase the young Marx, a material force that had a grip on the masses.

In Raymond Carr's words, Catalanism was turned 'from a minority creed into the vehicle for a generalised protest' (Carr 1966: 538). Carr sees the electoral success of the Catalanist parties in 1901 as the turning point for Catalanism, but the fact that what he calls Prat de la Riba's 'Catechism', written originally by E. Prat de la Riba and P. Muntanyola under the title of *Compendi de la doctrina catalanista* in 1984 (Prat de la Riba 1993), is alleged to have sold a hundred thousand copies in Catalonia (Carr 1966: 546) is a clear sign that the doctrine was no longer the exclusive patrimony of the Catalan intelligentsia.

I would like to introduce the idea of *Volksgeist*, which is essential for this text. The reasons for using a German term are obvious. I hope to avoid the rather psychologistic implications of the English expression 'national character'. Catalan authors are not always consistent in the use of the expressions *esperit nacional* and *caracter nacional*, though the former tends to have a more metaphysical quality than the latter. The reason for the inconsistency in the use of these terms may well be due to the conflation, in late nineteenth-century Catalonia, of different though related discursive formations: the Humean tradition, Herder's *Geist der Volkes*, Savigny's historical school of law and the Völkerpsychologie.

The idea of a *Volksgeist* as an active spiritual or psychological principle has been an unremitting feature in the history of the Catalan discourse on nationalism. Since the late nineteenth century the existence of a Catalan *Volksgeist* has been taken for granted and used as the explanatory principle by authors of different persuasions. Pi-Sunyer's *Aptitud economica de Catalunya* (1927–1929), Ferrater-Mora's *Les formes de vida catalana* (1944) and Vicens–Vives's *Noticia de Catulunya* are some outstanding examples of this unmistakably Catalan genre. In the late nineteenth century the ideologists of Catalanism, imbued with the spirit of positivism, were convinced that they had found, in the idea of *Volksgeist*, the scientific concept that would allow them to demonstrate that Catalonia qualified as a nation. For example, the full title of Almirall's book was: *Lo Catalanisme, Motius que el legitimen, fonaments cientifics i solucions practiques*. In the Catalanist discourse the *Volksgeist* acted, in the first instance, as a generating principle, that is to say, it was seen as begetting the language, art, law and thought that were distinctively Catalan. The *Volksgeist* was God's indirect creation insofar as it was the result of natural factors operating over a long period of time in a given territory. Hence the nation was of divine origin, and all its manifestations were sacred because they were a 'gift of God'. The *Volksgeist* became the mediating instance between the divinity and human beings. Catalan nationalism was originally formulated in a framework strongly permeated by traditional Catholicism, though not of the ultramontane variety. It was in the logic of the Catalan discourses on the nation to show more affinity with the idea of *Volksgeist* than to embrace the doctrine of the people's will.

As I have already mentioned, the *Volksgeist* was also envisaged as a psycho- logical principle that defined the Catalans in terms of a number of collective features of character which could be ascertained empirically by studying the history of Catalonia. As we shall see in more detail there is agreement among Catalan ideologists in emphasising common sense and industriousness as the two outstanding traits of the Catalan character. It is important to mention at this stage that from the eighteenth century onwards Catalonia had been in the lead in the process of economic development, and that by the late nineteenth century it was the only area within the Spanish state, apart from the Basque Country, to have experienced industrial capitalism on any significant scale.

It is thus important to see the *Volksgeist* as both a spiritual and a psychological principle if we want to understand the Catalanist discourse. As a spiritual principle the presence of the *Volksgeist* is attested by observing its empirical manifestations (language, art, law, thought, etc.), while at the same time the fact that it was conceived within a deist framework explains that it can act as a metaphysical guarantee for the survival of the nation. At the psychological level the *Volksgeist* is seen as requiring a certain type of social environment if it is to be able to display its creativity. It follows then that the enslavement of the *Volksgeist* is not only morally wrong (against God's law), but also socially and economically wasteful.

The image of the spirit of Catalonia subjugated within the Spanish state was dear to the ideologists of Catalanism. To justify the right of Catalonia to some form of separate existence two different types of arguments were used. At a general level, a metaphysico-political case was made for the preservation of Catalan identity threatened by extinction by the ever-growing encroachment of the Spanish state. In this context the reasoning was one of divine right: the Catalan spirit was God's creation and to preserve it was to follow God's will. But there was also an argument of socio-economic rationality: Catalonia's subordination to Castile was thwarting the enterprising spirit of the Catalans at a time when Catalonia was recovering from centuries of decadence.

The aim of this chapter is to map out the different constraints that shaped the Catalanist discourse into what it finally became at the turn of the century. At this stage of my research I cannot satisfactorily explain why the Catalanist discourse is centred on the idea of *Volksgeist* rather than on the idea of race or on the belief in the general will of the people. That Catalanism can be explained, to a certain extent, by reference to the history of Catalonia within the Spanish state is only to express the obvious. And yet this statement should not be interpreted as meaning that the Catalanist discourse is in any way the superstructural reflection of the interests of the Catalan bourgeoisie. This thesis has been widely defended by Marxists and non-Marxists alike and by both Spanish and foreign historians. It is worth noting the extraordinary appeal that vulgar Marxism (economism) has among people of different theoretical persuasions when political expedience requires it! J. Solé-Tura's *Catalanisme i revolució burgesa* is probably the best attempt to defend the thesis that 'this history of Catalan nationalism is the history of a failed bourgeois revolution' (Solé-Tura 1966: 7). In any case Solé-Tura only develops Pierre Vilar's known theory that 'It was the frustrated desire to mould the *Spanish* group in the image of the *modern nation*, with industry and a *national market*, that threw Catalan doctrinaires and men of action back into historic dreams of a state for *them* and of a Catalan *nation*' (Vilar 1980: 565). On the other hand, it is true that an important fraction of the Catalan capitalists did use the Catalanist discourse to further their class interests. For those who see in Catalanism the expression – in the first or the last instance – of the interests of the Catalan bourgeoisie, the form of many aspects of the content of the Catalan discourse is either irrelevant or nonsensical, or both. An immense scaffolding would have been erected to little or no avail: a product of human folly, exuberantly redundant, the unmistakable sign of a prolific and deranged false consciousness.

I believe that nationalism is a privileged semantic field that encapsulates the structure and dynamics of the Catalan social totality. The problem is how to interrogate this discourse, how to uncover the rules of its formation. Nationalism can be envisaged as a geological formation insofar as different ideological layers are deposited over time, but with the difference that past ideologies set constraints on present ones and that the latter may modify the former. The end product is an apparently motionless, but in fact continually changing, discursive formation.

## Catalonia within the Spanish State

In this chapter I have selected for my study a privileged moment in the history of Catalan nationalism, that in which, according to the expression of M. Hroch (1985), an ideology of a minority of intellectuals becomes a rallying sign of identity for a considerable part of the population. The factual information is based on a number of standard sources: Vicens-Vives and Llorens (1958), Vilar (1962), Soldevila (1961), Solé-Tura (1966), Linz (1973), Trias-Vejarano (1975) and Balcells (1996). I shall be looking at the historical formation of Catalanist ideology as the result of a variety of discursive and extra-discursive practices. For those who approach Catalanism as if it were an artificial construction conceived to fulfil the interests of the bourgeoisie, Stalin's dictum that this class learns its nationalism in the struggles to secure a national market surely appeared as a promising research programme. But the economic history of a country cannot unlock the secrets of nationalism any more than can an essentialist vision.

We are so accustomed to looking at late nineteenth-century Catalanism as a sudden ideological onslaught (which requires explanation) or as the result of endemic Spanish particularism that we have never seriously considered an alternative question: why did Catalonia fail to form a state of its own in modern times? The problem would be to show not so much how the bourgeoisie used the national potential that existed in Catalonia to improve their class position, but rather to consider which long-term and conjunctural factors, both within the Spanish state and within the world system, contributed to make impossible the crystallisation of a Catalan nation-state.

Catalonia is far from belonging to the category that Engels, following Hegel, called *geschichtlosen Völker*. It appeared as an autonomous state in the ninth century – an offshoot of the Frankish kingdom. At the beginning of the twelfth century Catalonia and Aragon were unified under the king of Catalonia, both states preserving their own institutions and autonomy. The economic and geographical expansion of the Catalan–Aragonese confederation, first in the Iberian peninsula (Balearic Islands, Valencia) and later on in the Mediterranean area, did not change its basically decentralised character although Catalonia developed a number of distinctive features: a language, a legal and political system, a philosophy and the rudiments of a collective psychology. Ultimately, dynastic union of the Catalan–Aragonese confederation with the kingdom of Castile in 1479 was to alter many of the features of Catalan identity.

Catalan was one of the many languages spoken in the Catalan–Aragonese confederation but it became for all practical purposes the most commonly used. Official documents were written in Catalan by the fourteenth century and an original literature (totally separated from Provençal after common beginnings) flourished by the thirteenth century. Catalan, which is much closer to Latin than either French or Spanish, had developed its main characteristics by the beginning of the fourteenth century. It has been suggested that, compared to other Latin dialects, Catalan is a rather coarse language. And yet Catalan writers, both medieval and of a later date, have considered that characteristic a source of creative energy and distinctiveness (Terry 1972). The incorporation of Catalonia within the Spanish Crown started a period of decadence for Catalan language and literature. Although Catalan was *de jure* the official language of Catalonia until 1716, the political hegemony of Castile within the Spanish state implied that Catalan ceased to be a language of culture much earlier. There followed a steady decline of Catalan literature and the progressive confinement of the spoken language to the sphere of everyday life. With the enthronement of the Bourbon dynasty there began a policy of open repression against the Catalan language (Carbonell 1977).

The union of the Crowns of Aragon and Castile, which took place in 1479, was originally a mere dynastic affair; it was not intended as a union of states, and much less as the formation of a new nation-state called Spain. It was taken for granted that each kingdom would preserve its traditional institutions; in fact the only thing that the kingdoms would have in common would be the ruler. At least this is the way in which the members of the Catalan–Aragonese confederation saw it, and for a while the kings were faithful to the original covenant.

In fact, the two kingdoms could not have been more dissimilar. As Elliot (1963: 6–7) has put it:

> The Catalan-Aragonese federation, orientated towards the Mediterranean, commercial in spirit, cosmopolitan in outlook, had little in common with a Castile whose social organisation was geared to the needs of a crusading warfare and whose mental horizons had been limited by centuries of political and cultural isolation. ... The *Cortes* of Castile, which had never attained legislating power, emerged from the Middle Ages isolated and weak, and with little prospect of curbing an energetic monarch. Those of

was deprived of its best elements due to the repression organised by the Inquisition against the most eugenically sound families. With the obliteration of the elite families both industry and the arts were paralysed. On the other hand, the celibacy practised by the members of the ever-growing monastic orders was denying the country the existence of a strong-willed progeny. Another source of eugenic drainage was the conquest of the Americas, which diverted across the Atlantic all the entrepreneurial and active characters of Spain. To sum up, the degeneration of the Spanish character can be partly accounted for by the fact that the 'natural aristocracy of the Spanish race disappeared' (Fouilleé 1903: 160).

There are, however, other reasons, not physical but sociological, which also help to explain the degeneration of the Spanish character according to Fouillée. The expulsion of the Jews (1492) and of the Moorish people (1609–10) deprived the Spanish economy of a rather active and industrious population. The discovery of America shattered the existing social relations in that it was a source of quick enrichment for a few and ruined many others. For Fouillée this was the main cause of the moral and social disasters of Spain. It radically changed the Spanish character in the sense that people came to rely more on chance than on hard work. This could not but engender laziness and, even worse, pride in being lazy. The Spanish character could not be creative because intolerance and fanaticism could at best produce only sophistry and rhetoric. The motto of the Spaniard is not know thyself but admire thyself; that is why he is so prone to 'donquixotism' and exhibits a superiority complex. A contemporary observer of the Spanish character concludes that, if by the end of the nineteenth century Spain had failed to modernise, this was due to the following factors: a tendency towards overconsumption; social prejudices based on birth without stain, the mania for ancestors (it is only in Spain that a man thinks himself dishonoured because he has no ancestors); scorn for productive activity (toil is considered a disgrace); and ignorance and scorn for knowledge (Bennassar 1979: 249–50). He also observes that the capitalist ethic developed only in Catalonia. Fouillée accepted the idea that, in some respects, the Catalan character was different from the general type that he attributed to the Spaniards. He praised in the Catalans the mental attitudes that have contributed to what Weber could call a capitalist spirit based on hard work, profit, accumulation and investment. It is worth noting that Fouillée's main source of information on the Catalan character was the work of Almirall, an author we will consider in further detail.

As we shall see, Catalan ideologists made extensive use of 'negative' foreign discourse on the Spanish character, while ignoring the more 'positive' statements made by Spanish or foreign authors. The mechanism was simple: it consisted in deconstructing the notion 'Spain' into an aggregate of loosely attached nations under the iron hand of Castile. What was being postulated about Spanish character by foreign observers might well have been true but did in fact only refer to Castile. The growing socio-economic gap between Catalonia and the rest of Spain helped to make this position more tenable.

71

## Background to the Idea of a Catalan Character

The re-creation of a national identity in late nineteenth-century Catalonia meant deconstructing a more or less established Spanish (Castilian) identity. In relation to certain key markers (language, literature, law, art, psychology, thought, etc.) Catalan ideologists emphasised the differences rather than the similarities. I have already mentioned that, in the process of constructing this national identity, the notion of *Volksgeist* was posited as the principle that generated the distinctive features of the Catalan nation, while operating as a guarantee equivalent to that of divine right. Finally, in the area of economic psychology it was claimed that the crucial difference between the Catalan and the Spanish (Castilian) character was the absence of the 'spirit of capitalism' in the latter. Common sense and industriousness were seen as the two basic features of the Catalan character.

How did the Catalans come to see themselves as different from the Spaniards? Part of the answer has to do with what we have called 'national potential'. The Catalans had a historical memory, no matter how numbed, of a past in which they were an autonomous country, with particular institutions and a distinctive language. Under the impact of Romanticism, a Renaissance started in Catalonia in the 1830s. There was a revival in the minds of the people of past glories, particularly medieval ones, while at the same time the vernacular was used for literary purposes. On the other hand, the sustained economic growth that Catalonia had experienced since the eighteenth century – while other parts of Spain were stagnant – was progressively perceived as a differentiating sign that had to be accounted for. It was assumed that factors like common sense and industriousness were uniquely Catalan, but that these characteristics could not find a fertile soil in which to flourish because Catalonia was part of the Spanish state. Moreover, if the Catalans were practical and hard-working people, this should manifest itself not only in their deeds, but also in the history of their thought. Hence the attempt to interpret the history of Catalan ideas in the light of this assumption. Last but not least, it was the idea of *Volksgeist*, as developed from Herder to Savigny, and later on to Lazarus, that was the conceptual framework which allowed the Catalan ideologists to organise all these disparate elements into a coherent and powerful doctrinal body. Needless to say this discursive formation was not static but dynamic, though, as Marx would put it, in any change the past lingers on in the present, shaping its direction and content.

The beginning of the eighteenth century meant the end of the last remnants of the Catalan medieval state: Catalonia became a province within the Spanish state and Catalan ceased to be an official language. These were the consequences of a military defeat, of a war in which Catalonia had sided with the vanquished. And yet the Catalans did not brood for long over the total collapse of the old polity. They seized the opportunity to look at and learn from Europe; they developed their economy, first in Catalonia, then in Spain and finally in the Americas. With the short interlude of the war against Napoleon, the commercial and industrial bourgeoisie of Catalonia succeeded in creating a prosperous country. The result was that the socio-economic structures of Catalonia and those of the rest of Spain became increasingly dissimilar.

Pierre Vilar has put forward a scheme of periodisation in which he has tried to identify the different 'national' roles played by the Catalan bourgeoisie in the eighteenth and nineteenth centuries. The early period, from 1720 to 1808, can be characterised by an integration of Catalonia within Spain. This process was accomplished by an increasingly affluent bourgeoisie. For the Catalans, fatherland, country, nation and state all seem to express the same reality: Spain. The second stage, from 1820 to 1885, Vilar calls 'regionalist-protectionist'. As he puts it: 'This was the period in which the leaders of Catalan industry, having captured the mediocre Spanish national market, and struggled to protect it, aspired without success to lead not a Catalan state, but, indeed the *Spanish nation*' (Vilar 1980: 550). The final period, from 1885 to 1917, is that in which 'a class aspired to the leadership of a state, and, when it saw itself denied the leadership of the Spanish state itself, fell back (without it always being possible to distinguish the role of illusion among its leaders) upon the demand for a politically autonomous, regional organisation' (Vilar 1980. 546).

This sketch has been very successful among researchers on the Catalan question but, unfortunately, it has been used in a rather dogmatic way. Many authors have operated a double reductionism: they have tended to see nations in terms of class, and class wholly in terms of economic interests. The nationalist discourses must then be, by definition, a 'misleading' discourse, a discourse concealing the interests of a class. And what is the meaning of the word 'class'? Marxists and non-Marxists alike often take a purely economistic view of what class is. Hence, when the expression 'the hegemony of the Catalan bourgeoisie' occurs, it is usually interpreted as meaning 'the material interests of the Catalan bourgeoisie'. In this way, the complexities of the nationalist discourse are completely lost, sacrificed to the gods of economic determinism.

The discursive formation of nationalism is the privileged locus where a variety of forces converge or are reflected. It is in this respect that from the standpoint of the philosophy of internal relations the nationalist discourse can be envisaged as the royal path that gives access to the social totality.

## The Catalan Renaissance

The Catalan Renaissance should not be identified purely with a literary movement, though this feature was particularly outstanding. In fact, it was a manifold cultural manifestation that affected history and the arts, philosophy and law, as well as many other aspects of the life of Catalan society. In a sense, the Renaissance was a successful attempt to recreate Catalan culture as a distinctive set of values, symbols and ways of thinking and acting, shared by the community. To say that the Catalan Renaissance was initiated and led by an intellectual elite is to state the obvious: how could it be otherwise? What is important is to stress the fact that the rest of the Catalan people gradually came to participate, and eventually took an active part in this cultural movement.

Romanticism has often been defined in terms of its strong sense of history (particularly of medieval history), its emphasis on popular poetry and its focus on the natural community. It is frequently remarked that the Catalan Renaissance can be explained as a result of the impact of European Romanticism. Yet the question of why there was a specific Catalan Romanticism, rather than a general Romantic movement for the whole of Spain, remains unanswered, unless we bring to the fore the question of the 'nationalist potential'. Romanticism was at its highest during the early period of the Renaissance, between the 1830s and 1850s. It is interesting to note that the Catalan language was not used widely or often during this time, although it was perfectly compatible with a love for the country and its medieval glories. In fact many writers were convinced that Catalan was doomed as a literary language. The climax of this period came with the publication of the masterpiece of romantic historiography: Victor Balaguer's *Historia de Cataluña y de la Corona de Aragon*. This work is an uncritical mixture of legend and fact, written with 'the patriotic objective of remembering a history of freedom and of progress unjustly forgotten' (Soldevila 1961: 657). Balaguer's work was extremely popular as a source of ideas for Catalan writers in the second half of the century.

The foreign author who provided the model for Catalan historical novels was undoubtedly Walter Scott. Some of his works were translated into Spanish by liberal Catalan exiles living in London as early as 1825 (Batista i Roca 1959). More important, though, was the impact that the Scottish philosophy of common sense had among Catalan thinkers. As we shall see, Catalan philosophers felt that the standpoint of the Scottish School was in consonance with traditional Catalan thought; furthermore, they maintained that this could be partly explained by the fact that Scottish philosophy was under the influence of the sixteenth-century Catalan thinker J.L. Vives. It must be remembered that the existence of autochthonous thought was one of the manifestations of the *Volksgeist*. Common sense would become an essentially Catalan philosophy, and at the same time a key feature of the Catalan character (Berrio 1966; Roura 1980).

The Scottish philosophy of common sense was introduced to Catalonia by R. Marti d'Eixalà. He was appointed to the first Chair of Ideology at the University of Barcelona in 1835. Marti d'Eixalà knew of the Scottish School through the Spanish and Catalan liberals, who had gone into exile in Britain in the 1820s, although his basic source of information was the French translators of the commentators on Reid and Stewart (i.e. Royer-Collard, Cousin and Jouffroy). This trend was continued by Marti d'Eixalà's successor, X. Llorens i Barba, who had a firsthand acquaintance with Scottish philosophy, and particularly with the work of Hamilton. Both Marti d'Eixalà and Llorens i Barba adhered to what might be called a psychological empiricism, and were still far from the shores of positivism. They found this philosophy to be in accordance with traditional Catalan thought (the last great representative of which was Vives, though the culture of common sense had persisted in seventeenth- and eighteenth-century Catalonia).

The doctrine of common sense, as a philosophical form of the traditional Catalan *seny* was a manifestation of the *Volksgeist*, one of its defining elements. Catalan philosophers had borrowed the idea of *Volksgeist* from Herder and Savigny, and it was used – particularly in the second half of the nineteenth century – to further the economic, spiritual and political needs of the Catalan people, threatened by the impositions of the Spanish state. By 1854, Llorens i Barba had already understood that the *Volksgeist* is what permits us to detect the whole of cultural life. Without it, there can be no language, no customs, no literature, no art, no institutions, no religious doctrine. The *Volksgeist*, however, is not produced by abstract reason, but by the historical conditions in which a country finds itself.

In conclusion, the philosophy of common sense, associated with the idea of *Volksgeist*, laid solid ideological foundations for the Catalan Renaissance. The idea of common sense, along with the idea of industriousness, which derived from the successful economic experience of the Catalans, came to dominate the definitions of Catalan character, as we shall see in the following section.

## The Catalan *Volksgeist*

After this somewhat perfunctory consideration of the economic, social, political and ideological conditions which resulted in the appearance of the discourse on the Catalan character, we are now in a position to describe and analyse its content in some detail. The first author who actually considered what was then referred to as the 'regional problem' from a political angle was the historian and essayist J. Cortada. As J. Molas has aptly remarked, Cortada might have been a romantic, but his treatment of the Catalan question was clearly modern. Cortada's work was openly polemical, and it had the avowed intention of redressing the balance in the way in which the Catalan character was presented at the time.

Cortada's initial concern was to explain how Catalonia, a country with a harsh and poor environment, had managed to become a fairly productive place. The reason must be, noted Cortada, that the Catalans have succeeded in developing a strong sense of resolution and constancy over the centuries. Another feature of their character, which Cortada considered to be the one that decisively explain the economic fortune of the Catalans, was the fact that they were hard-working people. This trait is not limited to one single class, rather it can be predicated of all the different social groupings. It would be misleading, though, to assume that this feature of the Catalan character was only projected into the economic field. In fact, it was also applied to technical inventions and scientific discoveries, as well as to artistic achievement and the pursuit of fame and glory. It may be more appropriate to talk of the Catalan existential philosophy, which emphasised that individuals should have an action-oriented life geared to concrete accomplishments.

From the initial premise that the Catalans were hard-working people followed, according to Cortada, a number of closely related features of the Catalan character. First, the Catalans had learnt to be self-reliant, to provide for themselves. Secondly, active and busy people were less tempted by worldly pleasures, so the Catalans were basically temperate. Finally, they were parsimonious: in relation to money, with respect to immaterial things and in their use of words. Cortada was somewhat contradictory concerning the question of the future of Catalan idiosyncrasy. At times, he seemed to give an absolute value to the particularism of the Catalan character, but more often he hoped that the differences among the peoples of Spain would progressively disappear. He was against any attempt whatsoever to efface regional peculiarities by force. In the final analysis, Cortada was a prisoner of the idea that Spain constituted both the state and the nation of the Catalans, while conceiving of Catalonia as the 'regionalist' fatherland (*patria*).

In the previous section, I briefly established that the idea of *Volksgeist*, in both its metaphysical and psychological dimensions, had penetrated the literary, historiographical and philosophical circles of Catalonia since the 1830s. Cortada's work was the first attempt to make a polemical and political use of this notion, but from what we might call a strictly 'regionalist' point of view. I mentioned at the beginning of this chapter that it was not until late in the century that Catalan nationalism appeared as a fully-fledged ideology. The period between 1886 and 1906 was rich in nationalist literature, and it might be argued that to limit the analysis to two texts – even if they are by wide agreement amongst the most significant and influential ones – may be construed as doing an injustice to Catalanism. My objective, however, is not to present a comprehensive description, analysis or explanation of the period, but to use these two texts in a symptomatic way, as an indication of a state of affairs which, if treated properly, would require much further research.

Valenti Almirall, a man with a republican and radical background and an early follower of the federalist doctrines of Pi i Margall, represented the transition from regionalism to nationalism. Almirall was well-read in the social scientific literature of the period, and accepted the basic stance of positivism. His starting point was the idea that Spain was a morbid organism and that the reasons for this state of affairs could be found in the fact that the Spanish state, dominated by Castile, was oppressing the different regions. More crucial for our purposes was the use that Almirall made in his key text *Lo Catalanisme* (1886) of the notion of character (*caracter*) in order to explain the decadence of Spain. According to Almirall, the Iberian peninsula had been inhabited since the remote past by different peoples (*pobles*). Disciplines like linguistics and anthropology were in a position to establish that there existed marked differences between the regions of Spain. It is clear, then, that, for Almirall, Spain should not be considered as a single nation, but rather as a collection of nations. As a result of its history, two basic races, peoples or groups were formed within the Iberian peninsula: the Castilian and the Basque–Aragonese or Pyrenean. Almirall considered the character of each of these two groups as polar opposites. On the basis of Almirall's work a table of binary oppositions can be drawn:

| Castilian Character | Catalan Character |
| --- | --- |
| (Semitic) | (Non-Semitic) |
| Generalising | Analysing |
| Imaginative | Reflective |
| Formalist | Positivist |
| Idealist | Materialist |
| Authoritarian | Freedom-oriented |
| Centralist | Particularist |

As a result of a historical conjuncture, the Castilian group had obtained hegemony within the Spanish state and consequently the authoritarian and generalising spirit prevailed. The Castilian discovery and colonisation of America consolidated and enhanced the hegemony of the Castilian character within the Spanish state. The conquest of America, argued Almirall, was an amazing feat of courage and arms that only a bold nation like Castile could have undertaken. With the collapse of the Mediterranean world at the end of the Middle Ages, the Catalan–Aragonese confederation lost its horizon; the Catalan character exerted too much caution in starting new endeavours. In the long run, the American adventure exhausted the energies of Spain. Then followed a period of rapid decline in which only the worst features of the Castilian character (authoritarianism, centralism, etc.) were preserved. During this time of Castilian hegemony, the best qualities of the Catalan character were kept at bay. In fact the Catalan character degenerated, acquiring not only some of the negative features of the Castilian character but, more importantly, not being able to put to good use the positive features of the Catalan character.

The *Renaixença* was seen by Almirall as the key realisation that the Catalan character needed a space of its own, that is, freedom to develop its positive features. The Castilian and the Catalan characters could never fuse because they were diametrically opposed. Any attempt of one character to dominate the other could only produce disastrous results: the degeneration of the social organism. Almirall did not contemplate separatism as a real alternative for Catalonia. He felt that Catalonia (sometimes referred to as a 'region', sometimes as a 'nation') was a firm part of the Spanish state and that the system he favoured – particularism – should be sufficient to 'regenerate' the different areas of Spain. At the political level, this meant an end to authoritarianism, centralism and the uniformity that the Castilian-controlled

Spanish had tried to impose on the different regions of Spain. A much more representative system should be created in which power was shared. In conclusion, Almirall believed that only a harmonious combination between the generalising Castilian character and the analysing Catalan character could give birth to a new state capable of occupying its rightful place in the international scene.

The period of twenty years which preceded the publication of Prat de la Riba's *La nacionalitat catalana* was rich in political developments, both in Catalonia and within the Spanish state. For one thing, political Catalanism, as distinct from a purely intellectual Catalanism, came into existence and became not only an important aspect of Catalan social life, but also an electoral force. Furthermore, the collapse of the remnants of the Spanish Empire in 1898 was the final proof the Catalanists needed to confirm that the Spanish state was in total disarray – a bureaucratic, inefficient and cumbersome machine which could hardly be regenerated. In relation to the national question, the traditionalist and conservative discourses of Manye i Flaquer, Torras i Bages and many others would be brought into play in Prat de la Riba's synthesis, while the more radically nationalist standpoints of Roca i Farreras and Marti i Julia went unheeded.

Enric Prat de la Riba was a lawyer, politician and statesman. He was one of the founders, in 1901, of the most important Catalanist party – the *Lliga Regionalista* – which he led until his death in 1917. He contributed more than anybody else to the coherence and appeal of Catalanism as a doctrine and its projection as a multidimensional social force in Catalonia. In Prat de la Riba, the idea that Catalonia was a nation was firmly established. He saw his own conception of Catalonia as a nation as the culmination of an evolutionary scheme with two preceding stages: Catalonia as a region, and, before that, Catalonia as a province. He accepted the idea put forward by Almirall that linguistics and anthropology provided a scientific basis for the definition of a nation, and that there were basic linguistic and ethnic differences between Catalonia and Castile. For Prat what really mattered were not the contingent manifestations of language, law, mores, institutions, etc. *per se*, but the existence of a Catalan nation, of a distinctive Catalan *Volksgeist*.

It is important to highlight the fact that Prat de la Riba was not always clear in the use of the expressions *esperit nacional* and *caràcter nacional*. Firstly, he used the expression *esperit nacional* in both a metaphysical and a psychological sense. As for the generating power of the notion of *Volksgeist*, it ranged from a comprehensive vision to one in which he maintained that it was only begetting the language and the manifestations of law. As to the expression *caràcter nacional* it was often reserved to explain artistic manifestations. In the final analysis he was inclined to uphold a rather comprehensive definition of the *Volksgeist* as 'an unknown and powerful force which is the same force which appeared engendering Law, giving birth to the languages with a distinctive stamp, creating an original art and circulating the warmth of life through the textures of the social organism' (Prat de la Riba 1977: 95).

Prat de la Riba had, on the whole, a well-worked-out conception of what 'Spain' and 'Catalonia' meant. For him, Catalonia was the nation, the fatherland, while 'Spain' referred to the assembly of nations that constituted the state. For Prat, it was a misnomer to talk of a 'Spanish' state because what received that name was a purely Castilian state in that it implemented Castilian policies, it had Castilian laws and it imposed Castilian as the official language. The distinction between nation and state was a crucial one that Prat helped to consolidate; in fact this distinction became the key element of political leverage that Catalanism managed to produce. He emphasised a definition of the state as an artificial and voluntary political entity. In contrast, he saw the nation as a natural and necessary historical community. The former was man-made, the latter was the work of God.

The synthesis of nationalist doctrine put forward by Prat de la Riba in *La nacionalitat catalana* was relatively explicit in acknowledging the intellectual affiliation of many of the notions that were used. To establish the idea that a nation was a social organism and that social evolution was organic evolution, Prat produced a long genealogy: Schäffle, Lilienfeld, Spencer, Comte, Krause, Schelling and De Maistre. He quoted approvingly Herder's dictum that language was an organic whole, and that it underwent the same processes as living beings: birth, growth and death. The language of a nation was its soul, but a visible and tangible soul. The language of a nation could not be changed without tampering with its *Volksgeist*. A revival of a language means also the revival of its people. Another important aspect of the nation was its law. In relation to that idea, Prat and the Catalanist ideologists in general owed a great deal to the thought of Karl von Savigny and the Historical School of Law. Two of Savigny's ideas were particularly influential. First, each nation had its own laws that were a response to its peculiar needs and idiosyncratic temperament. Consequently, wherever there was a distinctive juridical system there was a nation. In conclusion, for Prat de la Riba, the nation was a spiritual principle that manifested itself in different creations. The *Volksgeist* was formed historically by a variety of factors (territory, race, language, thought, etc.); once constituted it could only be destroyed if the people were physically annihilated.

As nations were spiritual principles, they could not be reduced to racial, geographic, ethnographic or even linguistic definitions. Prat de la Riba was particularly critical of those definitions which, by minimising historical factors, ended up by equating race and nation. Although there is little doubt that theories of the nation were a component of Catalan ideology, it is difficult to assess their importance. We may recall that Almirall's theory of the differences between the Castilian and the Catalan characters was anchored in the Semitic/non-Semitic principle. Some authors, like Pompeu Gener, went much further in developing an Aryan-cum-Gothic myth of origin for Catalonia (McCarthy 1975). In his book *Heregias* (1888) Gener maintained the following:

Only in the provinces of the North and North East have we seen in the race, and in the organisation of the country, reasons that allow us to think that there will be a development of a culture similar to that of nations of Indo-Germanic origin. In the Centre and the South (…) what predominates is the Semitic element and, even more, the pre-Semitic or Berber with all its features: moroseness, bad administration, disdain of the importance to life and time, despotism, exaggeration in everything, the harshness and the absence of medium tones of expression, the adulation of the language (p. 14).

On the racial question, he thought that the elements of the Catalan race were, in addition to the primitive autochthonous, Celtic, Greek, Roman, Gothic and Frank: in other words, strong, intelligent and energetic. Gener had a vision of Spain as a morbid organism and attributed its decadence to its racial debasement. The cause of the degeneration of the country went back to the mixture of races that followed the unification of the country, as well as to the continuous bleeding of the best genetic elements that Spain possessed. Spain had no other solution than that of a scientific dictatorship led by a Darwinian Cromwell grafted into a Louis XVI. A number of measures should be taken immediately: curtailment of the Church power, decentralisation and a progressive move towards a federal system based on geographic and ethnographic units, republican freedoms and education.

As to the Catalan character, Prat de la Riba had presented his main ideas in the *Compendi de la doctrina catalanista* published in 1894. In this pamphlet, he outlined a number of doctrinal propositions concerning the Catalan character: its practical and utilitarian spirit, the fact that it is inclined to entrepreneurial activities and that it is both liberal and traditional. Like Almirall, Prat was concerned with the degeneration of the Catalan character as a result of the oppressive nature of the Spanish state. In his own words: 'The vices which have denaturalised our national character are: the spirit of routine, frenzied utilitarianism, individualism and *flamenquisme*' (Prat de la Riba 1977: 88). If Catalonia was a nation (characterised by a collective soul, a *Volksgeist*), and if each nation had a divine right to self-determination, it then followed that Catalonia had the right to have its own state. In Prat's mind, this was not incompatible with the idea of a federation of Iberian states. On the contrary, for historical and political reasons, it was important to find a formula to keep the unity of the Iberian peninsula. Only, however, on the basis of freedom would Spain succeed in occupying its rightful place in the world.

## Conclusion

In this chapter, I have tried to show how central it was for the constitution of a credible Catalanist ideology to put forward certain criteria which would allow people to clearly differentiate Catalonia from Castile. In the intellectual horizon of the period, a number of empirical criteria were available: race, language, law, territory, art, etc. Catalan nationalists, however, did not focus their attention so much on specific factors, but on the rather more general, mediating, notion of *Volksgeist*. I have also tried to explain why this idea, in both its metaphysical and psychological dimensions, was particularly appropriate to the Catalan situation. There is no doubt that the notion of *Volksgeist* helped to strengthen the Catalan case. With hindsight, it is possible to say that, in the long run, the psychological aspect of the *Volksgeist* was to prove itself more effective than the metaphysical one. There is no evidence, though, that this was also the case during the time of its formulation at the turn of the century.

I should like to make two final points. First, I am aware that this approach raises too few questions, and certainly offers even fewer answers. The domain of Catalanist ideology, with the few exceptions mentioned in the course of this chapter, has yet to receive scholarly consideration. The task is certainly daunting because so much basic ground has to be covered, although Fradera (1992) and Riquer (2000) are of some interest. Secondly, a similar statement could be made about the *Volksgeist*. The reader will have observed that I have refrained from referring to the *Volksgeist* as a myth, although many current social scientists have little hesitation in using this label. In my view, this notion has received too little attention in the history of ideas. Our knowledge of the origins, formation and development of this conception is scanty. In addition, studies have not been undertaken to examine the place that this notion occupies in different discursive formations.

# 5
# GOD GIVETH THEM GLORY, FOR THEY SPEAKETH THE NATIVE TONGUE

❧❧❧

Has a nationality anything dearer than the speech of its fathers? In its speech resides its whole thought domain, its tradition, history, religion and basis of life, all its heart and soul. To deprive a people of its speech is to deprive it of its one eternal good (…) With language is created the heart of a people.

Herder, J. *Essay on the Origin of Language* (1772) 1966

## Theory

### Introduction

One of the reasons why social anthropology and the social sciences in general are unable to progress theoretically is because they are consumed by Byzantine discussions in which arguing at cross purposes is the rule of the game. This is particularly obvious in studies on nationalism. If such a litigious and unproductive atmosphere dominates our disciplines, it is important to ask why such a situation arises. There are a number of culprits that are recurrent, and hence predictable.

To start with, the constant intrusion of value judgements is a well-known feature of discussions on nationalism. Of course, many people are reluctant to admit them, but others pander to them unequivocally and without shame. Many people assume that nobody can enter the nationalist minefield without prejudices of one type or another. Self-styled cosmopolitans are quick to see prejudices in others, although rarely in themselves. At a different level, a factor that has an insidious and persistent influence is poor conceptualisation. It is bad enough when the concepts used are too fluid, but it is much worse when people take for granted that there is a univocal definition of a term. The word 'nation' is a case in point. Many typologies, and we shall examine the well-known distinction between civic and ethnic nationalism, are poorly conceived and hence ambiguous and open to manipulation. Finally, when it comes to theorisation, anthropologists and historians tend either to avoid it or to base it on a single case study. Sociologists tend to be more cavalier with facts and happily generalise from a thin veneer of data that are hardly more than illustrations.

## *Clearing the Field: Civic and Ethnic Nationalism*

Students of nationalism have repeatedly tried to fit the complex and variegated historical reality that they have analysed into simple dichotomies. Often, typologies have reflected a moral hierarchy, with one type of nationalism being morally acceptable and the other(s) unacceptable. Since Friedrich Meinecke (and Hans Kohn)'s classic distinction between political and cultural nationalism – the first envisaged as a rational pursuit and the latter as a mystical one – there have been plenty of attempts to capture reality in such a way.

In the 1990s, the most popular dichotomy was one that distinguished between civic and ethnic nationalism. A classic formulation is that presented by Liah Greenfeld (1992). She identifies civic nationalism with citizenship, and hence she equates it with an open kind of nationalism. Ethnic nationalism, on the other hand, is based on the principle that membership of the group is limited to those who have certain ascriptive qualities. As she puts it: 'their characteristics are genetic'. When it comes to defining ethnic nationalism more precisely, Greenfeld cites 'primordial or inherited group characteristics', traits such as 'language, customs, territorial affiliation and physical type' (Greenfeld 1992: 12).

If we turn our attention to a more popular writer like Michael Ignatieff (1994), we can see that he defines civic nationalism as that which maintains that 'the nation should be composed of all those – regardless of race, colour, creed, gender, language or ethnicity – who subscribe to the nation's political creed' (Ignatieff 1994: 3). As to ethnic nationalism, he contemplates the unity of the nation on the basis of 'pre-existing ethnic characteristics such as language, religion, customs and tradition' (Ignatieff 1994: 4). For Ignatieff civic nationalism is about choice, rationality and realism, while ethnic nationalism is about emotional attachments that are inherited and sociologically irrational.

Even accepting that these dichotomies are essentially ideal-typical, the inference that most authors make is that countries like the U.K., France and the U.S.A. can be characterised as having followed a civic nationalist path in which nationhood was defined in terms of common citizenship, while countries like Germany and most of Eastern Europe would fit into the pattern of ethnic nationalism.

It is somewhat surprising that most scholars should uncritically accept the dichotomy between civic and ethnic nationalism when there are grave inconsistencies both at the logical and at the empirical levels. To start with, at the logical level the category 'ethnic' is inappropriate and ambiguous. It is inappropriate because in its modern use 'ethnic' is not equivalent to inherited and genetic. It is ambiguous because the label subsumes traits of very different character. 'Race' is obviously genetic. 'Descent' and 'territorial affiliation' are ascribed (you are either born into a given group and in a given place, or you are not) and therefore can be said to be inherited. On the other hand, language, religion, customs, etc. are cultural and can be acquired (imperfectly in first-generation immigrants, as natives in second-generation ones).

At the empirical level, the countries that are presented as paradigmatic of civic nationalism often fall foul of the rules of the game. For example, the incorporation of non-white peoples into classic civic nations has been excruciatingly slow and problematic. It is in relation to language (and one could also add culture in general), however, that it is possible to demonstrate in detail that civic nations fall far short of the ideals that their propagandists have publicised for them. A comparative study of the policies of the U.K., France and the U.S.A. shows that these self-styled civic nations, whether in a forceful and clear way like France or in a more haphazard and uneven way like the U.K. and the U.S.A., have enforced monoglot policies throughout their history. The school system has been the main vehicle to achieve this monolingual objective (see Case Studies).

## Language and National Identity

There is a general agreement among scholars about the importance of language for national identity and nationalism. In this respect, it does not matter whether they are primordialist, evolutionist or modernist. But, while modernisers see language in instrumental terms, primordialists see it in emotional ones and evolutionists, of course, want the best of both worlds.

It is Ernst Gellner's contention that under the conditions of modernity people tend to move around and live predominantly in urban conditions. Work requires the sharing of the same language (in both its spoken and its written form) and an ethnic division of labour is incompatible with the dominant liberal-democratic political beliefs. In this type of situation the state promotes universal literacy in the dominant standardised language. Nationalism is the doctrine that requires the congruence between the political and the cultural (ethnic) group. The motto of modernity is one state, one culture. Subordinate cultural groups have two options: they either assimilate into the dominant culture (and language) or try to turn their subordinate culture (and language) into a dominant one through secession; autonomy is a halfway house. It is interesting that Gellner (1983; 1997) never mentions the emotional role of language in national identity, but then he only sees it as a means of communication. It is even more surprising to see that neither Benedict Anderson (1983) nor Eric Hobsbawm (1990), who refer to language extensively, gives much weight to the emotional dimension of nationalism, although Anderson (1993) has recently insisted that Gellner's dry functionalism could benefit from an immersion in the sentimental waters of cultural, including linguistic, expressivity.

An emphasis on language as a primordial attachment has a long history in the social sciences. It is perhaps through the work of Edward Shils (1957), Clifford Geertz (1963) and Harold Isaacs (1975), however, that primordialism has entered into contemporary discussions. It is not my intention to polemicise in general about the pertinence of either of these approaches. I am convinced, however, that, when we are trying to account for the attachment that people have to a given language, purely instrumental explanations are insufficient and some reference must be made to the emotional appeal of their language. In what follows, I intend to discuss three controversial propositions: that nations are linguistic groups, that language is not only a means to convey experiences but also shapes them and that individuals can have emotive ties only to one language (their mother tongue).

## Nations are Linguistic Groups

It follows from this assertion that there are as many actual or potential nations as existing linguistic groups. This proposition is often dismissed for one of the following reasons. First and foremost, it is a fact, we are told, that different nations share the same language. Within Western Europe, for example, Ireland and the U.K. share English, and Germany and Austria share German. Second, a nation may have more than one language – as in the case of Switzerland. Third, at a practical political level, a world with as many independent nations as there are languages would be totally unmanageable (as Gellner says). Before discussing each of these arguments it is perhaps pertinent to say that very few social scientists would defend the thesis that language is a necessary and sufficient condition for nationality. However, it may be heuristically useful to maintain that language is one of the key nationalitarian markers, if not the key one. The task, then, would rather be to account for the negative instances, that is, in Sherlock Holmesian terms, why didn't the dog bark?

1. *Many Nations Share the Same Language*. This appears to be an undisputed fact. Two points, however, need to be made. On the one hand, is it really true of all cases? On the other, if this is the case, can we account for the different instances? I should perhaps clarify that I am working within a theoretical framework that assumes that, from the beginning of the nineteenth century, nationalism (understood as the principle that holds that the political and cultural should be congruent) became a most powerful *idée-force*, with the effect that states aimed at becoming (cultural) nations and (cultural) nations strived to become states. It is an incontrovertible fact that, to ideologists of nineteenth-century nationalism in Western

Europe, language occupied a prominent place. If, however, the ideal was that each nation had a distinctive language, the realities proved more recalcitrant.

In a number of cases, for example, Ireland or Scotland, the language shift has proven to be irreversible. By the time that attempts were made to change direction, English was in the position of quasi-total domination. Neither Irish in Ireland nor Scots or Gaelic in Scotland have been able to occupy the place that nationalist ideologists had wished. However, it would be naive to assert that neither Scottish English nor Irish English is distinctive. Furthermore, even if spoken by small minorities, the symbolic value of Irish, or Gaelic and Scots, for Irish and Scottish national identity, respectively, should not be underestimated. Other cases point out the so-called cultural-linguistic nations split asunder by *realpolitik* and forming two or more states; Austria and Germany are a good example. The Dutch and the Flemish also share the same language, though they have been politically separated for over three hundred years. Do they form a single nation? Perhaps, but either the will to form a single state is not there or, if it is, the international order makes it impossible. As for examples from further afield, such as overseas colonies becoming independent but preserving the metropolitan tongue, this is a common occurrence. In this case, geographical distance plays a key role in minimising the conflictive role of language.

2. A Nation May have More than One Language. Switzerland is ritually and regularly offered as a paradigmatic case of a true, successful, conflict-free nation built on a number of languages and cultures. Two brief remarks. It is agreed that Switzerland is an exceptional case and that it works because it is 'cantonalised' to the extreme and the state is genuinely multilingual. Second, in what sense can we say that Switzerland functions as a 'nation'?

3. A World Consisting of as Many States as Linguistic Communities would be Unmanageable. It would be unmanageable only if each language had a bellicose army behind it. On the other hand, in the world as it is now, linguistically induced conflict and violence are rife. Perhaps an international order based on linguistic autonomy would be more manageable.

## Language Shapes Experience

This could be referred to as the Herder–Sapir–Whorf hypothesis. Each language represents a *Weltanschauung*. To deprive a people of its speech is to gag its spirit; it also deprives the world of an irreplaceable and unrepeatable cultural configuration. Many social scientists dismiss this proposition as romantic-nationalist claptrap. Language is a primordial indication of identity; it has a psychological immediacy for those to whom it is a mother tongue, in that it is the natural vehicle for thought and feeling. Derrida insists that it is extremely difficult to escape the prison of the native language. For many societies, the language problem is also the national problem.

Language, it can be observed, is often an essential ethnic boundary, and it is the defining element of national identity. It is also a way of expressing a difference

86

which applies to both dominant and subordinated nations. A decline of the native language is perceived and experienced as a decline of national identity. This is, of course, more acute when other diacritical signs of nationhood are weak or absent (Khleif 1980). Joshua Fishman (1972) has emphasised that oral or written literature has often symbolised the greatness of a nation. Tales or texts touch a variety of emotions and experiences that are untranslatable. Furthermore, it is the vernacular literature that makes possible the link between language and nationality at the level of the mass of the population.

### Individuals Can Only Have Emotive Ties to One Language: Their Mother Tongue

Of course, individuals may know other languages, but the proposition states that their relationship to them will be instrumental. When we speak of individual bilingualism or multilingualism it is assumed that by definition there is only one mother tongue, unless you are George Steiner (1997: 78) and then you are allowed three mother tongues. More seriously, two things should be asked about true bilingualism: Is it possible? and Is it desirable?

Is it Possible to be Bilingual? Authors like J.A. Laponce (1987) insist on the differences between the emotional and intuitive character of mother tongues and the instrumental, rational character of school languages. Mother tongues are languages of recognition (and hence of exclusion), while school languages are languages of communication (and hence of inclusion). It is one thing to be conversant in more than one language and another, a very different one, to be truly bilingual or trilingual. Perfect bilingualism is difficult to achieve because the two languages rarely have the 'same power of communication over the whole gamut of social roles' (Laponce 1987: 33). To reach perfect bilingualism, the quality of expression, creative ability and rapidity of mental recall should be equal for both languages. Now, in most empirical cases in which two languages are present in the same territory, one tends to be dominant and the other subordinate. The long-term tendency of dominant languages is to displace subordinate ones, especially when the latter are in a weak political position.

It is a truism to say that dominant languages always preach liberty and equality, while subordinate ones talk of borders, security, exclusivity and privileges. (Laponce 1987: 41). On the whole, dominant, universalist languages think that minority languages are not only worthless but also against progress. The irony, of course, is that some of the so-called universalist languages, say the official languages of France and Spain, dismissive as they are concerning the minority languages of their respective countries, adopt (particularly in the French case) an often pathetic policy of protectionism *vis-à-vis* English.

Is it Desirable to be Bilingual? I repeat that the issue is not that of monolingualism versus bilingualism. It is well-known that a sort of bilingualism is common if only because it is imperative to communicate with foreigners, and because human beings are constantly on the move. The presence of two languages in a territory may be peaceful or conflictual; the latter tends to occur when the two languages cover the same social roles and are used within the same context. The latter situation is unstable; it leads to unilingualism, either through the merging of the languages that are in contact or through the exclusion of the weaker language.

Concerning bilingualism, it may be of interest to look at neuropsychology. Some recent studies reported by Laponce (1985) suggest that bilingualism is inefficient and unnatural; it is also costly, as it causes interference, and in some cases may alienate the person from his/her own culture, or from his/her familiar ways of thinking and reasoning (Laponce 1985: 161). If people tend to form homogeneous linguistic groupings, this can be accounted for in terms of minimising the cost of communicating, and of the maximising the likelihood of communicating effectively. Some Japanese experiments suggest, perhaps more controversially, that greater involvement of the right brain hemisphere indicates that a change of language may involve a change of personality, not only because of the different cultural contents of the languages, but also because of the different brain wiring required for processing the various languages.

## Case Studies

The main objective of this section is to study in some detail the linguistic developments and state policies of the two Western European countries which are often presented as paradigms of civic nationalism: France and the U.K. Some reference will also be made to the linguistic experiences of other countries in Western Europe and North America (Hagège 1992; Baggioni 1997).

In the French and English cases, there has been a historical association of language and national identity over a long period of time. This is why it may appear that no conscious decisions were ever taken to promote the respective languages. It is true that, on the whole, the association of language and national identity was protracted and unplanned, though it was punctuated at certain moments in history with protectionist measures. In modernity these measures were more obvious and overarching. The end result was very much the same as that achieved by nationalist movements, and created an affinity between language and national identity over a shorter period of time and through rigorous planning. While it would be incorrect to state that in the French and English cases language was originally the cause of national consciousness, it should be noted that language was an important tool for expanding national consciousness to ever wider territories and to different social layers. Furthermore, there developed, at least from the sixteenth century onwards, a pride in the language and the literature of each of these nations, which was closely associated with national identity and with ideas of national grandeur (Seton-Watson 1981: 95–96).

## English in the United Kingdom

### Generalities

Obvious as it should be to any cultured person, England and the United Kingdom are different entities, and English is certainly not the only native language of the U.K. The history of the domination of English in the British Isles is part of what Braudel would have called the *longue durée*. It started before Norman times and proceeded unevenly and at times imperceptibly over the centuries. It is precisely because developments took place over such a long period of time that it may appear that the final domination of English was 'natural', not imposed.

The fact is, however, that already in the Middle Ages, but particularly during the Tudor period, specific measures were taken which laid the foundations for future developments. The present-day hegemony of standard English in the British Isles has been at the cost of marginalising the Celtic tongues (Gaelic, Irish and Welsh), Scots and an array of English dialects. Hechter's general model of internal colonialism is particularly suited to an understanding of the issue of language domination. The expansion of the English state into Wales and Ireland, and the incorporation of these territories into the orbit of the English monarchy, also meant the progressive presence of English at a variety of levels (military, civil service, judiciary, educational, etc.).

That English also became a lingua franca, a prestigious language: the language of economic progress was all the consequence of the presence of English power. The Union of Crowns between Scotland and England, followed a century later by the Union of Parliaments, sounded the death-knell of Scots, a variety of Anglo-Saxon which was spoken in south-eastern Scotland for many centuries, but which lost prestige after Scotland lost its independence. The immediate reason was that the kings of Scotland, who also became kings of England, preferred London to Edinburgh and ceased to patronise and cultivate Scots. Had it been otherwise, English and Scots would have probably survived to modern times as living, distinctive languages in the same way as Spanish and Portuguese, or Danish and Swedish, have done (Seton-Watson 1981: 96). When compulsory primary education was introduced in the U.K. in the 1870s, it was naturally offered in English.

### The Early History of English in England (Trudgill 1987; Wardhaugh 1987; Grillo 1989; Crowley 1996)

The earliest known inhabitants of the British Isles spoke Celtic languages. Of these original populations two major linguistic groups survive today: Gaelic languages (Irish, Scottish Gaelic and Manx) and Brittonic languages (Welsh, Cornish and Breton); Roman domination did not succeed in changing the linguistic map of the isles. From the third to the fifth century, different waves of Anglo-Saxon invaders settled in Britain; with their coming, the linguistic situation began to change quite radically. By the sixth century, Cornish and Welsh were separated, and a century later the Welsh were cut off from the Celts of Scotland. By the end of the sixth century the Anglo-Saxons controlled the British Isles except for Ireland, the Highlands of Scotland, Wales, Cornwall and the Isle of Man. Another language made its presence felt: Latin. It came with Christianity and survived for many centuries as a religious language and as a language of scholarship.

Although the Nordic, particularly Viking, incursions and invasions were unsettling and kept the affected populations of the British Isles in a state of fear, the linguistic effects were limited. By the tenth century, Old English became the language of a strong and centralised English state. The situation changed with the Norman invasion of 1066. Anglo-Norman became a serious contender to both Old English and the Celtic languages. The fact that Norman speakers were perhaps no more than 20,000 in a country with a total population of about 1.5 million inhabitants was not an obstacle for the official status of Norman in the sites of government, the courts and in intellectual life.

However, by the thirteenth century, English began to show its vitality and was already used in an official capacity both in parliament and in documents. Edward I was the first king to speak English. Other factors, like the wars with the French and the Black Death of the fourteenth century contributed to the decline of French, such that, by the end of the fourteenth century, English had established itself as the language of England. After English replaced French in parliamentary and legal systems, the growth and consolidation of English followed an ascendant path. At a later stage, when Henry VIII severed ties with Rome and printing presses came into existence, the Bible was made available in English and Latin was displaced from the religious sphere. It was, however, during the Tudor dynasty that English became one of the most important factors in the reinforcement of incipient English national identity. The insularity and strength of English nationalism originated in no minor measure with the events that led to the persistent monoglossia of the English.

### The Fate of Scottish Languages (Price 1984; Wardhaugh 1987; Grillo 1989)

It has been stated that Scottish Gaelic was doomed as early as the eleventh century, when Anglo-Saxon was introduced to the court and subsequently began to spread through the Lowlands. The fact that the economic, political and religious elites embraced Anglo-Saxon wholeheartedly was the beginning of the end of Gaelic in the Lowlands. Initially, only the aristocrats in the court and the burghers in the towns shunned Gaelic, but, by the sixteenth century, the entire Lowlands had become anglicised.

The powers in the Lowlands also dominated the Highlands and were able to impose the Statutes of Iona in 1609 and the Act of the Scottish Privy Council in 1616. These pieces of legislation instituted education in English. They also insisted that Gaelic was a barbarous and uncivilised language that must be abolished (Price 1984: 53). Similar measures followed later in the same century. The

Church of Scotland, suspecting that the Gaelic language was a refuge for recalcitrant popish supporters, was against its preservation. However, they had no alternative but to preach in Gaelic, because this was the only language understood by the population of the Highlands.

The religious denominations present in the Highlands were even more opposed to Gaelic, and were committed to its total disappearance. For example, the schools established in the Highlands in the eighteenth century by the Society in Scotland for Propagating Christian Knowledge preached only in English; pupils who were caught speaking Gaelic were subjected to humiliating punishments. After the Rebellion of 1745, the backbone of Gaelic resistance was broken for good. There followed, between the 1780s and the 1850s, the Clearances, which changed the 'linguistic geography' of the Highlands, marginalising Gaelic to the north-western fringes and to the islands (Price 1984: 54).

During the late nineteenth and twentieth centuries, the decline of Gaelic has continued unabated. The Education Act of 1872 made no provision for the teaching of Gaelic at primary school level. Today, some teaching of Gaelic takes place in schools, but is more symbolic than effective. With a population of about 80,000 speakers, all bilingual, Gaelic has low prestige and a minimal presence in the media. It is not used at all for official purposes. Furthermore, the current Gaelic-speakers are reluctant to transmit their language to their children because they no longer see it playing any role, either as a reservoir of emotions or as a means of communication (Wardhaugh 1987: 88–89). Not even in a hypothetical independent Scotland would Gaelic enjoy a higher chance of survival as a living language. It might have a symbolic status, like Irish in the Republic, associated with the historical memory of the origins of the Scottish nation. It is well known that this identity relies much more on other markers such as the specificity of Scottish law, religion, history, etc.

Another language spoken in Scotland is Scots or Lallans. It originated in the court of the independent kingdom of Scotland in the eleventh century; it was a dialect of Anglo-Saxon, which spread progressively all over the Lowland territory. Scots became a literary language, and in the fifteenth and sixteenth centuries a true national language. By the end of the sixteenth century, however, English began to displace Scots. As early as 1579, Scottish households of a certain socioeconomic standing were compelled to possess a Bible in English. With the Union of Crowns of 1603, Scottish dependence on England became more intense. Literacy in English rather than Scots became the norm. This can be seen in the fact that both the Bible and the Book of Common Prayer were made available in English rather than in Scots. After the Union of Parliaments, the Scottish nobility and intellectual class became easily anglicised due to the centralising pressure emanating from London. The school system also began to teach through the medium of English. In the long run, and despite the best efforts of some committed poets and writers, Scots was marginalised and was seen as a minor dialect of English.

In contemporary Scotland, Scots no longer constitutes a language with the potential to rival English in the hearts of Scottish people. Most people do not see the need for a separate language for Scotland, even though they may express a strong sense of Scottish identity. Only a minority feel that Scottish languages, be it Scots or Gaelic, are important for Scotland; how far they will be able to reverse the decline of these languages is a moot point. Some commentators have stated that neither Scots nor Gaelic will survive much into the next century (Wardhaugh 1987: 90).

### The Mixed Fortunes of Welsh (Khleif 1980; Grillo 1989)

Today, even though the Welsh language is the most powerful source of Welsh identity, only about 20 per cent of the people of Wales speak it. Many people seem to regret its decline, but they do not do much to stop it. A few people love the language deeply, while others despise it and find it useless. In Wales, linguistic policies changed over time. Conquered in the thirteenth century by the English, the language of the principality was not much affected for the next two centuries. After the Acts of Union of 1536 and 1542, however, Welsh was banned from the legal system, which operated only in English. The danger of religious separatism prompted the English authorities to encourage the translation of the Bible into Welsh in 1588 – Welsh being the only language understood by the majority of the Welsh people.

The strong anti-Welsh prejudices of the English authorities manifested themselves in a series of measures taken against the language of Wales in the nineteenth century. In the infamous Blue Books, prepared by the Committee of the Council of Education, Welsh was presented as an inferior form of communication, as a language that separated the higher from the lower layers of society. It was depicted as language that was a barrier to economic, social and spiritual progress. As to Welsh culture, and in particular the Eisteddfod, the best that could be said about it is that it oozed sentimentality and reaction. Welsh was seen as a culture that was in the antipodes of modern scientific civilisation (Trudgill 1987).

By 1800, the estimated proportion of Welsh speakers in Wales was about 80 per cent. Today there are practically no monoglot speakers of Welsh and the proportion of Welsh speakers has stabilised at around 20 per cent of the population, albeit they are concentrated in certain areas of the principality. The reasons for the deterioration of Welsh in modernity are well known:

1. The compulsory primary school system, which was introduced in the 1870s, was a deliberate tool to destroy both the Welsh language and Welsh culture, as all lessons were delivered in English. Only during the 1950s were some small counter-measures taken to stop the total Anglicisation of children, but by then the language shift had already reached major proportions. As Khleif (1980: 55–56) stated, languages do not die natural deaths, they are assassinated.

2.  A major influx of English speakers from England and Ireland from 1900 onwards. The different waves of migration into Wales were not assimilated, and in fact, the very opposite happened: the language of the newcomers engulfed the native language.
3.  Mandatory service in the Armed Forces in both world wars for all conscriptable Welsh men.
4.  Migration of Welsh-speakers as a result of the economic crisis of the 1930s. Many of those who migrated were Welsh-speaking teachers.
5.  The uprooting of Welsh-speakers from the Welsh valleys to provide water reservoirs for English cities like Birmingham, Bristol and Liverpool.

In conclusion, it would be fair to state that the U.K. authorities did not persecute Welsh in a spectacular manner. Nonetheless, the failure of the state to provide for the teaching of the language and the lack of institutional supports for this have meant that in the long run the Welsh language has become marginalised. Also, at an ideological level, Welsh-speakers have always been told by people in positions of authority that their language is only good for family and chapel. In short, in the presence of a world language like English, Welsh has historically been given no value and hence not much hope for its future survival.

### The Decline of Irish (Price 1984; Trudgill 1987; Grillo 1989)

Ireland was a Celtic-speaking country until the seventeenth century, in spite of the Statutes of Kilkenny of 1336, which insisted on the use of English surnames and of English speech. With the Protestant settlements of James I and Oliver Cromwell, Irish began to recede. The relationships between England and Ireland over the centuries were based on an attitude of cultural and linguistic superiority of the English over the Irish. The English presence was accompanied by strong anti-Irish propaganda, and progressively the Irish language was displaced from many areas of social life, particularly in towns. Between 1750 and 1850, Irish was practically abandoned in favour of English. Even the Catholic Church preached in English and their schools also used that medium. Dublin soon became an exclusively English-speaking town, and Irish was more and more confined to some western rural areas. Early Irish nationalists did not identify the Gaelic language with the Irish nation. A combined policy of secular harassment of the Irish language and the current appeal of English as a lingua franca made it unavoidable that the medium of nationalist expression would be English.

The linguistic alienation of Irish meant that certain sectors of the Irish population were the best enforcers of an English-only policy. They instituted a process of mockery and gagging, spying and punishment which was directed at all those who persisted in using the Irish language. Such behaviour can only be the result of a people who have been subjected to a long process of acculturation and of the loss of their own self-esteem. The founding of the Gaelic League in 1893 and their attempt to reverse the fortunes of Irish were unsuccessful. English was the language of those who fought against British domination. After Independence, Irish was declared the first official language, with English as the second official one. However, Irish was only spoken by a minority of the population (18 per cent), mostly in the counties of Mayo, Donegal, Galway and Kerry. At present, the *Gaeltacht* (Gaelic area) represents 2 per cent of the population of Ireland, although in surveys 19 per cent of the Irish claim to have some knowledge of Irish (Hutchinson 1987).

The causes for the decline of Irish are multiple. There is little doubt that the language was repressed and despised for many centuries by the English conquerors. To that, of course, must also be added that English domination was also 'the reflection of the economic vigour and cultural buoyancy of the English-speaking peoples' (Durkacz 1983: 214). It could technically be said that by the time the Education Acts came into effect, that is, from the 1870s onwards, the die had already been cast. This still leaves the issue of what would have happened if education had taken place in Irish rather than in English, or if it had at least been bilingual.

At the end of this brief survey of how English became the dominant language of the British Isles, a point should have become clear: this was not a spontaneous process; in fact, non-English languages were eradicated by stealth and direct action. And the reason is, as Grillo has remarked, 'the climate of opinion (...) was hostile to the languages and cultures of the Celtic fringe'.

## French and French-Speaking Countries (Certeau et al. 1975; Gordon 1978; Grillo 1989; Baggioni 1997)

### France

For French people, their language is the instrument by which the nation's personality is communicated, situates itself in history and affirms its creative uniqueness. 'An unusual concern for, and pride in, the French language is a characteristic of this culture' (Gordon 1978: 4).

By the seventeenth century, while Louis XIV (1643–1715) was the reigning monarch, the French language was standardised. By 1700, dictionaries and grammars of the language existed. At that time, the defenders of French already perceived it as a clear, succinct, pure, polite and simple language. However, of the 20 million people living in France at that time, more than half of them did not speak French, only two million were literate, and only about 200,000 took part in the cultural life of the country. Furthermore, the monarchy had neither the inclination nor the means to *franciser* the masses (Hagège 1992). A hierarchical society only requires that the elites should speak and be faithful to the national language (Baggioni 1997).

At the time of the French Revolution, the Abbé Gregoire published his famous *Rapport sur la necessité d'anéantir le patois et d'universaliser l'usage de la langue française* (January 27, 1794). From that moment onwards, there was a clear move towards linguistic unification of France; the state circles developed the belief that to be a true patriot one must speak French. In the same year, Bertrand Barrère, in his *Sur les idiomes étrangers et l'enseignement de la langue française* famously asserted that 'federalism and superstition speak Breton; emigration and hatred of the Republic speak German; the counterrevolution speaks Italian; and fanaticism speaks Basque' (Certeau et al. 1975).

Neither the money nor the teachers were available yet to 'Frenchify' the country. It was not until the Third Republic and Jules Ferry's legislation of 1881–84 that compulsory primary education was introduced that was in French only. Alsatians, Basques, Bretons, Catalans, Corsicans and Occitans were subjected to a process of ruthless assimilation and cultural deracination that started in school and was completed in the army (through obligatory military service). Ives Person has asserted that the French were the most ruthless 'cultural imperialists in history' (Gordon 1978: 31). In fact, the French language has the same word, *faute*, for both a moral fault and a grammatical error.

For France, the French language is an integral part of the nation; to preserve other languages was not only seen as cultural stupidity (since they were evidently inferior), but also as an attack on the prestige and the unity of the nation. The universalist project of the French Revolution was based on the implicit assumption that only the French language and culture were truly universal. According to Schnapper (1991), in the late nineteenth century, the French language was perceived as the soul of the nation. It was not until 1951 (Loi Deixonne) that the teaching of so-called regional languages was made optional in schools. By the 1970s, the 'regionalists' were widely dissatisfied; today they are not much better off. Neither Laponce (1987) nor Schnapper (1991) perceives the recent limited flourishing of 'regional' languages in France as a herald of change in their declining fates.

Laponce stated that:

> The objective of the movement to resurrect Occitan, which was started in the 1960s by totally assimilated Languedocians, was not to replace French by a regional language but to add an exclusive language – Occitan – to an inclusive one – French. If the intellectual of Aix-en-Provence went to the considerable trouble of acquiring the regional language of his ancestors (...), it was not in order to communicate to his grandparents in Occitan but rather to exclude the Parisian, the tourist and the foreigner. He used French as the language of national equality and Occitan as the language of regional privilege in order to exclude competitors seeking access to local appointments – as businessmen, teachers, councilmen, or mayors (Laponce 1987: 27–28).

As for Schnapper, she maintained that people no longer spoke the regional language not because they did not know French, but because they wanted to assert their identity or solidarity.

## Belgium

Belgium came to exist as a state only in 1830. The composition of the state comprised two main *ethnies* – Walloons and Flemish – and a German minority. At that time, and for quite a long period, the elites of both Walloons and Flemish spoke French, which became the dominant language; it was the language of the administration, the army, the judiciary and the universities. The problems started when, with modernisation, the non-French-speaking Flemish masses had to cope with a state that used only French as the official language.

In the past thirty years, Wallonia and Flanders have become separate entities, each with a different language and culture: the region of Brussels is a mixed area, with a growing influence of French culture and language. In this period, starting in the 1970s, Belgium was a linguistic battlefield. The Flemish were accused of using Nazi methods, mainly because they forced immigrants to use Flemish. On the other hand, the Walloons were interested in keeping the status quo and persisted in considering Flemish as a provincial language vastly inferior to French; they had vainly hoped that, with French education, the language would disappear. Many cultured Walloons (Simenon was a good example) were proud of being part of the French culture and language, and even hoped to unify with France.

## Canada

Lord Durham's *Report* of 1839 advocated the full assimilation of French Canadians into English culture to avoid divisiveness. Durham failed, both for sociological reasons and due to the will of the French Canadians. Montreal never became a melting pot, and after World War II half of the population spoke English. Although there were many bilinguals, French was spoken at home. French Canadians and anglophone reformers allied politically and so Quebec's identity survived because it was protected. In the 1970s, Quebec had 6 million people (of which 5 million were French Canadian); Canada as a whole had 21 million, of which 44 per cent were anglophone, 30 per cent were French-speaking and 26 per cent immigrants (who tended to become anglophone). Eighty-two per cent of all French Canadians lived in Quebec; in Montreal, with 2.2 million people, 67 per cent of the inhabitants were francophone.

## Switzerland

Switzerland is a confederation which consists of 26 cantons organised around the principle of linguistic territoriality; each canton, or portion of it, is linguistically homogeneous and has the right to defend its linguistic purity. Furthermore, Swiss citizens have the right to address federal authorities in any of the official languages (German, French or Italian).

In Switzerland one out of six people speaks French (about one million); they are concentrated in the monoligual cantons of Geneva, Vaud, Neuchâtel and Jura, and in the bilingual ones of Bern, Fribourg and Valais. Although the Swiss French speakers write in the language of Paris, they are loyal to the Swiss federation and are Protestant. The rest of the cantons, except Tizino, which is Italian-speaking, and Grisons, which is multilingual (German, Italian, Rheto-Romansche), are German-speaking. Based on the Swiss experience, Denis de Rougemont (1970) and others have stated a number of important and unusual features concerning Switzerland:

1. A single language is not necessary to define a nation-state.
2. A linguistic nationality need neither become a nation-state nor be subordinated by a larger nation speaking its own language.
3. National identity emerges in a multilingual state.
4. The emergence of a national sentiment is not accompanied by linguistic revindications.

Historically, the Swiss example is the one that comes closest to a political nationalism, that is, a nationalism in which the state is not based on a hegemonic culture and language, but which is defined in terms of a political project. The other examples of political nationalisms – France, the U.K. and the U.S.A. – fall very short of fulfilling these conditions.

## Conclusions

I have four general points that I would like to highlight from this chapter:

1. That, without a proper use of the comparative and historical method and of recent developments in biology and psychology, anthropology cannot expect to achieve any worthy generalisations.
2. That the dichotomy 'civic–ethnic nationalism' should be scrapped, because it is logically and empirically inconsistent.
3. That the force of language in national identity occurs not only at the instrumental level, as modernisers would have it, but also at the emotional one. This applies to all types of countries.
4. That in the 'purest' of the civic countries (U.K. and France) governmental policies have aimed, through the school system and other measures, at imposing the dominant national language (and culture), both on state citizens and on permanent immigrants.

In this chapter the rationality of ignoring a crucial fact may appear obscure: that the issue of the Catalan language is of the utmost importance to both those of Catalan origin and those of Spanish origin living in Catalonia. I would argue that my defence of the right of the Catalan language has been done indirectly by criticising the idea of bilingualism (which is presented as an effective Castilian/Spanish weapon). Another criticism was to remember that most nations were repressive, to say the least, of the non-official languages. Finally, in the last section of the next chapter, I will be dealing with the Francoist repression of the Catalan language and culture.

# 6

# THE STUFF THAT CULTURE IS
# MADE OF

ᒼᕞᔒᔕᕡᒉᔕᕡ

## Introduction

Culture is a concept so imbricated within anthropology that it is difficult to think
of this discipline independently of the term, although perhaps the situation is not
so Shakespeareanly dramatic as the title of this chapter might suggest. Traditionally, the concept of culture has been a constant point of reference in anthropology; in the past few years, though, many anthropologists have abandoned its use
or have been very critical of it. However, insofar as the concept of culture was
understood by anthropologists as the way of life of an ethnic group or a nation,
should it not have converted anthropologists into specialists of nationalism, that
is, of an important dimension of the modern nations? The failure of anthropologists to undertake such a conversion is not easy to account for.

It could be argued that authors like Marcel Mauss and Arnold von Gennep
wrote about the topic of nationalism in the early 1920s as a direct consequence
of World War I. There then followed a long silence, in which only the process of
colonial independence of the late 1950s and early 1960s brought a few contributions to this dimension of nationalism. It could also be argued that anthropologists were more concerned with ethnic groups than nations, even at a time when
many of the former became the latter, or at least part of one. The case studies
edited by Fredrik Barth in 1969 in the famous *Ethnic Groups and Boundaries* are
a good case in point.

Since the early 1980s, none of the most successful nationalist texts have been
written by an anthropologist: Anderson is a political scientist, Hobsbawn a historian and Gellner a social scientist. Examining the most impressive twenty volumes

of the period between the early 1980s and the present, none can be attributed to anthropology. At the same time, some anthropologists have become critical of the concept of culture, understood as the mode of life of an *ethnie* or a nation, while others have preferred to use the concepts of global culture or European culture.

In 1952, Alfred Kroeber and Clyde Kluckholn published a text entitled *Culture*. Their objective was to present a survey of the concept of culture and they found more than 150 definitions of the term. The book also attempted to present a synthetic definition of culture based on a scientific perspective. For them, culture consisted of explicit and implicit patterns of behaviour acquired and transmitted through symbols. Unfortunately, their attempt to unify the concept of culture was ignored; in practice, anthropologists followed divergent paths. More recently, the concept of culture has had an impressive impact, at least in the past twenty years, not only in anthropology, but also in the social sciences in general, in political language and also in the mass media. Does this signal a tremendous success for anthropology? In practice, it is only a pyrrhic victory because the concept has been denaturalised, and has lost precision and explanatory power; in other words, for many social scientists it has become a sort of mantra.

It is often remarked, as Claudia Strauss (1992: 1) says, that, in the past, anthropologists conceived cultures as integrated and stable wholes of meanings and practices reproduced in non-problematic form by socialised actors. In modern times, anthropologists became critical of this image and instead put emphasis on the conflictive aspects, contradictions, ambiguities and change within cultures; they also began to refer to negotiation and resistance. To using an analogy from the world of computers, one can say that culture ceased to be conceived of as a program that the individual has installed in his mind and that all the members of this culture share. Notwithstanding all this qualification, though, it is possible to agree with Claudia Strauss that, if we take at random two Americans, they would be more culturally similar than if the comparison were made between an American and a Nuer or an American and a Trobriander.

In the context of postmodernism, both from cultural studies and the extreme politicisation of this concept, the term culture is predicated of any human manifestation. This is the explanation for the interest in such a variety of issues: from drug culture to procurers' culture, as well as the culture of the internet pirates, and a long list of other cultures. It is obvious that the concept used in this way is extremely vague, flexible and relative, so that it means everything and nothing at the same time. Among anthropologists, an obvious and threatening danger is, without doubt, that the discipline is progressively dissolving into communities, especially in the analysis of literature and in the so-called cultural studies. It is a well-known fact that the latter are the dumping ground of critical studies of critical critics, of postmodernists, of political moralists, etc. It is quite correct to enquire, as some anthropologists do, what is left of the discipline as a scientific project? Perhaps the sad and blunt reply is: anthropology is no longer such an endeavour.

## The Concept of Culture According to Ernst Gellner

One of the anthropologists who has used the concept of culture as a basic principle in his works is Ernest Gellner (1983; 1997). For him culture is understood as a unique way of life, a series of features that a human group inherits and shares: language, values, facial expressions, etc. It is a fact that social actors are not always conscious of their culture. It is also important to realise that culture is not static, though there exists a certain temporal continuity. In certain cases, cultures change with great speed; there is also a great cultural diversity at the world level. Each human group not only has a distinctive culture, but is characterised by a social structure based on a great variety of organisational principles (age, class, gender, etc.). For Gellner, these are the two fundamental elements of social life, and they are present in all human societies. The relationships between culture and social structure vary from one type of society to another.

At the political level, Gellner believes that the importance of culture as a great mobilising power is a reality that occurs only in industrial societies. The reason is simple: this is the only type of society in which there is congruence between political unity and the cultural unity. This principle is known by the term nationalism. The basis that makes modern social life possible is cultural similarity; only those who share culture, that is, only those who form a nation, can legitimately constitute themselves as a political unity or a state. This was not the case, argues Gellner, in hunting and gathering societies – where the issue never arises – or in agrarian societies – in which this could happen but where culture has as its function the maintenance and reinforcement of a hierarchical system.

In the nineteenth and twentieth centuries, for the first time in history, 'cultured' cultures, that is, cultures that are codified, scriptural and transmitted through an educational system, were not the privilege of an elite, but came to dominate the whole society. This domination occurred not only through the formal capabilities of being able to read and write, to use a handbook to understand a machine, but more specifically through the fact that high cultures are articulated through one given language and not another: in other words, in English, not in Welsh, in Russian not Chechen, in Arabic not Berber, or in Castilian not Basque. Cultures also possess certain norms of social behaviour. Although it is certain that industrialisation followed specific national pathways (Japanese, Russian, German, etc.), those excluded from the new communities are not kept out because they lack the needed qualifications, but because they have learnt the wrong language.

Gellner also insists on the fact that the high culture of a modern industrial society is not colourless; on the contrary, it has clear ethnic and racial connotations. His cultural model therefore includes a series of conditions and prescriptions for the members of the community. An English person is not only somebody who must speak English and know the work of Shakespeare, but it is also assumed that he is white. The Poles and Croats have to be Catholic, while a Frenchman cannot be Muslim. When these basic conditions are not fulfilled,

Gellner argues, problems appear. For example, a black person who was born in England, who speaks perfect English and who is culturally English is not considered to be a fully 'English' person by the majority of the white population.

The unequal development of industrialism has the effect of excluding certain populations from wealth. If these populations are culturally different, culture can become an instrument of politicisation. Industrialisation tends to generate a set of units that constitute themselves as political and cultural units; that is, the states protect their own culture that symbolises and legitimates such a state. According to Gellner, not all cultures can achieve their objectives of constituting themselves as states; in fact, small cultural units tend to disappear because they are absorbed by larger ones.

Gellner insists that culture is not a romantic trick or an ideology of the privileged classes conceived to deceive or numb the masses. The attraction of cultural identity has profound roots in modern life and it will not disappear with good will or preaching universal fraternity; whether we like it or not we have inherited a plural and conflictive world in which wealth differences are totally unacceptable. Gellner's aim is to see an unequal economic world, with fewer cultural conflicts. This is perhaps an optimistic conclusion reached by Gellnerian materialism. That the social sciences had ignored nationalism for decades is a well-known fact; Gellner's work was short but comprehensive and cogently argued. It is perhaps not an exaggeration to say that Gellner's *Nations and Nationalism* (1983) was a seminal work

## Defining Culture

According to Immanuel Wallerstein (1990) culture can be viewed in two main ways, and one supplementary one. In the first place, as a set of characteristics which distinguishes one group from another. In this sense, culture is a set of values, symbols and patterns of behaviour that a person acquires as a member of a group. This is the widest definition possible, and is not always easy to operationalise. In the second place, as a set of phenomena which are different from and higher than some other set of phenomena within any one group. It is in this sense that we have elite and popular culture, a great and a small tradition, high versus low culture, etc. Finally, as a set of objects (material culture) or as a set of ideas (mental or intellectual culture).

The word culture, as specified in the first two meanings, refers back to the concept of group. There can be no culture without a group that produces or creates it and that is its carrier (*Träger*). Within these groups anthropologists have traditionally referred to tribes and ethnic groups; and in modern times we also speak of *ethnies* and nations as carriers of culture. It is obvious that this does not exhaust the concept of culture, because in contemporary parlance the word is used in many more contexts (the culture of the poor, gay culture, working-class culture, etc.). When we refer to culture, particularly in connection with the first meaning, we think in terms of the following characteristics:

1. Group self-awareness, with a more or less clear sense of the boundaries of the group.
2. Shared patterns of socialisation. Culture is learned within the family, in the school, etc.
3. A system to reinforce values or prescribed behaviour.
4. A certain organisation, which in the case of the nation-state is formalised, and in other cases may be more indirect.

It is obvious that in its everyday use, and even in the language used in the media and in the social scientific literature, we come across expressions such as, for example, Catalan culture, Spanish culture, European culture, global culture, etc. Does it make sense to speak of these different levels? It is obvious that culture means different things in each of these registers. If we contrast, for example, the expressions 'Catalan culture' and 'Spanish culture', most commentators would agree that they are incompatible, particularly if we take the expressions to mean national cultures.

The theorists of Spanish nationalism vehemently deny that there is something that can be called 'Catalan culture' in the national sense of the term. For them, the only national reality that exists is that of Spain; at most they will accept that Spanish culture has been forged on the basis of different ethnographic materials, but they insist that the fact that Spain has existed for over a thousand years has created a new reality: Spanish culture.

On the other hand, those who have theorised Catalan nationalism insist on the existence of a 'Catalan differential fact'. Catalan identity has always been expressed, with more or less vehemence, based on the idea that Catalan culture is something distinctive and original. Language is one of the essential features of Catalan culture, but so also are historical memory, law, national character, popular culture, etc. It is within the logic of any oppressed nation to want to free itself. That is why the ideologists of Catalan nationalism have always emphasised what separates Catalan and Spanish culture; they have actually insisted that so-called Spanish culture is only Castilian culture with imperialist pretensions.

From a descriptive point of view we could say, with Anthony Smith (1991), that the most important function of national identity is:

1. 'To provide a strong community of history and destiny to save people from personal oblivion and restore collective faith. It is a way of transcending personal oblivion through posterity' (ibid.: 161).

Other functions would be:

2. To restore collective dignity through an appeal to a golden age. It is for this reason that ethno-history has such an importance in nationalism in that it

generates national dignity. The idea of a glorious past is a basic element for 'personal renewal and dignity through national regeneration' (ibid.: 161).

3.  To be part of a family writ large which 'gives preeminence to realising the idea of fraternity' (ibid.: 162). The way to achieve and reinforce this ideal is through the use of symbols, rites and ceremonies which bind, in the words of Renan, the living to the dead and fallen of the community, the people of the past with those of the present and the future. 'The ceremonial and symbolic aspect of nationalism is the most decisive to the success and durability of national identity' (ibid.: 162).

Is it possible to defend this conception of the nation philosophically? In his *On Nationalism*, David Miller (1995) has maintained that to belong to a national community can be a rational form of conceptualising our place in the moral universe, provided that it is not based on rigid principles of descent or territorial affiliation. The fact that nations appear in modern times does not mean that their realities are ephemeral or illusory. Of course, nobody should be forced to belong to a given nation, but it cannot be said that to embrace a national identity is irrational. Nations are ethical communities towards which individuals have duties and obligations well beyond humanitarian rights. As Mazzini said, between humanity and the individual there is a need for intermediate social groups, and it is a fact that in modernity the nation has been the most successful one.

Miller refers also to the right of self-determination and insists that national communities have this right, from a classical as well as from a modern liberal perspective. However, the exercise of this right does not necessarily lead to the right to create a new nation-state. As to multiculturalism, Miller criticises the radical American version of it; he defends a flexible and changing national identity. His motives are clear: social cohesion is important to avoid the appearance of tyrannies and the loss of freedoms – ideas that originated with John Stuart Mill.

## Is There a European Culture?

To ask whether there is a European culture and, if so, what are its distinctive features has long been the concern of politicians and intellectuals. This is clearly an extremely politicised area. However, social scientists, anthropologists included, enter these discussions at their peril, due to an increased politicisation of this reality. We are constantly asked to take sides, to make pronouncements, but anthropology, at least the way that I understand it should be, must not enter into value judgements.

If there are different answers to the question of whether there is a European culture, it is largely due to the fact that people use different definitions of culture. There are those who, like the British anthropologist Cris Shore (1993; 1996; 1997), deny the existence of a European culture (an essentially empirical matter).

They think, however, that the European Union is trying to homogenise the different European cultures with the aim of creating a common culture. What the European Union is doing is just following the pattern used by European states in the past, which to say the least is a dubious assumption. Finally, Shore condemns these bureaucratic practices, as more imaginary than real, but his position clearly belongs to the field of value judgements.

If by culture we understand a form of collective life, with a repertory of beliefs, life styles, values and symbols, or, more simply, Gellner's idea of culture as a unique way of life, can we talk about European culture? Before answering this question we have to recognise that the limits of Europe are unclear. Are Russia and Turkey part of Europe? Not so long ago it was said that Africa began in the Pyrenees. In fact, neither geography, history nor any other discipline gives us a satisfactory answer.

I have defined culture as a set of characteristics that distinguish one social group from another. We have said that the idea of culture implies that of a group. It is important to emphasise that there is no culture without a group that produces it, creates it or adopts it. Groups, then, are carriers of culture, and that means there is a certain consciousness of the limits of the group, at least in the case of *ethnies*, and especially in the case of nations. Culture is learnt in the family and in the school, through the media and in many other banal ways. Finally, the group has at its disposal mechanisms to reinforce the prescribed values and patterns of behaviour.

Beyond the concept of culture, and encompassing a variety of closely related cultures, we have the concept of civilisation. This is a term indicating refinement or cultural superiority, but in the way used by Durkheim and Mauss (1913) it means a space that encompasses a certain number of nations, each national culture being a particular form of the whole. According to Durkheim and Mauss, the phenomena of civilisation are essentially international and extranational; they are social phenomena common to more or less similar societies.

The expression 'cultural area' used by some American anthropologists is similar to the Durkheimian definition of civilisation. It follows, then, that if by culture we understand the specific, the particular and the individual, the expression 'European culture' is inappropriate. Europe is a civilisation or a cultural area or space. As such, this civilisation is the outcome of long-term, non-intentional, unanticipated and indirect circumstances. On the other hand, this is very different from the European Union as an entity with a common will to build Europe at different levels: economic, political, legal, military and, to a certain extent, cultural. Most specialists deny the existence of a European culture qua national culture; however, in England, and perhaps other countries, European culture is envisaged as a sort of nemesis invented and propagated by the Brussels bureaucracy with the avowed aim of obliterating English culture.

The French anthropologist Edgar Morin, in his book *Penser l'Europe* (1990), distinguishes, in a similar way to that of Durkheim and Mauss, between culture and civilisation, although he is not always faithful to his own definition. When Morin refers to European civilisation, he emphasises what is cumulative and progressive. European civilisation has produced a number of values: humanism, rationality, spirituality, democracy, science and liberty. European nations share a civilisation, but they are different at the cultural level, precisely because culture is what defines each individuality. Culture, one should add, is singular and specific. The history of Europe is a history of discussions, conflicts and heterogeneity. The question is: can we talk of a certain European consciousness? The fact is that we do not share a past that is culturally and linguistically common; if there is a community of destiny it will be in the future, but it did not exist in the past. For Morin, the future can only be constructed by preserving cultural and linguistic richness: any future of Europe conceived with uniformity is destined to failure.

Certain authors who distinguish between elite and popular culture insist that elite culture is what unites Europeans, while popular culture is what separates them. In other words, the European elites share culture, while the masses follow their national cultures. According to Featherstone (1996), it makes sense to talk of European culture if what we refer to is a symbolic representation, a historical idea which has been developed beyond the nation-state, but which has not represented the elimination of national culture affiliations. In this context it is obvious that Featherstone follows the idea of George Simmel, who considered European culture as the adaptation of a tradition – the Graeco-Roman and the Judaeo-Christian – by a variety of cultural specialists (writers, artists, priests, etc.). In this sense, culture is what people like Dante, Shakespeare, Cervantes, Goethe, Michelangelo, Mozart, Dostoevsky, Descartes and many others produced. But why use the term culture and not the more appropriate concept of civilisation?

An area that appears to unite the Europeans is literature. In fact, many literary genres are pan-European, including poetry and theatre. However, according to Milan Kundera (1988), only the novel has accompanied *Homo europeus* in the past four centuries. The novel reflects a common experience that is the passion for knowledge; this is typically characteristic of Europe. According to Kundera, the 'imaginative kingdom of tolerance' may be an often betrayed dream, but it is sufficiently strong to unite Europeans. As a matter of fact, the European novel condenses the right of the person to a free life.

Other authors, such as the Hungarian sociologists Agner Heller and Ferenz Feher (1988), have maintained that the only thing that Europe has produced as an entity is modernity, and that it came into being between 1815 and 1914. These authors insist that modernity has little to do with culture in the strict sense of the word. Europe has been characterised by the existence of a great variety of cultures based on languages, modes of life and different peoples. These cultures competed, often violently, or they ignored each other majestically. Music, literature, arts, etc. are strictly national; while the English were famous in sports, the French succeeded in fashion and the Italians in opera.

On the theme of European culture we could conclude that the ambiguity of the concept of culture leads some authors to assert its existence, while others deny it totally. However, when we cautiously examine the reasoning of both groups we can see that the differences are not so marked as they initially appear. In fact, both groups accept that Europe is culturally diverse. Finally, it is possible to say that in some countries (England is a good example) European culture is seen as a nemesis invented and imposed by the bureaucracy of Brussels.

## Global Culture

I would like now to return to what I have previously called levels of culture. If by culture we understand a collective form of life, a repertoire of beliefs, styles, values and symbols, does it make sense to speak of global culture? Is global culture the same as cultural imperialism? How does the contemporary world function at the cultural level? Further, if global tendencies exist, are they the result of Americanisation or, as it is often called, a McDonaldisation of the world? A long time ago, Claude Lévi-Strauss asked himself if the whole world would become a single culture. The French anthropologist accurately observed that there were contradictory tendencies: what in today's terminology would be called globalisation (homogenisation) and localisation (diversification). It was not until the end of the 1960s that the world started to appear in the mind of some social scientists as an entity, as a whole.

Generally speaking, many anthropologists were interested to know whether economic and political domination at a world scale was translated into cultural domination. The response was affirmative and the U.S.A. was presented as a good example of cultural influence, as a result of its economic and political hegemony. On the other hand, during the long period of the Cold War, the Soviet Union, which was strong both economically and politically, did not translate this power into cultural domination, except in a rather limited form. This absence of correlation could be generalised, suggesting that, in the same period, France and the U.K. had a cultural irradiation at a world level much superior to that of Germany and Japan, which were much more powerful economic countries.

On the topic of global culture, one of the books that has become an important text, a framework of compulsory reference, is the collective work *Global Culture* edited by Mike Featherstone (1990). In the previous section we have already mentioned the contribution of Immanuel Wallerstein. There are also anthropologists, like Arjun Appadurai, Ulf Hannerz and Jonathan Friedmann, who contribute to the book. These authors made important anthropological contributions to global culture debates in the 1990s. Finally, an author who must be mentioned is Anthony Smith, who made a contribution that was critical and influential.

To the question of whether global culture is a reality, the editor Mike Feather-stone answers that in any case there exists a globalisation of culture; in other words, there exist processes that take place within a framework that transcends national cultures. One must take note, then, about the appearance of third countries, which go beyond the exchange between nations and that have a certain autonomy. For the time being, the present-day tendencies do not suggest that we are moving towards a world state, with a homogeneous and integrated culture. It is for this reason that one must use the expression 'global culture' with great caution.

It is as mythical to think of the past having totally isolated cultures as it is to describe a present of total global interdependence. Wallerstein's contribution refers to the existence of a world system since the sixteenth century; however, as we have seen, his defence of traditional culture as a set of features which distinguishes one social group from another is curious. In the past, the carriers of culture were tribes and ethnic groups, while at present the carriers are nations. Is this 'world of nations' that Wallerstein referred to a past reality because we have moved to global realities? Can we refer to a global form of life, to a series of beliefs, styles of life, values and global symbols?

When Anthony Smith (1990; 1991) refers to global culture, he lists a number of traits:

1. A cornucopia of standardised commodities destined for mass consumption, which are effectively advertised.
2. A patchwork of denationalised and out-of-context ethnic or folk styles and motifs.
3. A series of generalised ideological discourses on human rights, values and interests.
4. A scientific and uniform discourse on meaning: that is, a language of communication and appraisal which is presented as scientific.
5. An interdependent system of communication based on a computerised technology (Smith 1991: 157).

An important assumption about global culture is that it is universal and time-less, fluid and shapeless. It is an artificial culture, close to a pastiche, that is, capricious, ironical, non-emotive and shallow. If culture is always in the plural, does it make sense to talk about a single global culture? Further, is it possible to construct a global culture that does not consist of texts (that is, myths, memories, values, symbols, traditions, etc.) which do not have their origin in the discourses and cultures of concrete nations and *ethnies*? The answer seems to be in the negative (Smith 1991: 158).

On the other hand, ethnic styles and national discourses continue to have validity worldwide. The main problem for the construction of a global identity and culture is that collective identity, like images and culture, is always historically specific. A global culture is an artificial culture, without memory and emotion, and hence cannot constitute a historical identity.

In his critique of Anthony Smith, Ulf Hannerz (1996) accepts that the national dimension is undoubtedly more important than the global one. However, Hannerz emphasises the appearance of a series of people who are not faithful to places or organisations. Among these people he emphasises the presence of symbolic analysts, people in the transnational organisations and hybrids like Salman Rushdie. With these examples, Hannerz means to say that there is a growing number of people for which nation has a very limited meaning. At a more general level, the author refers to the fact that cultures are no longer autonomous and closed, that there is an asymmetric relationship (centre–periphery) affecting the distribution of culture at a global level. Generally speaking, it is certain that there is nothing that can be called transnational culture, but not all cultures are exclusively local. The nation, concludes the author, perhaps will not disappear but will change its skin.

Wallerstein's conceptualisation of the world in terms of centre and periphery has been criticised by Arjun Appadurai (1990), who thinks that global culture is complex and disarticulated. To that end, he postulates the existence of ethnoscapes (referring to people who are always in motion, like migrants, exiles, etc.), mediascapes (the variety of world news of communication), technoscapes (vertiginous diffusion of technology at a world level), financialscapes (instant mobility of global capital) and ideoscapes (the world expansion of Western ideas of freedom and democracy).

A preliminary conclusion that both Hannerz and Appadurai seem to defend, and which is shared with many other theoreticians of globalisation, is that an important feature of the contemporary world is the progressive deterritorialisation of the contemporary world. According to this concept, in this reality everything moves at a vertiginous rhythm: money, people, cultural objects, merchandise, etc. It is not easy to decide if Hannerz and Appadurai correctly grasp the current tendencies. In the first place, it is possible to say that they affect a limited number of people. The existence of cosmopolitan elites is not a novel phenomenon and it does not affect the importance and centrality of national cultures. Another question is that the idea of a melting pot or of the cultural assimilation of immigrants does not function in the same way as in the past. Are we now moving towards multicultural societies? There is no way of forming or holding a convincing answer because the process is not yet decided, indeed still rather undecided. In any case, this is an issue that is independent of the thesis of a global culture.

## Cultural Imperialism and Cultural Hybridity

The topic of cultural imperialism is perhaps a less attractive concept than in the past; in a way, it is clearly connected with the idea of a global culture. In reality, when we refer to a global culture it is often connected with the presence of

American culture as this has attained a worldwide presence. On this point we can all agree, but the problems begin when we try to interpret this fact. The answer to global cultural products, in other words, American products, is not something mechanical and predictable: the McDonaldisation or the Coca-Colaisation of the world. Cultures do not passively accept external influences, but they interpret them, modify them and integrate them in their own way. Recent studies show that responses to American TV products (the so-called soap operas) vary tremendously according to the receiving nation, ethnic group or even social class.

To a given population, the meaning of the most universal images derives from the experiences and social status of the group, as well as from the intentions of the authors of the cultural products. Recent studies of American products in such varied cultural countries as Holland, Egypt and New Guinea show that cultures are not passive receptacles of cultural messages. In other words, they are not a *tabula rasa* on which the invading culture writes its messages, but rather the identity of each nation is expressed in the way in which it integrates or assimilates the influence of the alien culture.

In this context, it is important to remember the anthropological concept of cultural traits, and to insist that one of the normal processes of a culture is to borrow alien cultural traits and to integrate them. A classic case would be that of the introduction of the horse, and later of rifles, within the cultures of the Indians of the Plains in the U.S.A. In the eighteenth century, this allowed them to hunt herds of bison more efficiently, and to resist, at least temporarily, the onslaught of white settlers in the nineteenth century.

Here it is important to emphasise that cultures change. This may appear obvious but it is sometimes forgotten, particularly when national cultures are understood in a somewhat essentialist way. Historical experience shows that cultures are not static, even if in the minds of many people they appear to be so. Cultural change can be endogenous (as a result of the interaction of culture with the environment) or, more often, as happens particularly in the conditions of modernity, exogenous, that is, as a result of voluntary or compulsory contact with other cultures. If we accept the premise of change, we must also accept that cultures are not the sum total of a certain number of traits, but that they are wholes characterised by the existence of a certain *esprit*. It is precisely this characteristic of cultures that allows them to integrate or assimilate alien cultural traits without losing their identity.

I am well aware that to postulate collective identities or culture, as I have just proposed, may create epistemological problems, particularly at a time when we live under the ideological dictatorship of postmodernism. It is obvious that in the past, organicism, functionalism and structuralism shared this kind of hypothesis without much trouble. But how do we justify it today? Here, the conceptual starting point is the polarity identity–difference. In a simplistic way, we could say that at the taxonomic level, the world is divided into cultures and that these cultures are different. The idea of collective identity is also fundamental. If, as I have said before, each culture represents a set of values, symbols and patterns of behaviour that a person learns as a member of a group, one should also add that a culture is a whole that shapes the ways of thinking, perceiving and feeling of each member of this culture. This configuration need not be interpreted in a rigid way, though it could be said that it is rooted in the mind of each individual; in other words, from a biological point of view, there are certain patterns moulded in the brain that sustain this specific cultural configuration.

Returning to the question of centre–periphery, it is naive to think that the U.S.A. is the only centre which irradiates culture at a global level. In addition to other countries like France, which exports high culture at a world level, including to the U.S.A., it is also important to remember the existence of regional cultural centres, so enabling us to explain the centrality of Egypt for the Arab countries, Mexico for Latin American and India for parts of South-East Asia. In addition, globalisation has produced the effect that certain cultural features of Third World countries have been adopted at a world level; this is the case, for example, of Indian cuisine, Jamaican reggae and the Latin American novel.

It is now time to introduce the issue of cultural hybridity. Some anthropologists, including Jonathan Friedmann (1997) in particular, suggest that the general process of ethnification that characterises the nation-state today can best be expressed within the reality that we know under the name of multiculturalism. In fact, ethnicity pervades all the different groups that can potentially be ethnicised (the dominant *ethnie*, the subordinate *ethnies*, ethnic groups and categories originating from immigrants, etc.) It is in this context that the new cosmopolitanism has made its appearance; it is also known by the labels of creolism, hybridity, métissage, etc. If the classic cosmopolitan was the person that transcended the world of cultural variety and insisted on universal values such as reason, science, human rights, etc., today's cosmopolitan is a postmodernist and hence conceives the world in terms of cultural mixture.

Authors like Clifford Geertz and others, who defend this kind of vision, particularly emphasise mass media products (TV, cinema, literature, popular music, etc.) These are areas in which it is easy to demonstrate the existence of mixed cultural roots. It can also be said that this is a kind of discourse addressed to a limited public (select intellectuals) with specific identity concerns. This modern cosmopolitanism aims at preserving the plurality of mixed cultures; the world is envisaged as in constant change, due to the migratory flows that exist at a world level. What is at stake is a kind of ecumenical pluralism that in reality can only be defended by the existence of a world political structure. This is a moralising discourse, bordering on the politically correct. It is a discourse that tends to equate ethnicity with racism, nationalism with violence. It abhors the Levi-Straussian pronouncements which state that ethnocentrism is not the same as racism and that strong cultural identities are a source of cultural creativity. The problem with this kind of cosmopolitanism is that it ignores the process of ethnification that characterises the present moment. It tends to demonise nationalism and ethnicity, and takes its desires as realities.

111

That there is currently a good dose of malaise within the anthropological discipline with respect to the concept of culture is quite certain. The reason for this is not clear, despite the widespread success of the term culture, or perhaps because of it. There are a number of anthropologists who feel uncomfortable with a concept which, according to them, objectifies the Other, which helps to construct and maintain cultural differences: a concept of culture which is presented in a static and oppressive way; a concept of culture which dehumanises because it homogenises; in other words, a concept of culture that exaggerates the borders between cultures. This is the way in which Lila Abu-Lughod (Ortner 1999) expressed herself – an anthropologist who, as Jonathan Friedmann said, confesses to embracing her hybridity. It must be remembered that her voice is typical of the postmodern generation of anthropologists in the U.S.A.

As for Britain, there is nothing new in saying that many British anthropologist are suspicious of, and hence distrust, the concept of culture. From Radcliffe-Brown onwards, British social anthropology has generally rejected the concept of culture. This author considered culture as something vague and abstract, preferring the concept of social structure. For Radcliffe-Brown, culture tells us very little about real relationships. At present, British anthropologists rarely use the term culture – very unlike the rank-and-file American anthropologist. In certain cases, eager anthropologists – and Tim Ingold is a good example – insist that culture is a concept that fragments the world and imposes unnecessary categories.

We have seen that a good number of anthropologists, at least the spokespeople of the new tendencies, criticise the concept of culture. The most radical members of the group wish to abandon the concept completely, perhaps to substitute it, as Marshall Sahlins (1999) has suggested through the Foucaultian concept of discourse. Is there, however, a more reified, essentialised, hegemonic and totalising concept than that of the discourse, with the idea of an omnipresent and mysterious power which penetrates all social relations and institutions? I tend to agree with the bright line of enquiry presented by Sahlins: the concept of discourse has been a fatal acquisition for the discipline. It would be more valuable to embrace the concept of culture, which is not only essential to account for nationalism, but has also, in spite of its limitations and contradictions, provided an important service to anthropology for over a century.

## Conclusion: The Catalan Case

The objective of this chapter was to investigate the complexity of the concept of culture in the context of a complex and changing reality. In many respects, the local, the regional, the national, the European and the global are presented as theoretical discussions in which anthropologists and other social scientists participate. It would be naive to present the Catalan reality from a purely internalist perspective. The reality of the country is multidimensional, and the implication of this fact is often ignored by the locals.

Having said that, it is important to look at the past realities of Catalan language and culture. In this respect, it is essential to remember that they were heavily persecuted under Franco. Franco's regime exhibited a totalitarian philosophy, which meant that any cultural, linguistic or national plurality was totally forbidden. It was characterised by the belief that any transgression or sedition had to be annihilated (Solé and Villaroya 1993: 8).

For the first decade of dictatorship, Francoism exerted a policy of total violence against the Catalan language and culture. The truth is that the repression of Catalan identity affected all the public spheres of Catalan society, from the school to publications, from the names of shops to cemetery gravestones. Francoism was an autocratic, authoritarian and dictatorial regime. The history of its first decade shows without any doubt that the objective of the regime was to demolish the Catalan language and culture. It may be suggested that the situation improved in the 1960s, but this only reflected the growing number of Catalan people who wanted to express their identity. It is a well-known fact that, as late as 1968, the then Minister of Information, the so-called 'progressive' Mr Manuel Fraga, wrote to a linguistic requester the following:

Catalonia was occupied by Philip IV and again occupied and defeated by Philip V. Later it was bombarded by the revolutionary General Espartero in the nineteenth century. We occupied Catalonia in 1939, and we are ready to occupy it again as many times as it is necessary. To that end I am ready to use weapons and have a gun ready for use again (Solé and Villarroya 1993: 217).

At present, it would be naive to believe that the Spaniards have emotionally and intellectually understood the realities of Catalan language and culture. In particular, the growing Spanish domination by the Popular Party (a right-wing and centralist party) shows a governmental policy which is against a decentralised vision of the Spanish reality. It is interesting, for example, that in 2001, even King Juan Carlos gave a public speech in which he denied the aggressive character of Spanish language and culture – a fact that Catalans, Basques or Latin Americans could not accept.

It is obvious that any concern about the position of Catalan language and culture today has to take into account the period following the Spanish Civil War. As we have seen, this was characterised by a period of approximately two scores years during which Catalan language and culture were subjected to a comprehensive and brutal repression. The survival of Catalan identity tells a great deal about its basic strength, which had developed since the end of the nineteenth century. The Francoist period not only aimed at suppressing the public manifestation of Catalanism in the language and culture, but was, if not active, at least sympathetic with a massive immigration into Catalonia that took place in the 1950s and 1960s from a number of Spanish regions (particularly Andalusia).

The return of democracy in 1978 enabled the reconstitution of the Catalan reality. However, the idealism that characterised Catalan politicians and intellectuals would eventually have to come to terms with the fact that approximately 50 per cent of the population who lived in Catalonia were of an 'alien' origin, both linguistically and culturally. At another level, Catalonia became more integrated within a number of different realities: Spain, the European Union and the world. To put it in a different way: it was difficult to maintain one's own linguistic and cultural identity in a changing situation, in a reality in which geography was no longer a barrier. To explore these realities, I will use the sociological research provided by Salvador Giner et al. (1996).

The process of industrialisation in the Francoist period created a homogeneous middle class for the whole of Spain. An additional factor in Catalonia was, as we have said, the immigration from the rest of Spain from the 1940s to the 1960s. A consequence of these two events was the progressive disappearance of the 'Catalan differential fact'. Two differential elements of the Catalans compared with Spaniards and Europeans in general are important: the language and politics (the legal system of the Parliament and the governmental action of the *Generalitat*). As Giner et al. say:

> The language maintains certain attitudes, symbols, traditions and myths which form the core of Catalan culture and that serve as an instantaneous sign to identify it and as a tool to provide cultural continuity for the future. The survival and prosperity of our civil society, of the civic cults, nationalism and language (without excluding certain characteristic Catalan popular customs) are the features which alongside an autonomous government, can guarantee a well-differentiated future for Catalonia (1996: 47).

Finally, another, more confused, element has to be added: social forms or conventions of Catalan life. As Catalan language is the key element with which to identify Catalan identity, there follows a process of language politicisation. The confrontation between the Spanish and the Catalan governments with respect to the linguistic factor is becoming more acute; the progressive characterisation of the people who live in Catalonia into two communities (Spanish-speaking and Catalan-speaking) is an increasing characterisation of a reality which was ideally conceived as bilingual. It should be added here that the linguistic diversity may also correspond to cultural diversity.

The survival of the Catalan language during the period of Francoist repression can partly be explained by the existence of the pre-modern conditions that allowed the survival of the language. However, the penetration of the modern media (radio, television, etc.) and the change in the composition of the population (a massive Castilian-speaking immigration) have produced a notable challenge to a situation in which not only rural people, but also the bourgeoisie, the middle class and the artisans of Barcelona preserved their identity until well into the 1930s. A well-known factor in this success was the weakness of the Spanish state (Giner at al. 1996: 50).

In the context of the European Union and the world economy, Catalonia occupies an area that is undergoing remarkable technological and cultural changes. How will the country be able to come to terms with these external pressures in the context of possessing certain governmental autonomy? In the more specific situation of Catalonia, as a part both of the Spanish state and of the European Union, its future is difficult to predict; it depends on whether primacy is given to small nations, the traditional states or the European Union. This is as far as the interesting ideas of Giner et al. go.

In the international social scientific literature on Catalonia, the Catalan model is referred to as a modern and satisfactory solution to the problem of nations without a state. In this model, Catalonia is presented as a country that is economically dynamic, with a vibrant language and culture, and an open and coexisting society which integrates immigrants, whilst respecting their linguistic and cultural characteristics (Castells 1997; Conversi 1997; Keating 2001). In a word, Catalonia is presented as a model of civic national culture. On the other hand, some local intellectuals have expressed a strong pessimism over the future of Catalan language and culture. They have announced a tragic death for Catalan language and culture resulting from the joint invasion of Spanish, European and global factors (Prats et al. 1990).

Who is right about Catalonia, the optimists or the pessimists? This is not an easy issue to decide. In any case, if Catalonia wishes to survive as a nation, but at the same time wants to have a presence and a projection, at both the European and the world levels, one must consider many of the issues discussed in this chapter. I am not sure of the reliability of the common critique given by, at least a part of, the Catalan intelligentsia, in the sense that it is very provincial and self-centred. If this is the case, they will suffer a serious social shock when they confront the changing world. I would, however, prefer to think that they are energetically preparing themselves to face the great adventure of this century.

# 7
# DISTANT SPLENDOURS, LATTER-DAY MISERIES: THE ROLE OF HISTORICAL MEMORY

Love thou thy land, with love far-brought
From out the storied past, and used
Within the Present, but transfused
Thro' future time by power of thought.
Tennyson

## Introduction

This chapter stems from a long and strongly felt uneasiness concerning two rather different situations. The first refers to the way in which a number of social scientists, active in the late 1960s and early 1970s, had written off Catalan national identity. The second deals with a theoretical fashion which has developed over the past few years among students of the national question, which consists of accepting the working hypothesis that nations are invented.

In some basic respect, both attitudes fail to understand the irreducible, *sui generis* character of national identity, and hence they cannot account for its amazing tenacity and resilience. What they tend to miss is what I would the call the materiality of culture, the materiality of the ideational. It is as if some contemporary scholars have not learnt the lesson beautifully inscribed in a passage written by Mauss and Fauconnet in 1901, which reads as follows: 'Sociological explanation assigns a preponderant role to (...) collective beliefs and sentiments' (Mauss 1968: 29). But, lest I be misunderstood, what the Durkheimian School is suggesting is not an ideational explanation, but merely a corrective to those (and they are still legion today) who give primacy to economic or social structures. 'There

116

is nothing more vain than to enquire if ideas create societies or whether the latter, once formed, generate collective ideas. In fact, these are inseparable phenomena, and it is nonsense to try to establish any kind of primacy, either logical or chronological' (ibid: 28).

Let us now return to the two situations that have triggered off my reflections. First, the concrete historical example of Catalonia. In 1977, a monograph entitled *Rural Catalonia under Franco's Regime* was published. The author, Edward Hansen, was then an up-and-coming American anthropologist who had done the standard fieldwork stint in the Catalan provincial town of Vilafranca del Penedès (the commercial centre of the *cava*-producing area) in the late 1960s. Hansen's general conclusion was that modernisation had eradicated Catalan national identity. Unfortunately for Hansen, on the 11th of September of 1977 one million Catalans demonstrated peacefully through the streets of Barcelona in favour of self-government, that is, the reinstatement of the 1932 Statute of Autonomy. Franco had been dead for only two years. In Spain, the political transition from dictatorship to democracy was a peaceful process that took place in a relatively short period of time. By 1978, the new Spanish Constitution had been approved, and, in 1979, a new Statute of Autonomy of Catalonia was in place. The force of Catalan nationalism had to be reckoned with in the shaping of the new Spanish state; and without the Catalan and Basque pressures there would have been no decentralised Spanish state.

What Hansen and many other observers of the Catalan reality had missed was that, under conditions of severe repression, nationalist sentiments are to be found at different registers from the usual ones appropriate for liberal-democratic countries. Where there is no free press and where political parties are banned, the culture of resistance will, by necessity, express itself in subtle ways. The ethnonationalisms that made their first public appearance in Eastern Europe in the late 1980s came as total surprise to the Western social scientific community. Communism, it was believed, had solved the national question. As Graham Smith has shown, however, for the Baltic countries, nationalism had never disappeared, it had just taken other cultural forms (Smith 1994).

The parallelism between the Catalan case and that of the Baltic countries in the transition from dictatorship to democracy has been emphasised by Hank Johnston, among others. He mentions seven main points of convergence: the vitality of nationalism after many years of repression, the memory of previous political autonomy, the crucial national role of the Church, the liberalisation of the state, the conflict between hegemonic and subordinated nations within the state, the presence of an important immigrant population and the progressive delegitimisation of the ancient regime (Johnston 1991: 202–3). It is interesting to note that Hansen had decided to ignore the evidence presented by a colleague, under the excuse that he was a petty-bourgeois Catalan nationalist. Oriol Pi-Sunyer, an American anthropologist of Catalan origin, had suggested, as early as 1971, that at least three levels of ethnonationalist affirmation could be observed in the Catalan case (1971: 130):

1. At the family level, Catalan national identity was preserved in a variety of ways. Speaking the native language was an act of Catalan affirmation, particularly as it meant fighting against the tide of Castilianisation. Reading books in Catalan was another. This was not easy in the early period of Francoism, but many middle-class families had preserved small Catalan libraries. At a more general level, the family was the only channel of socialisation into a sort of romantic and mythological history of Catalonia. Last but not least, Catalan lore (songs, proverbs, games, etc.) were also transmitted mainly through the family.

2. At a more formal level, a variety of groups (some social and recreational, others more intellectual and cultural) also contributed to the maintenance and transmission of Catalan identity. A good number of these organisations worked under the umbrella of the Catholic Church. These groups reflected a thriving civil society. Typical of such groups were excursionist clubs, choral societies, folk dance groups, cinema clubs, alumnae associations, literary organisations and gatherings, etc. Some sections of the Church itself played a decisive role in the first major movement of '*communitas*' (Turner) which took place in Catalonia in the postwar period. The ceremony of enthronement of the Virgin of Monserrat in 1947 was the first occasion in which Catalans of all persuasions had the chance to express their national identity, albeit through a disguised religious veil. Around 70,000 people attended the rituals in which a variety of symbols of Catalan identity were present. This episode became, in the long years until Franco's death, a reservoir of national strength; many resistance organisations which prospered in the 1950s and 1960s stem from this first popular re-encounter with the idea of a Catalan community (Frigolé 1980).

3. Underground political parties, although of different ideological signs, were all committed to a national (if not nationalist) vision of Catalonia.

It is possible to conclude provisionally that the Catalan case shows that while history was written by the winners, that is, a crypto-fascist Spanish national-Catholicism bent on eradicating Catalan separatism, the losers managed to preserve their ethnonational identity in the ways just described. However, the resilience of Catalan national identity would have been unthinkable had there not existed a reasonable degree of (ethno)national consciousness by the 1930s. This, in turn, was the result of one hundred years of (ethno)nation-building which had started with a cultural renaissance (*Renaixença*) between 1833 and 1885 and had continued in the movement for political autonomy – a process which culminated in the 1932 Statute of Autonomy.

Let me now focus on my second source of uneasiness, which is of a more general type. At the end of the introduction to *The Invention of Tradition*, Eric Hobsbawm writes about the following paradox: 'Modern nations (...) claim to be the opposite of novel, namely rooted in the remotest antiquity, and the opposite of constructed, namely human communities so natural as to require no definition other than self-assertion' (Hobsbawm and Ranger 1983:14). And then he adds: 'Whatever the historic or other continuities embedded in the modern concept of

"France" and "the French" – and which nobody would seek to deny – these very concepts themselves must include a constructed or "invented" component' (ibid: 14).

These are, to a certain extent, measured words, but the crucial thing is to determine whether the balance is towards continuity or invention (fictitiousness or artificiality in Hobsbawm's definition). In the course of the years since the publication of Hobsbawm and Rangers' seminal collection, and in the context of the demonisation of nationalism and the hegemony of postmodernist thought, it has become popular among a good number of social scientists to interpret the book as suggesting that history, and particularly the history of nations, is invented.

John R. Gillis, in a text inspired by Hobsbawm and Ranger, goes, I think, much further than the original when he states that 'National identities are, like everything historical, constructed and reconstructed; and it is our responsibility to decode them in order to discover the relationships they create and sustain. Today, the constructed nature of identities is becoming evident (...). By enquiring further into the history of similar constructions, we are beginning to learn more about who deploy them and whose interests they serve' (Gillis 1994: 4).

## History and Memory in the Recent Literature

This brings me to the main topic of this chapter: the role of historical memory in (ethno)nation-building. We have seen in the Catalan case, but also in Eastern Europe, that an ethnonation which has lived in a politically and culturally repressive state has a pronounced deficit of historical memories of its own nation, though it is fed with a diet of state history which ignores or perverts the ethnonational history. I shall return to this kind of state history later, but first I wish to note an interesting comment which throws some light on this issue. In B. Anderson's second edition of *Imagined Communities* (1991), there is a significant quote from Renan's *What is a Nation* (1882); it reads:

> The essence of a nation is that all individuals have many things in common, and also that they have forgotten many things. Every French citizen must have forgotten (*doit avoir oublié*) the [massacre of] St. Bartholomew, or the massacres that took place in the Midi in the thirteenth century (1991: 199).

Anderson remarks that, since Renan does not explain the details of the massacres, they must have been known to the French public (at least to the cultivated French people that he was addressing). The paradox here is how can have they forgotten and at the same time have remembered? The solution to this apparent mystery is that being reminded of what one has already forgotten is a typical device in the 'construction of national genealogies' (1991: 201). The Renan–Anderson equation seems to forget that there may be more than one memory in action; that multinational states that engage in historical reconstruction with a view to homogenising a given population with a dominant national culture and language may have to compete with alternative ethnonational visions – even if the latter may tend to project a weaker light.

What happens when, as is the case of Catalonia after 1979, with the coming of political and cultural autonomy, there seems to arise a need to connect with a suppressed past, which becomes the indispensable foundation of the *geistliche Gemeinschaft*? Does this mean a return to the era of romantic nationalism as some critics claim? In an ethnonationalism which is forward-looking, would not the idea of 'constitutional patriotism' (Habermas) or that of a 'community of citizens' (Schnapper) suffice? Or is there always bound to be at least a residual dimension based on the ideas of common history, common language and common culture? What has been the discourse of the Catalan Autonomous Government and that of the wider Catalan civil society concerning the (re)making of Catalan identity?

What kinds of theoretical tools do we possess to be able to look at the central issue of this chapter, that is, the role of historical memory in ethnonation-building? The modern literature on the topic seems to emphasise the invented, the fabricated character of this history. Even if this were the case, why are some invented histories more successful than others? Furthermore, perhaps there are other types of history. Bernard Lewis definitely thinks so. In a thin, but significant book, he identifies three types of history: remembered history, recovered history and invented history. Remembered history is the collective memory of a community: what the social group 'chooses to remember as significant, both as reality and symbol' (Lewis 1975: 12). It is common to all type of societies and 'it embodies poetic and symbolic truth as understood by the people, even where it is inaccurate in detail (…) It is preserved in commemorative ceremonies and monuments, (…) official celebrations, popular entertainment and elementary education' (ibid.: 11–12).

Recovered history is the consequence of a retrieval of past events by academic scholarship. These are events which for one reason or another have been forgotten and after a shorter or longer period of time are recovered by scholars studying archives, conducting archaeological digs, deciphering obscure languages, etc. Hence, a forgotten past is being reconstructed: an activity that is fraught with dangers. What separates recovered history from invented history is that, while both imply a reconstruction of the past, the latter (when necessary) fabricates facts to suit a political purpose.

A look at the literature of the past few years shows a growing interest in the issues of history and memory (Lowental 1985; Namer 1987; Connerton 1989; Middleton and Edwards 1990; Fentress and Wickham 1992; Hutton 1993; Gillis 1994; Nutall and Coetzee 1999). All these developments are tributaries of the work of a leading French Durkheimian – Maurice Halbwachs – who in three classic studies (*Les Cadres sociaux de la mémoire* (1925)), *La Topographie légendaire des évangiles en Terre Sainte* (1941) and *La mémoire collective* (1950)) did the essential groundwork for a sociology of memory.

A major contribution to the study of historical memory, inspired by Halbwachs's method, is a collection in seven volumes directed by Pierre Nora and entitled *Les Lieux de la mémoire* (The Sites of Memory); it was published between 1984 and 1992. It deals with the representation of the French national memory. An array of specialists offer us an inventory of the different traditions that have shaped the French national memory. Nora and his contributors follow the diverse paths (republican, national and cultural traditions) which provide a key to French national identity. For Nora 'the memory of the past is central to the identity in the present' (Hutton 1993: 89). This is even more apt after the demise of the communist utopia.

In an earlier work, Nora had distinguished between collective memory and historical memory. By collective memory he meant what 'is left from the past in the actual experience of groups (including nations) or that which these groups make of the past (…). Collective memories evolve with the groups and constitute an inalienable asset which can be manipulated; they are both a tool for the struggle for power, as well as a symbolic and affective stake (*enjeu*)' (Nora 1978: 398). Historical memories are the 'result of a scholarly and scientific tradition; they are the collective memory of a specific group: the professional historians. Historical memories are analytic and critical, precise and distinctive. They have to do with reason – which instructs without convincing (…) Historical memories filter, accumulate, capitalise and transmit' (ibid.: 399).

This distinction between collective memory and historical memory reminds us somewhat of Lewis's remembered history and recovered history. Some recent critics have strongly objected to Nora's idea that memory and history are different, and more importantly to the implication that the latter is superior to the former. Elizabeth Tonkin, for example, does not accept that history is 'just reconstruction of what no longer exists' and insists that 'however carefully and critically historians reconstruct, they have also been formed by memory. This means also that their choice of topic is unlikely to be independent of social identity, a historical construction rich in the imaginary, which claim us all' (Tonkin 1992: 119).

What is important in Nora, whether we agree or not with his distinction between historical memory and collective memory, is his creation of a history of France through memory. His crucial theoretical tool is that of '*lieu de mémoire*' (site or place of memory). The history of any modern country is made of an 'array of sites of memory that have been invested with enduring and emotive symbolic significance'. A *lieu de mémoire* is 'a meaningful entity of a real or imagined kind, which has become a symbolic element of a given community as a result of human will or the effect of time' (Wood 1994: 123–24). However, 'all that we refer to today as memory is not really memory but already history (…) The need for memory is a need for history' (Nora 1984, I: XXV). As to the *lieux de mémoire*, they are 'memories worked over by history, – which is to say, worked over by professional historians who are concerned to respond to the felt emotional and psychological needs of their fellow citizens' (Englund 1992: 305).

## A Catalan Case Study

We can now return to the issue of the role of historical memory in the (re)making of Catalan national identity after Franco's death. There is little doubt, as I have already implied, that historical memory is one of the central components of contemporary Catalan identity (language being perhaps the most important one). The point of departure of my enquiry are the sites where the Catalan nation 'places voluntarily its memories or rediscovers them as a necessary part of its personality' (Nora 1978: 401). Following Nora, I shall be distinguishing four types of sites of memory: symbolic sites (commemorations, pilgrimages, anniversaries, emblems, etc.), functional sites (manuals, autobiographies, associations, etc.), monumental sites (cemeteries, buildings, etc.) and topographic sites (archives, libraries, museums, etc.). The study will, of necessity, be selective, but I hope that it will be comprehensive enough to give a good, overall vision.

### *Symbolic Sites: Two Key Anniversaries and a Centenary*

The reason commemorations are so important from the perspective of nation-building is because they strengthen what Halbwachs called the 'habits of mind', bringing about specific recollections of the past in the form of images. Commemorations tend to be selective, structuring time and space in a certain way. Only a few events and places can profitably be remembered (Hutton 1993: 79–80). Commemorations are particularly useful when the sense of continuity of a nation has been lost through conquest or occupation (and later recovered) or has been changed through revolution. In these cases, a commemoration signifies a rupture with a certain undesirable past. Furthermore, commemorations are also useful when divergent representations of past times exist and where a unitary version of national identity is required. Finally, fragile nations and new nations are in special need of commemorations (Gillis 1994: 8–9). To conclude, human societies in general, and nations in particular, seem to have an irrational fear of historical emptiness, hence, a connection with the past appears as extremely desirable (Llobera 1994: X). This 'possession in common of a rich heritage of memories' that Renan referred to seems to be a constant point of reference of national commemorations, but also of celebrations – which are perhaps more festive in character, but nonetheless as important.

#### A Key Commemoration: 11th September

The 11th September is at present Catalonia's National Day (*Diada Nacional*). It commemorates the fall of Barcelona to the troops of Philip V (the Bourbon contender to the Spanish throne) in 1714. The defence of the city was led by Antoni Villaroel and Rafael Casanova, two names that are remembered with streets in Barcelona's *Eixample*; Casanova also has a monument in the city centre. The defeat, in addition to the ferocious repression that followed, meant the end of autonomy for Catalonia and the beginning of the political centralisation of the Kingdom of Spain (*Decreto de Nueva Planta*, 1716).

During the period of the *Renaixença* (1833–85), the 11th September began to acquire a certain meaning by making its appearance in some of the historical novels of the period. In fact, however, the tradition of commemorating that date began in 1901, when a group of young people decided to place a wreath on the monument to Casanova in Barcelona (*Arc de Triomf*) on 11th September; they were rudely interrupted by the police and sent to jail. There followed an act of protest organised by the *Unió Catalanista* (a political association created in 1891 with the goal of promoting Catalanism) against the detentions; and another wreath was placed on the monument to Casanova (Albareda 1991: 62–3).

It is from 1901 onwards, then, that we can say that a tradition of patriotic commemoration of the 11th September started. The state authorities tended to repress these patriotic demonstrations, particularly during the dictatorship of Primo de Rivera (1923–30). During the short Republican period, in the 1930s, the commemorations were legal and were encouraged by the Catalan Autonomous Government. With the coming of the Francoist dictatorship demonstrations were completely banned and the monument to Casanova was withdrawn (though the street name was preserved). Nonetheless, the 11th September was always marked in a more or less public way by a small but active minority. From 1964 onwards, the number of people demonstrating grew noticeably; however, it was only in 1971 when the Catalan national anthem (*Els Segadors*) was sung publicly for the first time (Albareda 1991: 63).

The tradition of commemorating the 11th September was once again allowed in 1976. There followed a mass demonstration in Barcelona, which proceeded to Sant Boi de Llobregat (Casanova's death place), in the periphery of the city. As I have mentioned above, on 11th September 1977, there was a mass demonstration of about one million people in favour of the Statute of Autonomy. In 1980, the Parliament of Catalonia unanimously passed a bill declaring 11th September the National Day of Catalonia (Albareda 1992: 757–58). It had been customary since 1980 that the President of the *Generalitat* (Jordi Pujol) addressed the country on the occasion of the National Day. Before analysing the content of his speeches, which are I think essential to an understanding of the whole process of nation-(re)building in the 1980s and 1990s, I would like to briefly discuss the other key anniversary of the Catalan calendar, that is, the 23rd April, which celebrates St George's Day.

## A Key Celebration: 23rd April

What does St George's Day mean for the Catalans? It is essentially a day on which all those who either are Catalans by birth or live and work in Catalonia and want to be Catalans feel a certain sense of pride in themselves. The 23rd April is not only a celebration of the patron saint of Catalonia; it was also chosen because it coincides with the anniversary of the death of two great writers: Shakespeare and Cervantes. The image projected by the day's events is fundamentally a festive one. The towns of Catalonia, but particularly Barcelona, awaken to hectic cultural activity, which will last until late in the day. To the superficial observer the 23rd April will appear as just another, perhaps glorified, book fair – which the innumerable street bookstalls confirm. In fact, the 23rd April is much more than a book fair because, alongside books, red roses and Catalan flags are present. On 23d April, it is customary to buy a book and a rose (decorated with a small red and yellow ribbon) for loved ones. St George's Day is an extremely popular festivity that brings together natives and immigrants. In Barcelona, thousands of people participate in the ritual struggle through one of the crowded street, the *Ramblas*, to choose the right book (and rose) for loved ones (including oneself).

The celebration contributes in no minor way to the creation of a sense of community, even if diffuse, which is focused not on past values but on perennial ones. Two essential values are enhanced here: cultural sensibility and amity. These are features that are typically based not on the principle of ethnic exclusion, but on the idea of integration: they generate what has recently been labelled civic nationalism. By focusing on universalist values (literary appreciation and love of others) it is possible to transcend the dangers of chauvinism which are present in all nationalisms (Durkheim dixit). The success of Book Day (*Diada del Llibre*) prompted the *Generalitat* of Catalonia to undertake two initiatives at the international level: first, to send a book by a Catalan author in translation, as well as a rose, to a select list of world heads of state on 23rd April; second, to suggest to UNESCO that the 23rd April should become International Book Day.

The contrasts between 23rd April and 11th September could not be more striking, and can be expressed in the following list of opposites:

| 23rd April | 11th September |
| --- | --- |
| Popular | Official |
| Universalist | Particularist |
| Present-oriented | Past-oriented |
| Non-heroic | Heroic |
| Profane | Sacred |
| Civic | Ethnic |
| Culture of leisure | Culture of resistance and love and grievance |

### The 11th September Speeches of Jordi Pujol

I have mentioned above that, in the context of the commemoration of the National Day of Catalonia, I would refer to the speeches of Jordi Pujol (1993). In many respects Pujol is no ordinary politician. He presided over the *Generalitat* (the Catalan Autonomous Government) from 1980 until at least 2001, having won five successive elections – which is no mean achievement. A medical doctor by training, he was always a man of strong religious and nationalist convictions. He was active in the resistance movement against Franco from the 1950s, and he spent some three years in jail for his political activities. In the 1960s, without abandoning politics, he was involved in policies of nation-building (*fer país*) at economic and cultural levels.

Pujol represented the political centre, and evolved later from a social democratic positions to a more liberal one. He was the unchallenged leader of CiU (a coalition which governed Catalonia at least from 1980 to 2003). Concerning the Catalan national question, Pujol pursued a policy of both firmness and compromise *vis-à-vis* the Spanish state. Although not in favour of immediate independence, he was still in favour of taking the Statute of Autonomy to its virtual limits. An astute politician, Pujol had a clear European vocation and saw in the European Union a Europe of the regions in which small stateless nations like Catalonia could flourish and be free. Although neither a prolific nor an intellectual writer, his books and his collections of speeches were politically cunning and historiographically sophisticated; they are also an indispensable tool for the understanding of contemporary developments in Catalonia

What were, then, the leitmotivs of Pujol's 11th September speeches? At one immediate level, the 11th September commemorated not a defeat, but the heroic deeds and sacrifices of the Catalans nearly 300 years ago. In the face of an overwhelmingly superior army of foreign invaders, the Catalans defended the will to survive as a people, as a nation. Hence, the 11th September honours the brave ancestors of the Catalan people of today. From a more contemporary perspective, the commemoration implies the will to maintain a country with a millennial history, a common culture, a common language and common institutions. Of course, each historical period has commemorated the 11th September in different ways: the 1940s to the 1960s was a time of resistance, the 1970s a time of popular mobilisations and the 1980s and 1990s a time to consolidate Catalan autonomy.

The heroic register was not the only one mentioned by Pujol. In many of his speeches he asked rhetorically what happened on the 12th September 1714. The answer is that on that day the Catalans went back to work; that is, they channelled their energies in productive directions. This was not a betrayal of lofty ideals, but a reflection of Catalan pragmatism. In this way they reconstructed, through their own efforts, a country which had been ravaged by a cruel war. This can only be done by a people that is self-confident and that is willing to keep its language and culture in the face of adversity. This was a collective effort undertaken by a hard-working people with a civic spirit.

These two features of heroism and tenacity, which constitute the essence that can be distilled from this episode of Catalan history, are not all that Pujol wanted

125

to emphasise. He also looked at three current variables: economic progress, social integration and autonomic development. In relation to economic progress, the speeches obviously reflected the vagaries of the growth and decline of the GNP, the level of unemployment, the degree of competitiveness of the country, etc. Perhaps the main message here was the attempt to infuse self-confidence in the historically demonstrated economic abilities of the Catalan people. As a convinced European, Pujol also believed that modernisation means Europeanisation: that the country has to prepare itself to compete advantageously in the EEC.

Social integration, that is, the fate of the immigrant population in Catalonia, was another leitmotiv of the speeches. As I have mentioned before, this was an old concern of Pujol, who, in 1965, had already stated that 'a Catalan is whoever lives and works in Catalonia and wishes to be Catalan'. The danger of the creation of two opposed communities is what prompted Pujol's attempt to integrate the immigrant population in a democratic way. Concerning autonomic development, the speeches reflected the constant battle with the central government over the speedy implementation of the Statute of Autonomy. This was a theme that appeared every year and that reflected the frustration of the stop–go policies of the state. However, Pujol did not disappear; rather he showed an amazing amount of tenacity in pursuit of higher levels of autonomy short of independence. According to Pujol, the events of 1989 in Eastern Europe gave a boost to the rights of peoples to self-government. In this sense, he asserted the right of the Catalan people to see in recent events a new justification and a reinforcement of its national claims. On the positive side, the Statute of Autonomy guaranteed the Catalans a number of achievements. Linguistic progress was an obvious one, following on from the Law of Linguistic Normalisation of 1983 as it did (by 1986, of the people living in Catalonia, 90 per cent understood Catalan, 64 per cent spoke it, 60 per cent read it and 31 per cent wrote it). The Law of Linguistic Politics of 1998, however, was much more controversial (Argelaguet 1998).

A final point is worth mentioning. Pujol was well aware of the importance of commemorations as a means of preserving identity and enhancing patriotism. He often emphasised the importance of origins, using organic metaphors (trees, roots). History is essential for the making of the nation. In his speeches, there were often references to other commemorations sponsored by the *Generalitat*: the one thousandth anniversary of the birth of Catalonia out of the Carolingian matrix in 1988, the centenary of the *Bases de Manresa* in 1992, etc.

### A Centenary Commemoration: The *Bases de Manresa*

The Centenary of the *Bases de Manresa* (First Convention for Catalan Autonomy) was celebrated in 1992. Although there was an official initiative for the commemoration which stemmed from the *Generalitat*, there were also active voices arising from the Catalan civil society. The Managing Committee of the Centenary consisted of a variety of literary, recreational, sporting, cultural and political organisations; more than seven hundred non-governmental groups adhered to the commemoration and signed a document putting forward a number of demands, which essentially amounted to a manifesto for the self-determination of the Catalan nation. The fact that the Centenary of the *Bases de Manresa* coincided with the year of the Olympic Games meant that the celebrations of the former were largely eclipsed by the multitudinous repercussions of the sporting event. In any case, the Olympic Games could hardly be instrumentalised as a purely Catalan happening, while the *Bases de Manresa* could.

Independently of the way in which the *Bases de Manresa* have been historically interpreted, it is clear that there is a tendency to see them, in the words of Rovira i Virgili, as a conservative combination of federalism and traditionalism. Nonetheless, the document represented the starting point of the Catalan claims for self-government that would eventually lead to the Statutes of Autonomy of 1932 and 1979. It is in that sense that the document constitutes an important milestone in the annals of Catalan historiography. In spite of its limitations, the document came to symbolise the nationalist demands of Catalonia.

It would, of course, be historically naive to expect that the *Bases de Manresa* were unanimously accepted, although they were the political platform of the *Unió Catalanista*. Indeed, a leading Catalanist like Valentí Almirall did not participate in the production of or contribute doctrinally to the document. Nonetheless, the participants represented a wide range of middle class opinion; in addition, the most influential Catalan intellectuals of the time were also present. The political moment was also appropriate because the 1890s were a period of expansion for the Catalan political press. An initiative like the *Bases de Manresa* was bound to have an echo through the media. Doctrinally, many of the statements on Catalan nationalism uttered in the 1890s and later are concrete reflections of the general principles exposed in the *Bases de Manresa*. It is also worth remembering that the famous *Compendi de doctrina catalanista* (a catechism of Catalan nationalism), written by Prat de la Riba and Muntanyola in the form of questions and answers, was published in 1894 and that 100,000 of copies of this were printed.

On the other hand, the reactions of the Spanish politicians were predictably hostile, rejecting the moderate home rule programme of the document. For many years, the *Bases de Manresa* were envisaged by the Spanish centre as the first well-articulated manifestation of a dissenting particularism. However, from the point of view of the Spanish state, the project was more utopian than illegal. The animosity against the *Bases de Manresa* continued unabated during the first third of the twentieth century: when the Francoist troops conquered the city of Manresa in 1939, the Falangist press reminded its inhabitants of the negative role that their city had played in the 'deplorable political process' of Catalan separatism (Figueres 1992: 48).

The commemoration of the *Bases de Manresa* consisted essentially in an itinerant exhibition, a series of lectures and a number of publications (Figueres 1992; Termes and Colomines 1992; Ferrer 1993). The media covered these events, which culminated in a formal ceremony, presided over by Jordi Pujol, on the 25th March 1995. Perhaps the pinnacle of the commemorations of the centenary was the roving historical *pièce de résistance* display, which was visited by more than 100,000 people. The catalogue printed to accompany the exhibition was divided into four major sections: origins of Catalanism (1868–1914), Catalan society (same period), biographies of illustrious Catalans and symbols of Catalan identity. It is plain that the catalogue's objective is to enlighten, perhaps at a rather crude level, a population which is largely ignorant of Catalan history. Ethnonation-building is the term that comes to mind when assessing the content of the exhibition. On the other hand, some critics (Martinez-Fiol 1993: 48) have suggested that the whole thing should be seen as an exercise aimed at glorifying Pujol and his nationalist policies.

It may well be the case that the exhibition portrays the Catalan past in a selective way, but the purpose of commemorations is not strictly academic, rather political. The question is whether what is conveyed is an invented history or a recovered history – to use Lewis's terms. In the present circumstances, nationalist mythology may be both unacceptable and counter-productive. On the other hand, to highlight certain episodes of history for political purposes may be permissible, provided that it does not involve blatant distortions.

### *Functional Sites: Spanish and Catalan History Textbooks. The Catalan* Historikerstreit *(a Dispute Among Historians)*

From what I have said previously, it is already well-established that in the Catalan case Prazauskas' statement that 'historical memory is generally the central component of national identity' (Prazauskas 1994: 159) holds well. In modern societies, a crucial aspect of historical memory is incorporated into history textbooks or manuals. Pierre Nora, in his *Lieux de la mémoire*, offers a number of examples of such texts from the history of France: from Lavisse's *Histoire de France Cours Moyen* to Bruno's *Le Tour de la France par deux enfants*. The role of these texts cannot be overemphasised: millions of copies were sold and many generations of French children were brought up with them.

Under a culturally repressive and uniformist system, such as the one that characterised Franco's Spain, history textbooks reflect a rigid vision of the past which in Spain was seen through what I have called before a quasi-fascist, national-Catholic conception of Spain. There was no room for a counter-history, except in the recesses of the family or in small informal groups. An examination of the history textbooks used in the Spanish secondary school system through Franco's dictatorship showed a remarkable thematic and ideological persistence, well into the 1960s.

How was history taught during the early Francoist period, that is, between 1939 and 1959 (Valls 1984)? In the secondary school system the core of the teaching of history was essentially focused on the History of Spain, though World

History was also part of the curriculum. Textbooks reflected a strictly traditional, conservative and reactionary standpoint. The ideological axis was an ultramontane Catholicism for which Reform and Enlightenment, as well as liberalism, democracy and socialism, were the anathema. The sources of such history were nineteenth-century authoritarian, ultra-Catholic Spanish thinkers such as Donoso Cortés and Menéndez y Pelayo, and twentieth-century proto-fascist ones such as Ramiro de Maeztu.

The ideological bias for the teaching of the History of Spain was essentially Catholic fundamentalism, and only subsidiarily fascism (perhaps the centrality of the idea of 'Empire' was the main contribution of fascist origin). The History of Spain was presented as centred on two main ideas: that of 'Catholicism' – which is what constitutes the essence of Spanishness – and that of 'nationalism' – considered as a mentality, as a collective mind which transcends the will of the individuals; the fatherland (*patria*) was conceived as a precipitate of history, and hence tradition was a central concept. Alongside these two ideological elements there was also a chauvinist and xenophobic distrust of all that is foreign; European ideas (and by that was meant particularly the Enlightenment) were seen as a threat to the 'eternal essence' of Spain.

In this conception of Spain, which is seen as the result of embedded historical traditions, there is no room for political and cultural pluralism. The idea of an integral, unitarian and centralised state is firmly entrenched in the Francoist conception of things. As the enemies of Spain were liberalism, communism and separatism, their defeat meant that they could be obliterated. The History of Spain taught at secondary school level conveyed a teleological conception of Spain as the fundamental and unrenounceable feature of Spanishness.

Although Roman Spain prefigures the future reality of the country, by focusing on the Visigothic period as the founding of Spain, the two key elements of Spanish history were emphasised: the conversion to Catholicism of King Recared and the territorial unity of Spain. The idea that the Spanish character (*Volksgeist*) was shaped at that time is typical of late nineteenth-century and early twentieth-century conservative thought, and was incorporated into the history curriculum. In this conception, the will of the people is irrelevant; what matters is the objective existence of a fatherland with a 'spirit' that dominates. In this way, there was no room for any separatist region/nation trying to constitute an independent state or to reorganise Spain along federalist lines, because the idea of a unitarian Spain was unchallengeable. The period of Muslim domination tended to be glossed over, and in any case the multiplicity of Christian Kingdoms (Northern versus Pyrenean) in the peninsula is not envisaged as a factor of dispersion, because they shared Christian religious ideals and they were united in their attempts to overthrow Muslim rule. The distinctiveness of Catalonia and the Basque Country were generally ignored.

The period of Ferdinand and Isabella, the so-called Catholic Kings, was central in all school textbooks. They were presented as having created the territorial unity of Spain (conquest of Granada and the annexation of Navarra), the national unity of Spain (the union of the Crown of Aragon and the Kingdom of Castile) and the religious unity of Spain (expulsion of Jews and *Moriscos*). From that moment onwards (fifteenth to sixteenth centuries), Spain becomes a 'unity of destiny' (*unidad de destino en lo universal*), with an imperial mission that was the defence and spread of Christianity, as well as a sense of grandeur (justification of Empire).

Spanish history textbooks account for the decadence of Spain in terms of the loss of idealism and as a result of poor government, without forgetting foreign conspiracies. In modern times, the culprit of the Spanish disasters is always the Enlightenment in general, and liberalism in particular. The history of the nineteenth and twentieth centuries is presented in a quasi-paranoid frenzy, as a concerted attempt from different quarters to destroy the essence of Spain. Separatism is one of the many enemies of Spain, but so are liberalism, democracy, Marxism, Judaism, the Masonic movement, etc. With Franco's victory we see a return to the essence of 'eternal Spain', namely a Catholic world-vision.

To establish the maximum possible contrast, after having considered how the History of Spain was taught at a secondary school level during Franco's era, I propose to analyse how the History of Catalonia is now portrayed in the secondary school textbooks. The first thing to say, perhaps, is that the teaching of the History of Catalonia is rather recent, as it has been part of the curriculum only since 1988. More important is the fact that the subject-matter itself has been far from unproblematic; it is not only that different versions of such a history are offered, reflecting diverse methodological and theoretical standpoints, but also that the very possibility of such a history has been challenged.

Prior to offering a distilled précis of what the dominant images are that emerge from the Histories of Catalonia, I think it relevant to enter into what I have called the Catalan *Historikerstreit* (or dispute among Catalan historians) concerning the feasibility of a Catalan national history. The controversy started in 1982 with a special issue on 'Myths in the History of Catalonia' published by the monthly history magazine *L'Avenç* (a sort of *History Today*) and has continued unabated until the present. The arena of debate has been mostly the aforementioned magazine, but it has also spilt over into the daily Catalan press. A somewhat partisan compendium of the debate, with some of its documents, can be found in Balcells (1994). It is possible to assert that in the context of the struggle against the decaying Francoist dictatorship in the 1960s, the writing of Catalan history was a political act, even if it was done from a scholarly perspective and as a way of counteracting the official histories of Spain. This task was performed by local historians following the lead of Jaume Vicens-Vives (who died in 1960), and by an array of foreign researchers, among whom the most influential has undoubtedly been Pierre Vilar through his *magnum opus La Catalogne dans l'Espagne moderne* (1962).

The article that started the polemic was entitled 'On Catalan Historiography' and was penned by three respectable historians (Barceló, De Riquer and Ucelay de Cal 1982). It suggested that Catalan historiography had entered a period of crisis after 1978. The crucial issue at stake was whether it was possible to write a proper history of Catalonia, or whether Catalan history was inevitably bound to be a regional history. After all, a Catalan national history can only be envisaged as that of the history of the failure of Catalonia to become a nation-state; at best Catalonia would be a nation without a state, always trying to keep its specificity in front of an often intolerant centralising Spain. Furthermore, the institutional framework in which research on Catalan history could have developed was non-existent. The Spanish university system allowed only for World History and the History of Spain, with the occasional concession of a chair of the History of Catalonia. The article also criticises the remnants of romanticism present in contemporary Catalan history. To a certain extent this can be explained by the fact that, under Franco (and particularly in the 1960s), historians played a key role in providing a sense of historical continuity between the present generation and the past. Since Franco's death there has been a proliferation of local history (and of the history of special groups), with few serious attempts at providing a global and interdisciplinary synthesis.

The crucial issues to be considered are: (1) What are the implications of other special relationships between the Catalan nation and the Spanish state? (2) What is the relation between social hegemony and Catalan nationalism (the issue of class and nationalism)?

In the end, the question at stake is whether, in the Catalan case, a national history necessarily means a nationalist, mythological one. From a wider perspective, it is possible to say that the crisis of Catalan historiography in the 1980s, which is referred to in the article discussed, also reflects the beginning of the end of the dominance of the model of materialist historiography in Catalonia. To a certain extent, the confusion that appears to characterise the historians' garden is simply a reflection of the different political visions of Catalonia available after 1978: from moderate to radical nationalism, from communist to socialist views, etc. The precarious 'national' homogeneity which existed in the years of the struggle against the Francoist dictatorship disappeared with the politically negotiated transition to democracy.

The reply to Barceló et al. came from three other leading, and perhaps more established, historians and was published in the prestigious monthly magazine *L'Avenç* in 1985 (Balcells, Martí and Termes 1985). Their answer to the perceived dilemma was to restate the vitality of Catalan national history, not as a nationalist endeavour, but by presenting a 'history of Catalan society that shows the process of construction of Catalonia as a nation, but avoiding both an organicist perspective and the anachronism of projecting the present into a distant past and the past into the present. In a word, it is a national history of the Catalans in their experience as a people who gives itself successive models of social coexistence' (Balcells 1994: 45).

In the second half of the 1980s a number of prestigious historians, social scientists, writers, etc. petitioned the *Generalitat*, to which many educational prerogatives had been devolved from the central government, to make sure that the teaching of Catalan geography and history would find a place in the school system (the suggestion was that one third of what was taught under the rubric of 'social sciences' should be dedicated to Catalonia). Interestingly enough in terms of the discussion on history and memory, the petition of 1986 concluded in the following way:

> A nation which has struggled for self-government and does not wish to lose its identity can only see with extreme concern the fact that the majority of its future citizens ignore the history of the country; after all, the collective memory is part of the consciousness of identity of a people and to a great extent the efficient functioning of the institutions of the country depend on such a memory, as does the national creativity which is necessary for successful autonomous growth (Balcells 1994: 77).

Finally, another important factor in the reflections on the history of Catalonia have been the yearly meetings which, since 1987, have taken place in different parts of the Catalan Countries under the generic title 'Catalan Nationalism at the End of the 20th Century'. These symposia have gathered a variety of specialists on the national question and have to a great extent once again put Catalan nationalism on the intellectual horizon with a view to articulating a committed but scholarly vision of the issues at stake. Perhaps most important in the rarefied environment of the political compromises of the post-Franco period is the fact that in these meetings the issue of Catalan self-determination is openly discussed.

The ideological battle concerning Catalan historiography has continued unabated; it has only turned more bitter over the years. The issues at stake are very much the same. Perhaps the most important one is whether Catalan history should play a role in the shaping of national consciousness. The fact that since 1988 the History of Catalonia has been part of the secondary school curriculum means that, to a certain extent, it is an idle pursuit to argue about its feasibility. As could have been expected, Catalan history textbooks, reflecting different methodologies, pedagogies and theoretical perspectives, started to appear on the market. After all, in a liberal-democratic and diverse society, such as Catalonia today, the idea of a unitary history would not only be undesirable, but unthinkable. This should not be misconstrued as meaning that anything goes. It is important to realise that there is essential agreement about the basics, though different authors may provide alternative interpretations of given historical situations and accentuate or minimise others.

I have chosen Varela et al. (1989) as a representative textbook of the History of Catalonia. As with all good textbooks, it presents a synthesis or digest of the standard academic books on the topic, and it does so in a pedagogically modern way. The manner in which the materials are presented perhaps reflects the current hegemonic vision of the past of Catalonia. If anything the emphasis is on the political, while, for example, Casanova et al. (1993) offer a more socially oriented type of history.

For the sake of brevity, I have tried to focus on what I believe are the key points that, according to Varela et al., contribute to creating the specificity of Catalonia *vis-à-vis* the rest of Spain in the course of history. They are the following:

1. The Frankish origins of Catalonia, though the substratum of the country was Roman and Visigothic. The birth of Catalonia dates to 988.

2. The Middle Ages shaped Catalonia, giving it features  different from those of other Iberian kingdoms. Feudalism, pactism and federalism are distinctively Catalan. The peculiarity of the legal system is also emphasised.

3. The union of the Crown of Aragon and the Kingdom of Castile in the fifteenth century is seen as essentially dynastic, and not as the creation of a unified country called Spain. The emphasis is placed on the autonomy of each of the kingdoms of the Crown of Aragon within the unified monarchy. The union was forced by the economic weakness of Catalonia and the existence of a Castilian dynasty in Aragon (*Compromis de Casp*, 1412).

4. A culture of resistance against the centralist and unifying tendencies of Castile is emphasised. High points of such resistance are : (a) The Revolt of the Catalans (1640–59) or the War of the Reapers, which ended in the defeat of Catalonia, the loss of the Pyrenean counties to France and the tightening of the Catalan political institutions by the Spanish monarchy, and  (b) The War of Succession, in which the Catalans (and the Crown of Aragon in general) sided with the Austrian pretender against the French Bourbon one, the reason essentially being the distrust and hatred both of French absolutism and of Castile, but also the belief that the Austrian rulers would be in favour of decentralisation. The triumph of the Bourbon cause (due, among other things, to the perfidy of the English Crown) meant the end of the self-governing Catalan institutions (1714–16).

5. The eighteenth century and part of the nineteenth are presented as centuries in which Catalan identity took a dive (politically after 1714, but also later culturally and linguistically). However, this is a period in which the country thrived economically (Pierre Vilar's thesis).

6. The *Renaixença* (1833–85) is a period of cultural, and subsequently linguistic, revival of Catalonia. Later, between 1885 and 1905 the foundations of Catalan nationalism (*Catalanisme*) were laid. A number of key political events and publications are highlighted in this context: *Memorial de Greuges* (1885), Almirall's *Lo Catalanisme* (1886), *Bases de Manresa* (1892), Torres i Bages' *La tradició catalana* (1892), Prat de la Riba and Muntanyola's *Compendi de doctrina catalanista* (1894)  and Prat de la Riba's *La nacionalitat catalana* (1906). The whole period is seen as a reflection of a thriving Catalan civil society in general and of the Catalan bourgeoisie in particular.

7. In the next period, the main emphasis is placed on the *Mancomunitat de Catalunya* (1914–25), that is, the union of the four Catalan provinces as an administrative step towards the achievement of the *Estatut de Catalunya* (1932–38/9), which constituted Catalonia as an autonomous region within the Spanish state, albeit with limited powers (bilingualism emphasised).

8. The Francoist period is generally presented as one in which a severe repression against the Catalan nation took place, tantamount to a quasi-genocide attempt against the culture and language of the Catalans.

9. The *Estatut d'Autonomia de Catalunya* (1979) recognised Catalonia as an autonomous nationality within the Spanish state and allowed the country a number of exclusive competences in the areas of culture, tourism, urban development and education; further future transfers were contemplated. At the linguistic level the Statute established bilingualism with the formula that Catalan was Catalonia's own (*propi*) language, while Spanish was the language of the whole state.

## Monumental Sites: The Streets of Barcelona

Since the mid-nineteenth century Barcelona has offered a remarkable, perhaps unique, example of having its history imprinted by conscious design in the names of the streets of one of its modern quarters (*l'Eixample*). As with other sites of memory, it is not easy to ascertain the effectiveness of monumental sites. But even if 'the impact of the names of the streets on the collective memory is ambiguous, it will inform us on the representations that the establishment has had of the national memory and of the great men, as well as on the ways of promoting these representations' (Milo 1986: 286). In any case, what is fixed in space and has a physical presence – the physical props that Durkheim referred to in *The Elementary Forms of Religious Life* – may be of great help in sustaining identification and recognition. However, the passage of time may dent the symbolic meaning intended, particularly when the social milieu is no longer sympathetic to the original message (as happened during Franco's dictatorship).

The naming of the streets of the new quarter of Barcelona in the mid-nineteenth century was a momentous event. The project for the *Eixample* (meaning essentially extension or enlargement of the city) came at a time when the Catalan bourgeoisie had reached both a socio-economic and a cultural peak. It was put forward by the civil engineer and politician, turned urban studies specialist, Ildefons Cerdà in a number of books between 1855 and 1859. The purpose of Cerdà was to provide Barcelona with a rationally designed space that would allow the city to cope with the demographic changes that had accompanied industrial and commercial development. To that end the defensive walls of the city had to be destroyed and urban growth was to be allowed in the empty space between the old city and neighbouring villages (Permanyer 1990: 28–9).

In 1865, one of the leading intellectuals of the *Renaixença*, Victor Balaguer, published a book in two volumes entitled *Las calles de Barcelona*. This was the project he had submitted the previous year to the Town Hall of Barcelona for the naming of the streets of the *Eixample*. A romantic and progressive historian, Balaguer chose from the history of Catalonia a list of illustrious persons, heroic deeds and historical and old kingdoms. This is how Balaguer envisaged his endeavour:

When it came to having to christen the streets of the new Barcelona, the author of this work sent to the Town Hall a long list of names referring to historical events all related to the Principality of Catalonia. Most of them were accepted; only a few were substituted (…) It was the original intention of the author to name all the streets of the *Eixample* with reference to events, glorious deeds and institutions belonging to the history of Catalonia, with the the the objective of creating a historical and harmonious general setting or plan (Balaguer 1888, Vol. 21 (II): 29).

How did Balaguer organise his plan of the *Eixample*? An important component was made up of the political entities which either through federation, conquest or annexation were connected with the Crown of Aragon, with all its power and importance during the medieval period. It was represented by the following streets: Catalunya, Aragó, València, Mallorca, Rosselló, Provença, Sicilia, Nàpols, Calabria, Còrsega and Sardenya.

The origins of the Catalan fatherland (*patria*) are remembered by streets with the names of the counts of Urgell (a fifteenth-century failed pretender to the Crown of Aragon) and that of Villena (a famous writer, the last descendant of the family who occupied the throne of the Crown of Aragon). The popular and civic glory of the Catalan nationality and its free institutions were celebrated with medieval military leaders such as Roger de Flor, Roger de Llúria, Vilamarí Entença and Rocafort and political institutions such as *Corts Catalanes* (Parliament), *Diputació* (self-government) and *Consell de Cent* (municipal goverment). Other streets recollected magistrates and great leaders of the early modern period such as Pau Clarís, Tamarit, Casanova, Villaroel and Fontanella. Literary and scientific figures were also present: the poets Ausiàs Marc, Ramon Llull and Aribau, philosophers like Vilanova and Balmes, the painter Viladomat, etc. The resistance against Napoleon was celebrated in the street names of Bruc, Girona and Tarragona. Finally, *Comerci* (Trade), *Marina* (Navy) and *Indústria* (Industry) celebrated the entrepreneurial spirit of Catalonia. There are some street names that reflected Spanish glories (Trafalgar, Pelai, Lepant, Bailèn, etc.), while others obey geometric considerations (Diagonal and Parallel).

On the whole, Balaguer's choice was a useful and instructive historical lesson, which survived (with a few exceptions) even the Francoist period. During Franco's dictatorship the two main avenues of the city – Corts Catalanes and Diagonal – were respectively rechristened Avenida José Antonio Primo de Rivera and Avenida Generalísimo Franco, while Pau Clarís was turned into Via Layetana; Casanova survived allegedly because the civil governor of 1939 assumed that it referred to the Italian romantic adventurer, and not to the Catalan patriot. After Franco's death, the old names were recovered, and, of course, the twentieth-century presidents of the *Generalitat* (Macià, Companys and Tarradellas) and other Catalan personalities were also allocated streets, though not always in the *Eixample*.

Franco's dictatorship lasted 35 years. This may not be a long time in the history of a millenarian nation like Catalonia, but it certainly shaped the national perception of those who were socialised in this period, even if fragments of the collective memory of families and others were conveying counter-images. What was the effect of the nationalist grid of the streets of the *Eixample* at a time when the history of Catalonia was not being taught in the schools to reinforce its symbolism? Obviously it was very limited. No doubt a certain connection with the Catalan past was made, but the overall original objective of sustaining Catalan national identity was lost, because many of the names had no meaning at all and, when they did, the association had no significant nationalist undertones. With the return into the open of the repressed Catalan identity, and in the context of a progressive familiarisation of the Catalans with their national history, it would not be far-fetched to assume that the streets of the *Eixample* are, to a certain extent, once again nationally alive.

## *Topographic Sites: The Archives of the* Generalitat

This section will receive only a very brief treatment. It refers to an episode that occupied the Spanish and Catalan media in 1995. The Council of Ministers had decided some time ago to return to the *Generalitat* of Catalonia all the documents that belong to this institution and that had been expropriated by the Francoist troops when Catalonia was defeated in 1939. These documents had been kept in the Archives of Salamanca since that time, alongside documents from other organisations (political parties, trade unions, etc.) that lost the war. The original purpose of the archive was repressive and the data kept there were used to persecute Republican supporters for many years. The decision to return the documents was taken by the socialist government following a request from the *Generalitat*. This moved was backed by all the political forces of Catalonia. It was agreed that the documents would be microfilmed and that a copy would remain in Salamanca. When the *Generalitat* had built an appropriate repository for the archives, the Town Hall of Salamanca and the population as a whole objected vigorously to the transfer.

What followed in the Catalan media was not only an attempt to justify the return of the archives on a variety of grounds (most importantly that the documents had been stolen *manu militari* at the end of the Civil War), including the fact that there was a strong symbolic argument for their return. It was suggested that the archives ensured the continuity between the present and the past; that they were an essential part of the historical memory of Catalonia. On the Spanish side, the media defended the idea that the crucial point was to preserve the unity of the Archives of Salamanca, as the national archives of the Civil War. What seems to be at stake here is that there are two different, incompatible concepts of nation (Catalan and Spanish), and that there is no way of fudging this issue. It is true that it can be alleged that the Spanish Constitution encourages a certain degree of ambiguity (by introducing the term 'nationality' to account for realities such as Catalonia), but the problem lies in that, in practice, there exist two national projects with, as we have seen, different historical memories and ethnic markers (language, culture, etc.). This is not a controversy that can easily be solved, as the passing of years has not solved the problem to the satisfaction of the Catalans.

## Conclusions

That historical memory seems to be one of the central components of (ethno)national identity seems to be amply demonstrated by the recent experience of stateless nations in both Western and Eastern Europe. Indeed, the phenomenon is much wider as can be shown by the case study of nation-states such as France (Nora 1986–92). What is perhaps less clear is how effective the different sites of memory are in securing the intended national anchorage. Unfortunately, we do not possess adequate and precise instruments to measure, for instance, the results of the specific policies of (ethno)nation-building of the Catalan *Generalitat* or of the variety of voluntary associations of the Catalan civil society. By 1995, twenty years had elapsed since Franco's death, and no doubt great strides had been made in rekindling the hidden Catalan national identity that had eluded some foreign researchers in the early 1970s. For what they are worth in ascertaining the degree of national identity, both regular elections and surveys confirm that nation-building has proceeded at a steady pace.

The specific sites of memory that I have presented for consideration are a very small part of the possible range of instances. For better or for worse, in contemporary societies the role of the mass media is paramount in shaping, but also in diluting, national identity. Both the press and radio and television echo in multitudinous ways nationalist initiatives that have arisen either at the official level or at that of voluntary associations; this, of course, is within the context of their political and cultural agendas. Indeed, there is a constant reminder of Catalan commemorations, anniversaries, celebrations, etc. in all the media. On the other hand, the mass media are also the carriers of constant messages that refer to the Spanish nation. All this is taking place in the context of the increasing media presence of an American-inspired global culture. By mirroring foreign models, it is alleged that national cultures are being emptied of their original contents. The dangers of being swamped by the process of Americanisation of the world (both at the linguistic and at the cultural level) are all too real to be brushed off. Even the French do not any longer believe that their precious cultural and linguistic castle is impregnable. In the Catalan case, however, the main danger is that of being acculturated by the powerful and ever-present Spanish culture.

What is the role of historical memory in such a situation? I have maintained elsewhere (Llobera 1994) that, for reasons that are not altogether clear, the idea of historical continuity appeals to nations. The search for origins, particularly if they show a separate political entity with clearly defined cultural and linguistic features anchored in a more or less distant past, is a generalised pursuit of (ethno)nations trying to make their presence felt. This exercise in historical memory may be fraught with romantic and essentialist traps (Martinez Fiol 1993).

This is not to say that a sense of national identity may not only be a necessary corrective to a prior political situation that was experienced by the majority of the population as oppressive, but also provide the needed energy to give dynamics to a society. The crucial issue is whether the right kind of balances between civic and ethnic nationalism can be established. Equally important is the time frame and the means used to implement the policies of national redress. It would be naive to expect that situations that require compromise from the different participating actors will not be conflictual. Language, culture and national consciousness are often highly valued assets, hence the entrenched positions. What matters, however, is how to minimise the conflictivity, that is, how to develop procedures to manage conflict in a properly democratic and tolerant way.

Only in rarefied intellectual atmospheres can nationalist historians get away with their myths and fables. Unfortunately, this is what has happened in ex-Yugoslavia, where extremely skewed national histories have been used to justify horrendous crimes. There is no panacea to human folly except a free, vigorous and vigilant civil society. Totalitarian regimes of whichever persuasion (fascist, communist or those derived from religious fundamentalism) will tend to monopolise historical memory with the avowed aim of creating and imposing a certain type of uniform national identity; as a consequence, ethnonational identities will be at best ignored or repressed, and at worst obliterated.

# 8

# DOES NATIONALISM INEVITABLY LEAD TO CONFLICT AND VIOLENCE?

cୟୢ୭୧ଽ୨

## Introduction

This chapter deals with topic of the psychological and political nature of nationalism. In the course of the book it has clearly emerged that nationalism is at times peaceful and at times violent. In the case of Spain, very different realities have emerged on ethnonationalism in the period between the 1960s and the present (2001). It is a well-known fact that in Catalonia the level of political violence is low, while in the Basque Country it is at a high level. It is one of the purposes of this chapter to consider, among other things, how one can approach the reality of violent nationalism at a general level. It should be said in advance that there is no easy solution to this problem. As David Laitin (1995) has pointed out, when dealing with national violence it is important to accept the importance of non-predictable events.

The main empirical purpose of this chapter is to deal with the recent Catalan political reality. One of the issues that has intrigued researchers working on post-Francoist Catalonia is the degree of consensus politics that has operated for over twenty years among political parties as ideologically diverse as Christian democrats, socialists and communists. Some scholars have attributed this pattern to the traditional 'pactist' nature of Catalan politics. Without discounting this historical element, the chapter purports to show the importance of two other factors. First, the ruling elites of these parties were forged in the anti-Francoist struggle, where participants shared a number of major political objectives (democracy, autonomism, etc). Second, and possibly more important, the elites were mostly recruited from the Catalan-speaking, progressive bourgeoisie.

What will occur when the political life of the present elites comes to a natural end, as is bound to happen in the near future? The possibility of a more confrontational type of politics is not to be excluded, particularly as the socialist leadership, exemplified by the Jacobin 'local barons' who are the children of the working-class, Castilian-speaking immigrants, progressively take over. Furthermore, with the decline of the Catalan communist party, the radicalisation of the hegemonic nationalist party (CiU) and the political rise of the '*españolista*' right represented by the PP, the era of consensus politics may be over.

## Explaining Political Theory and National Violence

### *Introduction (In Lieu of Theory)*

In *Economy and Society* Max Weber provides us with two slightly different definitions of power (*Macht*). Power, he first says, 'is the probability that one actor within a social relationship will be in a position to carry out his own will' (Weber 1978, I: 53), Later on in the book, power becomes 'the chance of a human being or a group of human beings to realise their own will in a social action even against the resistance of others who are participating in the action' (1978, II: 926). To be successful, however, a group of human beings must be centralised, cohesive and well organised; this is when the group becomes a power elite. As Gaetano Mosca remarked, it is a fact of political life that in most known societies 'minorities rule majorities, rather than majorities [rule] minorities (…). The power of any minority is irresistible against each single individual in the majority, who stands alone before the totality of the organised minority' (Mosca 1939: 53).

While in the past the so-called elite theorists (Pareto, Mosca, Michaels) were dismissed as little else than proto-fascists, recently they have been largely rehabilitated as important political theorists. In concluding their review of elite theory published in George Marcus's *Elites*, Edward Hansen and Timothy Parrish assert that 'a revised version of Pareto's and Mosca's elite concept might be useful in resolving the ancient controversy over who rules in capitalist society' (Hansen and Parrish 1983: 273), and they add that this perspective enriches Marxist analysis. Whether we call them minorities and majorities or elites and masses, there will always be top achievers (a few) and low achievers (the mass). Pareto argued that there were two ways through which the elites could maintain power: coercion and persuasion. For others, in a more psychological way, leaders were either lions or foxes. Of course, Pareto suggested that elites were also recruited from the masses.

It has often been repeated that elite theorists, and this would also include Max Weber (1978) and Joseph Schumpeter (1950), operated in very different societal conditions from the ones affecting us today. I believe, however, that based on the work of these authors it is possible to formulate a very general framework for research that is valid for advanced capitalist societies of the liberal-democratic type. The key propositions, inspired partly by Marger (1981) and Albertoni (1987), are:

1.  There is an asymmetry of power in the sense that it is always exercised by a minority over a majority. The fact that a society is liberal-democratic and has a multiparty system does not change the nature of power, though it obviously modifies it.

2.  As Michael Mann would put it, there are different sources of social power, and that is why there are economic, political and cultural elites (and military ones in some types of societies). Within each sphere different elite groups compete for supremacy by peaceful means. Although there may be an overlap between economic, political and cultural elites, it is methodologically sound to assume that each type of elite is autonomous.

3.  It is in an open society, where the principles of competition and meritocracy are ingrained, that the 'circulation of the elites' (Mosca) can be maximised.

## *The Relevance of Political Elites in the Study of Nationalism*

In the past few years, and as result of an apparent increase in ethnic/national conflict, violence and war, social scientists have tried to answer the question of why some nationalist movements turn violent while others pursue their ends through peaceful means. There is no absence of so-called explanations of ethnonational violence in terms of irrational, emotional factors. It is often assumed that blood ties, a common language and territory, shared myths of origin and religious beliefs, and a common 'invented' history among other factors are sufficient reasons to account for the violence against a designated enemy. In the 1990s the tragic events in the former Yugoslavia have often been accounted for in these terms. On the other hand, sociobiologists have suggested that the ethnonational bond is just an extension of the principle of inclusive fitness which induces humans to favour their genetically closest relatives.

In a recent article, Michael Hechter, has maintained that ethnonationalist 'violence can be best explained instrumentally' (1995: 57); that is, 'it can be a means to valued ends' (ibid.). The ends can be economic (wealth), political (power), but also cultural (prestige). This is an important departure from earlier economistic interpretations of the author and others who had shared the 'internal colonialism' paradigm. Nonetheless, it is not easy to offer empirical proof that things do occur as predicted by the theory, that is, that actors wish to maximise 'some combination of wealth, power or prestige' (Hechter 1995: 59).

Based on his 'solidaristic theory of social order' Hechter assumes that individuals join ethnonational groups with the aim of achieving goals that cannot be attained individually. Violence is a by-product of different ethnonational groups competing for their goals. The state can be understood as an institutional framework in which inter-group conflict can be managed. However, conflict may still be present as long as opposition groups reject the legitimacy of the state, that is, if there are 'groups that see themselves as potential political units' (Hechter 1995: 59).

Violence is one of the options that ethnonationalist groups have to obtain their objectives. In the final instance, their aim is to achieve self-determination. On the other hand, the state also engages in violence with the aim of destroying the opposition groups that challenge its survival in its present form.

## *Is Violence Universal?*

Psychologists tell us that there are two kinds of violence: emotional and instrumental. In emotional or hostile violence the objective is to hurt the victim; from this aggression the perpetrator derives pleasure. This inclination towards violence is provoked by a psychological state that it is called malaise. On the other hand, in instrumental violence the objective is to preserve power, domination or social status (Berkowitz 1993: 11). Although violence is more a capacity than an instinct, it is here to stay. And the reasons are: violence pays off, so people learn to be violent; and emotional aggression will always exist, because it is not possible to avoid distress and unhappiness in the human condition (Berkowitz 1993: 431).

Is violence, in general, and tribal/ethnic violence in particular, a generalised phenomenon in human societies? It would appear that the simpler and smaller the society is, the lower the degree of violence. With increased sociocultural complexity, that is, from bands to tribes, from tribes to chiefdoms and from chiefdoms to states, the frequency of violence and war increases, and reaches a peak in contemporary industrial societies. Even in hunter-gatherer societies it has been pointed out by Woodburn and others that immediate-return societies tend to be more peaceful than those characterised by delayed return. With the Neolithic revolution, territory and durables became the object of dispute (Van der Dennen and Falger 1990: 242–43).

The appearance of the state 7,000 years ago represented the institutionalisation of violence, as Pierre van den Berghe has reminded us. The state has a monopoly of force and is not shy in killing people if it is necessary to defend itself against internal or external enemies. The modern state exhibits three new features (van den Berghe 1990): it has a murderous technology of destruction; it has shifted from external to internal violence; and it kills in the name of the statist ideology of nationalism.

Many modern anthropologists have difficulty in accepting the reality of human violence. For example, the famous Seville Statement on Violence was endorsed by the AAA in 1986. The propositions stated in the document are (Tiger in Van der Dennen and Folger 1990: 1):

1. It is scientifically incorrect to say that we have inherited a tendency to make war from our animal ancestors.
2. It is scientifically incorrect to say that war or any other violent behaviour is energetically programmed into our human nature.
3. It is scientifically incorrect to say that in the course of human evolution there has been a selection for aggressive behaviour more than for other kinds of behaviour.
4. It is scientifically incorrect to say that humans have a 'violent brain'.
5. It is scientifically incorrect to say that war is caused by instinct or any other single motivation.

In my opinion, this is neither a scientific statement nor a research project: the points are too general to be meaningful. On the other hand, the history of mankind was a bloody history long before scientists had expressed any ideas about human evolution. This list is essentially a political manifesto; furthermore, it insists on an old hobby-horse of cultural/social anthropology: that evolutionary biology may well, as Lévi-Strauss put it, apply to ants (Wilson) or ducks (Lorenz), but not to humans. The human mind is a *tabula rasa* on which culture writes all the best tunes, but also the worst. Robin Fox says that it is somewhat ironic that this document on violence should have been produced in Seville, which was for centuries the sordid centre of the Holy Inquisition.

## *Does Ethnicity/Nationalism Inevitably Lead to Violence and War?*

The modern media present the world as 'a seething ethnic cauldron' (Brubaker). Is it, however, like this? We all know about the appalling ethnic violence, ethnic cleansing, ethnic wars, etc. of the 1990s in ex-Yugoslavia (Bosnia, Kosovo), in some parts of Russia (Chechnia), in Ruanda (Hutu/Tutsi), in India (communal violence between Hindus and Muslims) and elsewhere. Let us, however, look more carefully at the situation. The collapse of the Soviet world between 1989 and 1991 was an event of major political significance, comparable only to the French Revolution of 1789 or the Russian Revolution of 1917.

Between 1989 and 1991, it was not only the communist system that faded away; the events of this period also led to the freeing of many countries from the iron rule of Moscow. In this sense, it would be correct to describe the process as one in which a large number of countries gained or regained political sovereignty. The potential for ethnic national violence, if by that we understand the presence of multinational states and the presence of different ethnic groups, was there, at least in the abstract. The Baltic countries contained large numbers of ethnic Russians, the Czechoslovak state split in two, there are Hungarian minorities in at least seven states, etc. The same is also true of other parts of the world.

It is clear that the idea that nationalism leads inexorably to violence is imprinted in the mind of many a contemporary, and that both the media and many intellectuals have contributed to it. Many people only see the nationalism of others, while they, of course, bask in legitimate patriotism. To them I have only this to say: nationalism is the patriotism of the others. I think we should recognise, with Tom Nairn, the Janus character of nationalism: its good and its dark side. We should also carefully distinguish between democratic and undemocratic forms of conflict. Ethnic/national consciousness, ethnic affirmation, ethnic movements, ethnic competition and even ethnic conflict can be kept within peaceful boundaries. There is qualitative change when we enter into ethnic violence, cleansing, war and annihilation.

What characterises ethnic violence is either the use of physical force to inflict bodily harm or the threat to use physical force (Brubaker and Laitin 1998: 247). More contentious is the idea of symbolic violence developed by Bourdieu, because the recipient is not conscious of it, since it is inscribed in the social and cognitive structures of society, in what he calls 'the order of things' (Bourdieu 1982: 143). Nonetheless, there are forms of cultural violence (myths, memories, representations, etc.) which dehumanise and demonise 'the Other' and open the way to the use of physical violence, including killing.

Returning to the image of the world as a seething ethnic cauldron, we must remember that, because nationalism and ethnicity are popular conceptual frameworks for thinking contemporary political realities, events which in the past would have been looked at through ideological or class binoculars are today tinted with nationalism. A final point. As many commentators have described what happened in ex-Yugoslavia and elsewhere as 'tribal wars', this led a leading British historian, John Keegan, to utter the following words: 'These are primitive, tribal conflicts that only anthropologists can understand.' Rhetorically, I would like to ask the following question: have anthropologists been better than other social scientists at explaining ethnic violence?

## *Instrumental Versus Cultural Theory of Ethnic/National Violence*

To explain national violence the contribution of Michael Hechter (1995) is quite relevant, though perhaps not altogether convincing. His assumption is that nationalist violence is more instrumental than emotional; and by instrumental he means the maximisation of material (wealth), political (power) and cultural (prestige) objectives. The satisfaction of these goals, which are egotistic but rational, is a necessary but insufficient assumption for nationalist violence. For such an explanation what is needed is a theory that explains human solidarity or, as he calls it, a solidaristic theory of social order. The basic assumption of this approach is that human beings join groups to attain objectives that cannot be achieved individually. Conflict between groups which want to achieve the same goals is not inevitable, but it tends to happen.

The state is an institution that appears as a result of inter-group conflict. The legitimacy of the state can always be challenged by one or another group; violence against the state can result in changes that favour (in terms of rewards) the violent group. Hechter's theory looks at both the state and the nationalist group. There follow four major propositions:

1. If the state is strong and inhibited internationally it is likely to engage in violent repression of the nationalist group (e.g. Russia).
2. If the state is weak the nationalist group is likely to engage in violent action against it (e.g. some African states).
3. If the nationalist group exhibits solidarity, violence will be controlled by its leaders (e.g. Northern Ireland and Euzkadi).
4. If the nationalist group does not display solidarity, violence is likely to be greater because it will be uncontrolled by its leaders (e.g. Lebanon).

The conclusion reached by the author is as follows: violence is likely to break out when a weak solidarity nationalist group confronts a strong state apparatus having high domestic and international autonomy, but it is likely to escalate and to be sustained only in the context of a weakened host state facing a high solidarity nationalist group.

Culturalist approaches envisage ethnic violence as 'meaningful, culturally constructed, discursively mediated, symbolically saturated and ritually regulated' (Brubaker and Laitin 1998: 441). The question is how to make sense of senseless violence? Is there logic to ethnic violence? Culturalists maintain that violence makes sense not instrumentally, but in terms of meaning, because it resonates with other elements of the given culture. Much ethnic violence is preceded by a 'culture of fear'. Through rhetorical processes, using symbolic resources, representational forms, narratives, myths, rituals, commemorations and memories, 'the Other' is dehumanised and demonised. In this category fall the beliefs of Serbs about Muslims or Croats, the Hindu beliefs about Muslims, the Sinhalese beliefs about Tamils and the Hutu beliefs about the Tutsi. These fears, when properly manipulated by ethnic activists, may lead to violent pre-emptive strikes against 'the Other', as the Serbians behaved towards Croatians and Bosnians, and the Croatians towards the Bosnians.

The problems with culturalist explanations are twofold (Brubaker and Laitin 1998: 443). First, it is not always easy to produce the appropriate kind of evidence. In reality we do not know if the people who participate in ethnic violence believe in cultural constructions or if this is a *post facto* rationalisation on the basis of nationalist propaganda tracts. It is often the case that researchers do not have firsthand evidence and rely on newspapers, pamphlets, etc. Second, culturalist approaches, although vivid, do not really explain ethnic violence. In other words, they are too general and overarching. They do not account for why ethnic violence occurs in some places and not others, why some people participate and not others, or why ethnic violence takes place at a certain moment in time and not at another, etc.

## *Long-Term and Immediate Causes of Ethnic/Nationalist Violence*

For many years, we have lived with what could be called the permafrost theory of ethnic conflict/violence/war. According to this theory authoritarian regimes keep ancient ethnic/national hatreds frozen and out of sight. When these dictatorships collapse, as happened in the Soviet Union and ex-Yugoslavia, hatreds become visible once again and ethnic conflicts are given a new lease of life. Is this explanation satisfactory and complete? As we have seen, theories that emphasise the irrational basis of nationalist violence have been challenged by Michael Hechter with his suggestion that there is an explanation for such behaviour.

Is there a more comprehensive theory that provides us with the basic conditions, both long-term and immediate, that account for the phenomenon of nationalist violence? Recapitulating the literature of the past years, I have found in the articles written by Michael Brown and Stephen Van Evera (Brown 1997) a number of ideas that have come to the forefront and which have been conveniently presented in the following way. Among the long-term causes of ethnic violence we should consider the following factors: structural, political, socio-economic, cultural-perceptual. As for the proximate or immediate causes, it is useful to distinguish the following: internal, mass-level factors; external, mass-level factors; and external, elite-level factors. Another important issue is how to account for the escalation of hostilities. The final issue deals with the prescriptions that can help to avoid ethnic/national conflict and war. Generally speaking, it must be said that only an attempt has been made to provide a rather schematic viewpoint of a reality that is extremely rich.

Which are the most important structural factors? Both Brown and Van Evera believe in the importance of the state. For Brown, the main reason arises if the state is weak, particularly when there is a power struggle between ethnic/national groups to become dominant. As to Van Evera's perspective, what is relevant is the presence of a situation in which both the central state and the stateless nationalities are quite strong and trying to achieve their respective and different objectives. As is well-known, the existence of a weak state is open to domination by strong neighbouring states. A classic example of these features is Lebanon.

Another factor that accounts for tension and conflict is what is usually called ethnic geography, that is, a situation in which nationalities are mixed. In reality, only about 10 per cent of states are ethnically or nationally homogeneous. Most societies are multinational, sometimes they exhibit homogeneous regions, sometimes intermingled ones. An important point emphasised by Van Evera is that the more densely nationalities are mixed, the greater the risk of conflicts and, in some cases (like the ex-Yugoslavia), the greater the risk of violence and war. Clearly, the risks are greater if the intermingling of the national populations occurs at the local village level, rather than the provincial or regional level. However, the congruence between the ethnic and political boundaries makes the risk of violence less likely to occur. This would explain why in Western Europe there are fewer ethnic/ national conflicts than in Eastern Europe.

As to the political factors that account for violence, it is possible to refer to a number of them. Perhaps a quite important framework is that which is characterised by a long-term political discrimination of one ethnic/national group by another. This situation may enforce a reality in which the rights of the subordinated ethnic/national groups are vastly inferior. In extreme situations the politicians of the dominant group may engage in a policy of 'ethnic bashing' or scapegoating. It is obvious that somebody like the Serbian leader Milosevic played a central role in this type of policy. The case of the ex-Yugoslavia is a powerful example of another dimension: the revival of the past. The Serbs in particular developed a conception of their past in terms of the negativity of their neighbours. These enemies were vividly remembered as unforgivable criminals, both in the past and present of the Serbs; they were read in terms of oppression, victimisation and elimination. All these factors were powerful enough to justify ethnic violence and physical elimination.

How important are economic and social factors in accounting for ethnic violence? There is no doubt, as Brown emphasises, that economic crises in the forms of slow-down, stagnation, deterioration or collapse of the economy can have important destabilising effects. Another important factor is the inequality of opportunity that exists between the different ethnic/national groups in access to land or capital. Finally, there are situations in which the political institutions lag behind the economic ones. It is difficult to assess the importance of the socio-economic factors because their impact on the political tends to occur in the long run.

The last structural element worth mentioning can be referred to as the cultural and perceptual factor. Perhaps the most obvious situation is that in which there exists a pattern of cultural discrimination. Under this concept there are a variety of practices against ethnic/national minorities: from political freedom to educational opportunities, from the use of language to the freedom of religion. What is at stake is a political situation in which total assimilation is the major objective. As mentioned before, the existence of past grievances, real or mythical, tend also to be present. In this sense, recent experience in many Eastern European countries shows that, if the different nationalities of a state tend to present divergent and confrontational national liberties, the risk of war is greatly increased. This cause may not of itself be sufficient to cause war, but in combination with a disastrous economic situation and an aggressive mythical history could be. In this sense, negative effects might be unavoidable.

There are other factors that Brown and Van Evera consider as proximate or immediate causes of ethnic/national violence. In fact, it is not so clear that it is easy to separate long-term from proximate factors. Brown presents a long list of elements which are internal to the state and at a mass level, and that generate domestic group problems. They go from rapid economic development to discrimination at various levels (political, cultural and economic), from an acute

147

social uncertainty to fear of what the future can bring (cultural assimilation and survival) and from the misrepresentation of 'the Other' (information failure) to not trusting that the other group will respect the agreements. As for external mass-level elements, having bad and aggressive neighbours is a potential disaster; Palestinians in Lebanon was a good case in point. On the other hand, the occurrence of elite-level 'nasty neighbours' tends to affect small or weak states. The cases of China and Russia as troublesome to their respective neighbours are well-known examples.

Summarising, one can mention four main reasons for the escalation of hostilities: the increase of economic problems (inflation, unemployment, resource competition, etc.); confrontation among groups which combine the past and the present; the fact that the ethnic and national elites have entered into intense competition; and, finally, the presence of ethnic activists who can manipulate people's consciousness and of political entrepreneurs, that is, individuals who seek political office and power, who polarise society by using ethnic markers.

It is Van Ewera who deals with specific situations that account for a greater risk of war, as well as prescriptions that help to avoid ethnic/national conflict and war. The first type of proposition is explained by reference to a number of situations:

1. The greater the proportion of stateless nationalities seeking secession, the greater the risk of war.
2. The more that states pursue the recovery of national diasporas or annexionism, the greater the risk of war.
3. The more hegemonic the goals that states pursue, the greater the risk of war.
4. The more states oppress their minorities, the greater the risk of war.

The measures that can help to end violence are based on democratic and peaceful factors. The most general measure is that of opting out of the use of general force. On the other hand, the national rights of minorities, including secession, have to be guaranteed. As part of the democratic framework, there should be political parties, freedom of the press, etc. Also important is a commitment to a balanced teaching of history in schools and an attempt to refrain from extremist propaganda. Finally, the state has to respect the existing borders or reach an agreement to settle contested ones peacefully and by negotiation.

## Catalonia and the Basque Country

In the context of the Spanish state, a number of recent texts (Johnston 1991: Diez-Medrano 1995; Conversi 1997; Guibernau 1999) have been trying to account for the different paths followed by the Catalan and the Basque nationalist movements. If we look at the history of Catalonia and the Basque Country within the Spanish state – and that means approximately the past 500 years – it would probably be correct to state that violence has been more endemic in Catalonia than in the Basque Country. In the twentieth century this is certainly the case up to the 1930s, including the Spanish Civil War – and even in the 1940s.

Most scholars would agree that during the Francoist period the ethnonational and class cleavages were much more pronounced in the Basque Country than in Catalonia. The Basque bourgeoisie was much more integrated within the Spanish state than the Catalan one, while the working classes, largely of immigrant origin in both countries, behaved very differently. In Catalonia they were co-opted by left-wing parties (socialists and communists) which shared with Catalan nationalists the basic assumption that Catalonia was a nation and that it was entitled to political autonomy if not self-determination. In Euzkadi this was not the case: the socialist party was largely Jacobin and centralist, while the communists were not that influential. Furthermore, Basque nationalists were much more essentialist and maximalist than their Catalan counterparts. Following David Laitin (1995) it is possible to add that the cycle of violence of ETA was based on multiple events: repression and killing by the Spanish government in the 1970s, the successful assassination of the Spanish Prime Minister in 1974 by ETA, execution of ETA prisoners in 1975, etc.

Many authors have pointed out that the fundamental political differences between Catalonia and the Basque Country appeared in the years immediately preceding Franco's demise. While Catalonia developed unitary, underground oppositional structures like the Assembly of Catalonia (Batista and Playà 1991), which brought together all political parties, religious and cultural groups, as well as working-class associations, in the Basque Country, the opposition to Franco was much weaker and was not based on a single platform. In Catalonia, the existence of unitary organisations from the late sixties onwards created a widely based elite network with people from all shades of the political spectrum. Out of that, there developed personal friendships and an *esprit de corps* (Johnston 1991: 160). This was largely maintained in the transitional period to democracy (1975–79), through the 1980s and to a certain extent in the 1990s. In the Basque Country, the nationalist parties, especially the PNV, were also in power during the democratic period. However, the confrontational situation of the Basque nationalist parties with the AP and PSOE has been on the increase, to the extent that, immediately prior to the elections in the year 2001, the situation was extremely tense, and it deteriorated afterwards.

## The Role of Political Elites in Catalonia

### Catalan Political Elites and the Spanish State: A Historical Excursion

In his classic *Noticia de Catalunya* (A panorama of Catalonia), Jaume Vicens-Vives (1954) noted that the participation of the Catalan elites in the tasks of the Spanish state had been rather limited. From its very inception in the late fifteenth century, the Catalans have felt that the Spanish state was an alien body that they were sucked into by the forces of history. They surely had to find accommodation within it, but their attitude was always distant and diffident. Furthermore, their experience taught them that the Spanish state was essentially a Castilian affair and that it was inevitably bound to erode the political autonomy of Catalonia.

According to Vicens-Vives, from the twelfth to the fourteenth century Catalonia developed a political system called *pactisme*, which can be defined as a covenant between the upper classes (nobility and bourgeoisie) and the king. The purpose of this agreement was to protect certain freedoms; it was a way of controlling the growing power of the monarchy and of introducing a modicum of democratic freedoms in the political system. However, in the long run these arrangements became rather rigid and did not stop the progressive encroachment of first the Habsburgs (sixteenth and seventeenth centuries) and later the Bourbons (eighteenth century onwards). Even during the high points of rebellion against the centralising state (1640, 1714), the Catalans were not able or willing to find an alternative to their political predicaments.

In any case, the military defeats forced the alien state on them. This was particularly the case after 1714 with the suppression of the traditional constitutional framework and the introduction of the Decretos de Nueva Planta, which gave the centralised monarchy the upper hand in the control of Catalan affairs. It is interesting to note that during most of the eighteenth century not a single Catalan served in the courts of the different monarchs, although things improved slightly towards the end of the century.

It was not until the Napoleonic invasions that Catalonia managed to create a skeleton of an autonomous government (*Junta Superior de Govern del Principat*). It performed reasonably well and even made good use of the vernacular for military and political purposes. This experience was of short duration (1808–12). With the restoration of the monarchy in the figure of Ferdinand VII, centralisation continued unabated and so did the Catalan reluctance to participate in state affairs in a subordinate position. All Catalan attempts to organise themselves politically and economically in the context of a more progressive and liberal framework were foiled, often by military force.

In the second half of the nineteenth century, Catalonia, despite being the most economically developed area of Spain, refused to participate in political life, hence abandoning the running of the state to elites from other areas. There were some exceptions, particularly during the revolutionary period between 1868 and 1874. However, the experiences of the Catalan elites were rather negative because they tried to implement a set of modernising policies (federalism, secularism, internationalism, socialism, etc.) which found no support either in Castile or in Andalusia. In this sense, one could say that the Catalan political elites that participated in the tasks of governing the Spanish state were rather naive.

On the whole, during the second half of the nineteenth century Catalans perceived the corruption and 'clientelism' of the Spanish state as an evil to be

avoided. That does not mean that the industrial bourgeoisie did not have to compromise with the regime in its efforts to secure the Spanish market. While absent
from the Spanish arena, the Catalan elites, led by Enric Prat de la Riba, became
interested, between 1890 and the late 1910s, in the *res publica* – but at the level
of Catalonia. The *Mancomunitat* – an embryo of autonomous government – was
the model of an honest and efficient administration, but when Primo de Rivera
became a military dictator in 1923, it was immediately dissolved.

It is interesting to note in passing that the diffidence and mistrust felt by the
Catalan bourgeoisie towards the Spanish state was experienced to an even higher
degree by an important sector of the Catalan proletariat (both authochthonous
and of immigrant origin). There developed a strong libertarian movement, bordering on millenarianism and mysticism, which rejected any form of authority.
By the 1930s, this movement had taken a prominent role, having also influenced
a number of intellectuals of petty bourgeois origin.

Both Catalanism and anarchism, which came of age towards the end of the
nineteenth century, were the products of the inability of the Catalans to find
accommodation within the 'modern' Spanish state. However, these movements
represented two diametrically opposed political projects. While Catalanism was
essentially reformist, anarchism was uncompromisingly revolutionary; while the
former was nationalist, the latter was internationalist; while Catalanism was
mainly a middle-class movement, anarchism was on the whole a working-class
one. In the years leading up to the Civil War, no bridges were built between these
two extremes; the name of the game was rather confrontation – open, often violent, class warfare. Catalanism, however, progressively constituted itself into two
major wings: a left, republican, secular one (ERC) and a right, monarchist, Christian one (LRC).

I would like to conclude this section on a quantitative note. Between 1875 and
1902 there were 175 ministers in Spain, of which only five were Catalan (compared to 35 Castilians and 26 Andalusians). Between 1902 and 1930, there were
182 ministers in different Spanish cabinets, of which only 13 were Catalans,
while there were 51 Castilians and 43 Andalusians. According to Genieys (1997),
this meant that the Catalan elites were not properly institutionalised in the power
structure of the Spanish state. It is not surprising that there emerged a peripheral
elite opposed to the state (1997: 79).

The period of the Second Republic (1931–36) and of the Civil War
(1936–39) was the first modern period in which there was an important presence
of Catalan ministers in a Spanish government. Out of 89 ministers, 13 were
Catalans, 14 Andalusians and 14 Castilians. This was the first time that the
Catalans were not only well represented, but actually over-represented (14 per
cent of ministers out of a population of Catalonia that was only 12 per cent of
that of Spain). The reasons for this strong integration of the Catalan peripheral
elites in the power structure of the Spanish republic were: the defence of the economic, financial and political interests of Catalonia and in particular of the

Statute of Autonomy; and the fact that Catalan republicanism was very strong, particularly up to the period of the Civil War.

During Franco's dictatorship (1939–75) the elites were mostly either born or centred in Madrid, they belonged to the middle classes and adhered to traditional values. Up to 1956 many were of military or fascist extraction, while after that date civilians (mostly civil servants) predominated. Altogether there were eight Catalan ministers out of a total of 114 (Jerez-Mir 1982; Botella 1995).

## The New Democratic Order and Elite Settlement

Before dealing with the topic of elites in Catalonia in any detail, it is perhaps useful to say a few words about the transition to democracy in Spain in general. A long quote from a noted specialist will give us the tone:

> The successful democratic consolidation in Spain [between 1978 and 1982] was primarily the product of a profound transformation of Spain's political elites from disunity into consensual unity. For the most part, the transformation involved the processes of an elite settlement. All significant nation-wide parties [with the Basque Country excepted] were induced to acknowledge the legitimacy of the regime's institutions and respect for its behavioural norms through extensive rounds of negotiations from the second half of the 1976 through the end of 1978, culminating in the overwhelming endorsement of the new Constitution in the December 1978 referendum. This elite settlement also helped forge a high and unprecedented level of structural integration among national elites (Gunther 1992: 40).

Among the features of this elite settlement that are worth pointing out are:

1. A mutual respect of opponents.
2. A noticeable degree of ideological convergence.
3. The moderate, democratic, Euro-friendly outlook of the Communist Party.
4. The conversion of large sections of the old Francoist elite to liberal democracy.

These events did not happen in a vacuum, and certainly the mass mobilisations of 1975 and 1976 against the attempts to perpetuate the Francoist order were an important catalyst for the future constitutional changes. Adolfo Suarez came to power in 1976; he was far from the stagnant character of his predecessor Arias, who had been appointed after Franco's death. Suarez, however, was still a child of the old order, though his will to change was obvious from the very start. How far he would have gone, though, without the unrelenting pressure of the political parties, the working-class organisations and the civil society in general is a moot question. In any case, the first democratic elections took place on 15 June, 1977.

It is important to remember that in the previous democratic experience of the 1930s the elites in Spain were disunited and polarised and their behaviour was rancorous. At that time Spain was a country of severe cleavages between the bourgeoisie and the workers (but also between landlords and peasants), between centralising and peripheral nationalisms, between the extreme left and the extreme right, between Catholic fundamentalism and militant atheism, etc. After the war, the Francoist experience represented a total suppression of ideological conflict; the Francoist political elites were recruited from three major pools: the army, the Fascist party and the Catholic Church.

Two of the most controversial decisions taken by Suarez were to legalise the Communist party and to grant a pre-autonomy statute to Catalonia (which involved the return of the President of the *Generalitat* in exile, Josep Tarradellas). The decision to reinstate the *Generalitat* was largely a symbolic act, given that its political content was rather limited. However, this brought Catalan political elites into the transition process as active collaborators. Among the seven men who drafted the Spanish Constitution, two were Catalan: one represented Catalan nationalism (Miquel Roca) and the other the communists of both Catalonia and Spain (Jordi Solé-Tura). The final agreement between the different parties was not easy; it took fifteen months of intense negotiations, and it required important concessions from all groups.

As Gunther has put it: 'the constitutional agreement of [October] 1978 represented an elite settlement among all politically significant parties outside Euzkadi' (1992: 61). An important point to make at this stage is that the main reason for the reluctance of Basque nationalists to participate in the process was that the future Constitution did not allow for the right of self-determination and secession. In this sense, the Basques were more faithful or stubborn to their original political project than the Catalans. After all, the right to self-determination was one of the key demands of the unitary Assembly of Catalonia, and this goal was shared by communists, socialists and nationalists alike.

### Elite Competition in Catalonia (1979–99)

From the beginning of a Catalan parliament, Catalan politics was characterised by the hegemony of a nationalist party (CiU) (Convergence and Union), which is essentially a centre, catch-all party; the success of CiU cannot be dissociated from the role played by its leader Jordi Pujol (Walker 1991). He was not a charismatic leader in the ordinary sense of the term and he was certainly not a prophet or a demagogue. On the other hand, he fits into one of Weber's categories – that of a person with a strong vocational sense (which goes back to his opposition to Franco in the 1950s) and an appeal focused on his person and his qualities.

Pujol was an extremely able political entrepreneur, with a sophisticated grasp of economic and political realities, not only at the Catalan level, but also at the

Spanish and European ones. In the elections to the Catalan parliament (1980, 1984, 1988, 1992, 1995 and 1999) CiU was always the most popular party. The autonomous community of Catalonia had only known one government – that of CiU – though in the parliament that followed the elections of 1980, 1995 and 1999 they had formed minority governments.

It is important to emphasise that, although CiU is the Catalan nationalist party *par excellence*, there are other parties which share, to different extents and with somewhat different implications, the belief that Catalonia is a nation. The Catalanist constituency, understood in this wider sense, would include approximately 80 per cent of the electorate. There is also a small party (ERC) (Catalan Republican Left) that is more radical, both socially and politically, than CiU. It is the heir of the nationalist hegemonic party of the 1930s. However, its recent electoral results are only around 10 per cent of the vote. In the 1990s, ERC came out openly in favour of full independence for Catalonia.

In the aftermath of the Francoist dictatorship, the two main parties of the left in Catalonia were the socialists (PSC) (Socialist Party of Catalonia) and the communists (PSUC) (Unified Socialist Party of Catalonia). They were both strongly committed to Catalan national identity and transmitted, with reasonable success, a Catalan sense of identity, or at least an understanding of the Catalan national realities, to many of their members and voters who were immigrants from poorer Spanish regions (mostly Andalusia). Through a civic definition of Catalan identity – Catalans are those who live and work in Catalonia and wish to be Catalan – autochthonous and new Catalans shared in the struggle against Franco under the banner of the famous rhyming slogan, which was chanted in many demonstrations: *Llibertat, Amnistia i Estatut d'Autonomia* (Freedom, Amnesty and Statute of Autonomy). It is important to emphasise that both socialists and communists were in favour of Catalan autonomy and federalism.

PSUC and PSC were relative newcomers to the Catalan political scene. The PSUC, formed during the Civil War as a result of a merger of four different left parties, was a communist party which maintained, to a varying degree depending on the historical period, an amount of independence from the PCE (Spanish Communist Party). It was perhaps the most active and successful underground party in the opposition against Franco.

The PSC came into existence in 1978 from a fusion of at least three nominal socialist parties – PSC (Congress), PSC (Regrouping) and PSOE (Catalan Socialist Federation) – and a variety of smaller groups, including anarchists and Trotskyists. The PSC (C) was by far the largest of the socialist parties. While the PSOE (Spanish Workers Socialist Party) was firmly established in many Spanish areas, including the Basque Country, this was not the case in Catalonia. The PSC, while maintaining its autonomy, chose to integrate itself within the PSOE. However, the relationships between the two parties have not always been easy, but the PSC has survived the test of time. During the period of socialist hegemony in Spain (1982–96) members of the PSC have participated in socialist cabinets in

Madrid, both in senior and in junior positions; particularly important was the role played by Narcís Serra, first as a Minister of Defence, and later occupying one of the two vice-presidencies of the Spanish government.

As to the other major left party (PSUC), it suffered a serious electoral erosion in the early 1980s, after having done reasonably well in the late 1970s (although not as well as expected, given its strength in the late 60s and early 70s). The reasons for its decline are varied: lack of appeal of the traditional communist message in a society that by then was economically developed, vote transfer to the triumphant socialists, internal squabbles, etc. In 1986, they re-emerged with a new name (IC) (Initiative for Catalonia) and later on, in 1995, they entered into an electoral pact with the Green Party. Although they have managed to improve their electoral results, they are no longer the third political force. In fact, with less than 10 per cent of the vote they trail behind the conservatives (PP) (Popular Party) and even ERC (at least for the elections to the Catalan parliament).

Finally, completing the party system in Catalonia, the Spanish right, with different political guises over the years – UCD (Democratic Centre Union) up to 1982, AP (Popular Alliance) up to 1989 and PP from then onwards – has always behaved as a centralist party, with minimal concessions to the Catalanist national demands. If it were in their power they would like to roll back the autonomic process and curtail many of the recent developments, particularly in the area of Catalan nation-building. Their electoral support in Catalonia (for the Spanish elections) has oscillated between 15 and 20 per cent of the electorate; in the Catalan elections their latest level of support was about 10 per cent.

A final general feature of the Catalan political system is what the specialists call the dual vote (Montero and Font 1991). From the very inception of the new democratic system in 1979, there has been an important floating vote, that is, people who change their party preferences depending on the type of election (municipal, autonomic, legislative and European). It has mainly affected, although not exclusively, the two main parties (PSC and CiU) and two types of elections (autonomic and legislative).

The end result of this vote transfer has been that, while the PSC has a majority vote at the elections for the Spanish parliament, the CiU has been hegemonic in the Catalan parliament. At the municipal level, the major Catalan cities, including Barcelona, have been controlled by the socialists, sometimes in coalition with the other left-wing parties (PSUC, ERC). Two main reasons explain the dual vote: firstly, many socialist voters of immigrant origin abstain at the autonomic elections. It appears that these voters are not terribly concerned with or aware of the important decisions taken by the Catalan parliament. Secondly, there is an autochthonous Catalan floating vote which prefers to support CiU for the Catalan parliament and PSC for the Spanish one. These voters believe, rightly or wrongly, that CiU will be better for Catalan affairs, while the PSC will represent them better in the Spanish arena. Furthermore, when people voted for the Catalan parliament the most prominent and best known figure they saw in the electoral contest was the leader of the CiU, Jordi Pujol. Conversely, at the level of the Spanish parliament they would tend to identify (until 1996) with Felipe Gonzalez.

The pattern of dual voting also occurs, but to a lesser extent, in the Basque Country, but not in any other autonomous community. It will be interesting to know what will happen in Galicia if the nationalists (BNG) (Galician Nationalist Block), which by the end of the twentieth century were the third party, with about 15 per cent of the vote, continue to make progress in the future. However, the solidity of the PP (with 50 per cent of the vote) and the strong position of the PSOE appear unassailable.

At this stage it is possible to conclude that the strategies of the two main parties of Catalonia (PSC and CiU) obey a different logic. For the PSC (autonomous insofar as Catalan affairs are concerned but subordinated to the PSOE in the general affairs of the state) the socialist victory of 1982 in the legislative elections meant that the *crème* of its elites were catapulted to Madrid and were asked to participate in the tasks of central government. During the years of socialist government (1982–96) five Catalan ministers were part of the different cabinets. Especially important, as I have hinted before, was the presence of Narcía Serra, first as Minister of Defence (1982–91) and then as Vice-President (1991–95). Other Catalan ministers were: Ernest Lluch, Minister of Health (1982–86), Joan Majó, Minister of Industry (1985–86), Josep Borrell, Minister of Transport (1990–93) and Jordi Solé-Tura, Minister of Culture (1990–93).

Perhaps more important than the above-mentioned ministers was the fact that the PSC also provided dozens of junior ministers and civil servants to the socialist administration. If a word defines their collective stance, it is that of 'modernisers'. Most of them had been dogmatic Marxists in the 1960s and even 1970s; by the 1980s they had been converted to the virtues of capitalism. Many of them were economists, and were concerned with contributing their managerial skills and their financial expertise, acquired in foreign universities, and exercised in the private sphere and in local government, to the tasks of running Spain. Their political philosophy can be encapsulated in the slogan 'what is good for Spain is good for Catalonia'. Or, to be more precise, only an economically developed, fiscally efficient, politically stable, European-oriented Spain would allow the development of Catalonia to its full potential.

There was, of course, a price to be paid. It is a well-known fact that European socialists have, on the whole, been Jacobin. The PSOE is a case in point. Its history is that of a centralising party and nobody should be taken in by its federalist trappings, which are mere concessions to the gallery. Insofar as the autonomic development of Catalonia as a nation was concerned, the PSOE of the 1980s was not only largely insensitive to the calls from the PSC, but in fact practised an involutional policy.

This state of affairs gave ample ammunition to the critics of the PSC, who maintained that the Catalan socialists had contributed, through their silence, if not their less than wholehearted backing, to the regressive autonomic policies of the PSOE. Things changed in the 1990s, and, while the PSC maintained that it was due to the influence of their leaders, less charitable interpretations, pointed to the fact that the PSOE no longer had an absolute majority in the Spanish parliament and needed the support of the Catalan and other nationalist parties.

In so far as CiU is concerned, what can be factually stated is that during the twenty years of democratic rule in Spain, CiU did not participate with ministers in any coalition government in Madrid. There were plenty of opportunities to do so, both in the early years when UCD, led by Suarez, had no majority, after 1993 when the socialists lost their absolute majority and at present when the PP is in power, but with an insufficient majority. However, CiU, along with other nationalist parties within Spain, had entered into agreements to support the survival of different minority governments, namely the socialist one in 1993 and the conservative one in 1996. An attempt in 1986 to create a Spanish-wide reformist party of a non-centralist kind led by Miquel Roca (CiU's second in command) failed miserably to obtain support.

On the whole, the policy of the Catalan nationalists over the past twenty years has operated at two levels:

1. At the general level of the state, the CiU became an influential political pressure group which, through lobbying, and by offering support to minority governments, exacted important concessions in the sense of a transfer of power from the centre to the Catalan autonomic institutions. This was seen by the CiU as an exercise in state-building, that is, the creation of a Catalan regional state, with an increasing economic, political and cultural content.

2. At the Catalan level, the CiU presented itself as the party of government *par excellence*, as a genuine Catalan party, that is, independent of any bonds or servitude to the centre. Only in this way could the national interests of Catalonia be best served. Recently, the nationalist discourse of the CiU has become more radical, although it is still short of demanding self-determination as the Basque nationalists do. The message, however, is that the model of the Spain of the Autonomies has not solved the Catalan national problem.

## Looking at the Future of Catalonia

Are the socialists, due to their schizophrenic attitude towards the national question, destined to be kept away from the *Generalitat*, from the Catalan Autonomous Government? Of course, as we have mentioned above, the Catalan socialists have managed to obtain good results in the local elections, particularly in the big cities. Either by themselves, or in alliance with the Catalan communists, they have successfully run Barcelona in the past twenty years, regenerating a city in decay and bringing the Olympic Games of 1992. In the

Catalan parliament, the PSC, as the second most popular party with the electorate, played a pivotal role in supporting the process of Catalan nation-building, including the at the time controversial linguistic legislation.

From 1982 to 1997 the mayor of Barcelona was Pasqual Maragall. A man with an impeccable Catalanist pedigree (his grandfather is the best-known poet of Catalan modernism), he is generally seen as an honest and efficient administrator. After much hesitation, he decided to put forward his name as the official socialist candidate to the *Generalitat* in the elections of autumn 1999. Without the support of other parties and, more importantly, without an important vote shift from loyal nationalist supporters, he did not win the elections. What will happen in the next elections, perhaps in 2003, is not clear, but the chances of Maragall are perhaps higher.

To have a wide appeal he has to convince a large part of the electorate that he will be faithful to the Catalan national project, while being careful not to alienate the traditional socialist supporters of immigrant origin, who may view him with suspicion if he goes too far in his Catalanism. Furthermore, at the Spanish level the PSOE is led by people who espouse a rigid centralism and are openly against Catalan nationalism. More or less open clashes between Maragall and some of the Spanish socialists are perhaps inevitable.

At this stage of the political game, it is difficult to predict what sort of changes a socialist victory would bring to the *Generalitat*. Maragall's political programme has been hitherto rather vague. It would appear that the administration would be inclined towards managing the Catalan institutions more efficiently; it would also be less ideologically charged in the nationalist sense of the term. The latter would reflect the changes in the PSC, particularly at the level of the intermediary cadres but also at the level of the leadership. While in the past, and to a certain extent even today, the ruling elites of the party were recruited from the autochthonous middle classes, the future trend is towards a domination by people of immigrant origin, whose sense of Catalan identity is more nuanced, if not ambiguous.

# 9
# THE FUTURE OF NATIONS IN A
# UNITED EUROPE

## Introduction

In this chapter, I deal with the implications of European unification. As the European Union moves inexorably towards higher levels of economic, political and cultural integration, states, ethnonations, transnational ethnic communities and regions ponder the advantages of such developments. The attitudes that each of these types of units display are obviously diverse, reflecting different interests and agendas. Ethnonations tend to see in the overarching institutions of the European Union a potentially more sympathetic and flexible framework in which to realise their objective of shared sovereignty, rather than the traditional state in which they find themselves at present. A 'Europe of the regions' – the ambiguity of the word 'region' notwithstanding – is one of the possible outcomes of the current process of unification, though the likelihood of such a development will depend on the strength that ethnonations and regions can muster in their confrontation with the state and with the emerging European bureaucracy.

Social scientists have recently observed, although not really explained, the apparent paradox that, at present, while there is an impetus towards the building of large economic and political units, there is, at the same time, a strong assertion of small-scale regional, ethnic and national identities. This has been taken to signify the death-knell of the nation-state and the coming of a future configuration of Europe in which ethnonational and regional identities dominate the scene in the context of large-scale, European-based institutions. Is this wishful thinking on the part of those who espouse such a thesis or are there real trends in this direction?

To say that the present is a momentous period in the history of Europe is to utter perhaps a *lieu commun*, but at present we can only have a hazy picture of what is likely to happen in the future. As social scientists, we have had to confess to two major inadequacies: an inability to predict the collapse of communism and the disintegration of the Soviet bloc, and the absence of sociological categories which would allow us to think in European terms – all our concepts being appropriate only to the national state. In the present circumstances, at a time of incessant change, the danger that we are facing as social scientists is that our short-term analyses, perhaps closer to glorified journalism than to painstaking sociological enquiry, are already dated by the time of their publication and medium-term and long-term projections are difficult to muster when no clear trends seem to have emerged.

Much has been made of the hegemony of the nation-state in modernity. There appears to be a consensus that the dominant, if not the sole, form of political organisation in the post-1789 era, and even before that, has been the nation-state. This thesis contains two very different assumptions. Firstly, it conveys the idea that, while in the medieval period a variety of state forms flourished (empires, city-states, theocracies, federations, etc.), modern times have seen the emergence, consolidation and final domination of a medium-sized, territorial, centralised, sovereign type of polity. Secondly, this new political unit is also characterised by national homogeneity – hence the expression 'nation-state', which means one state, one nation. Both assumptions are problematic, particularly the second one. While there is little doubt that there has been a tendency towards the consolidation of medium-sized, 'modern' types of states in Western Europe, the presence of the Austro-Hungarian and Ottoman empires until World War I, of the German Reich from 1933 to 1945, and of the Russian empire until recently qualifies the idea of the dominance of the nation-state in the modern period, if we refer to Europe as a whole. In addition, the persistence of small states in Western Europe challenges the assumption of the medium-sized nation-state as the vessel of modernity.

A much more important critique of the concept of nation-state is that it is regularly used to describe states which are meant to be nationally, that is, ethnically, homogeneous, when in reality they are not. The idea of a world consisting of states the boundaries of which coincide with the homelands of cultural groups is a myth. In a well-known article, W. Connor (1996) remarked that only 9.1 per cent of the world's existing states were ethnically homogeneous, and hence deserved the label 'nation-states'. It would appear, then, that the uni-national state is not a common occurrence, but rather a rarity. There are, of course, different degrees of heterogeneity: from the existence of a small national minority within a state to truly multinational states. The point to be emphasised here is the misnomer of the expression nation-state when referring to the realities, not the ideals of modernity.

To return now to Western Europe, none of the medium-sized classical examples of nation-states (e.g. France, Great Britain, Spain) fit the bill; the newcomers (Italy and Germany) hardly qualify either, because the nation is wider than the state (Germany) or because the nation itself is an invention without roots and what has salience are the local identities (e.g. Italy). Of course, the word 'nation' is often used in a political sense as equivalent to citizenship, to signify the democratic incorporation of the population of a country to the political tasks. The word 'state', however, should suffice to indicate this reality, particularly in the twentieth century. It is true that there is some ambiguity in the word 'state', which can also mean, as in the case of the U.S.A., a federal union; in this eventuality the constituent units are referred to as 'states', and hence the use of the expression nation-state to refer to the whole. But these so-called states lack one essential characteristic – total sovereignty. It is inescapable that the term 'nation' should have a political and cultural dimension. Only ideally do countries converge towards the perfect congruence between the political (state) and the cultural (nation). As K. Aun has remarked, 'the paradox is that both nation-building by the states and state-building by the nations have the same root – nationalism; and they have the same goal – the nation-state; but as processes they collide with each other' (1980: 72). In fact, the objective of achieving true nation-statehood has proven a slippery, not to say an unattainable aspiration.

The process of clarification of the concept of nation-state has indicated an unavoidable ambiguity in the use of the term. It is naive to expect that the expression 'nation-state' will ever be used to reflect a univocal reality. The reluctance of social scientists to coin and to agree to the use of new technical terms, with precise definitions, is notorious; they prefer to stick to everyday language, to redefine old terms and hence to contribute to the ceremony of confusion. In addition to this, however, multiple meanings also result in the possibility that a term may be used by different groups to defend different political models in the cultural arena. In other words, terminological ambiguity may mask attempts to monopolise the symbolic capital of certain ideas which are considered extremely valuable in modernity. This is the case of the concept of nation. Many social scientists, particularly in the French tradition, are reluctant to label as 'nations' entities that are not politically independent: Durkheim, Mauss, Dumont and more recently Schnapper (1994) all seem to agree.

The insistence of multinational states such as the U.K. and Spain in calling themselves 'nations' should alert us to the appeal of the idea of nation. From the perspective of the submerged ethnonations, there is also an insistence in asserting their nationhood by the use of the term 'nation' to refer to themselves. Furthermore, the process of cultural struggle is completed by each group labelling its opponent with a term considered unacceptable by the other – ethnonations do not like being called 'regions' and self-styled nation-states object to being referred to as states.

To some rigid commentators, wherever state and nation do not coincide there is bound to be a clash of loyalties; it is argued that one cannot serve two masters. Raymond Aron put it the following way: 'Chacun de nous a une patrie et une religion, mais nul ne saurait avoir deux patries' (1969: 41). This is true insofar as both states and nations try to become nation-states, which is precisely what happens in the era of nationalism. As expressed above, it is fair to say that, on the whole, the idea of a world in which nation-states would be the predominant political type is a mirage. The practice of nationalism in the past two centuries (both state nationalism and nationalism against the state) has shown how illusory the dream is, and how often it can turn into a nightmare. The first fact to be faced is that the reality of any unit, no matter how many subdivisions a state might be subjected to, is still likely to be multinational and multiethnic. This is, of course, a generalisation and, as such, it should be qualified. Even if we can agree that, at least in Europe, the nationality principle has radically changed the political map of the continent in the past two centuries, the end is nowhere a set of homogeneous states. A number of reasons account for this:

1.  The nationality principle is eminently ambiguous and open to instrumentalisation by any group that has an axe to grind. All the key elements involved in the definition of a nation (language, culture and history) can be easily manipulated. Insofar as a national project can gather a degree of popular support, it has a de facto reality. In other words, there is no end to potential fissiparity, though in practice it may be restricted.
2.  Once the notion of homogeneous states has been dispelled, the next myth to be challenged is the idea that there exist homogeneous territorial ethnonations. The uneven development of capitalism in the different European states has produced population movements that have undermined the traditional homogeneity of these areas.
3.  Some parts of Europe, particularly the East, are traditionally areas of great national and ethnic complexity.
4.  Recent migratory processes have brought into Europe, particularly Western Europe, transnational ethnic communities from different parts of the world.

## Spain and the United Kingdom: Nation of Nations?

It is interesting to note that the expression 'nation of nations' has made its recent appearance in the literature to account for such realities as Spain and the U.K. This brings the issue of multiple identity and multiple loyalty to the fore. If it were possible to separate loyalty to the state (a political matter) from emotive attachment to the nation (a psycho-cultural phenomenon), the problem of congruence between state and nation would not be of much consequence. The problem arises because the state tries to become a nation, so that it has to elicit sentiments of belonging, that is, love from its subjects; this is the modern pre-condition for loyalty.

To succeed in that it has to attempt to homogenise a multiethnic reality. This is achieved by erasing, with a mixture of coercion and inducement, all cultures other than the dominant one. On the other hand, the nation, in an attempt to preserve its identity, has no other option but to try to become a sovereign, self-governing entity, that is, an independent state. This is a rather ideal typical presentation of a much more complex historical reality. In fact, states and nations often compromise and accept solutions that are far from their intended objectives. Furthermore, it should already be understood that deviations from the ideal norm are overdetermined by a structural variable hitherto unmentioned – the regional or global interstate system.

It is precisely as a result of this fuzziness between state and nation that a concept such as that of 'nation of nations' could be coined. This expression seems to indicate a supranational reality, usually formed over a long period of time around a cluster of nations which share a state. The new entity would emerge in the context of a sort of pooling of cultures, each essentially preserving its identity, but giving rise to a higher level, national reality. Now, this model can only work if the state is the result of a pact of equals, and is organised on a federal basis, respecting the national characteristics of the constituent parts. Historically, this is an extreme rarity, with only perhaps Switzerland approximating the model. In the historical context of Europe, even if some states were initially the result of a union of crowns (usually engineered by monarchs in league with sections of the aristocracy), what happens in the long run is that they become centralised, unitarian types of state, with a dominant nationality which tries to impose, to various degrees, its own language, culture, sense of history, religion, etc. on the others. Insofar as this process is successful, the expression 'nation of nations' may be appropriate, but it implies that the second part of the equation refers mostly to the past. France, originally an 'ethnic mosaic' (Strayer), would perhaps best conform to this model, although one should not forget that the end product is recent and contains imperfections.

So what can be said about realities such as Spain and the U.K.? Can they be envisaged as nations? The two cases are not necessarily the same, although they offer interesting possibilities of comparison. The problem with the U.K. is that there is no single word to designate the members of the supposed nation – although Tom Nairn (1988) has suggested, somewhat jokingly, the term Ukanian. British is, of course, the usual word, but it excludes some of the peoples of Northern Ireland. Leaving aside terminological problems, can we say that the English, Northern Irish, Scots and Welsh all feel the same towards the U.K.? It is obvious that, for the English, the U.K. is England writ large or a Greater England. British culture is essentially English culture, with some minor colourful concessions to the cultural peripheries. The English shamelessly refer to the U.K. as 'England' (a practice which is even more widespread among foreigners). This should come as no surprise, even if the Scots tried, after the Union of Parliaments, to popularise the expression 'Britain' (and even 'North Britain' to refer to themselves). Scots, Welsh and Irish have lived under the spell of English culture, and have to a certain extent been 'anglicised'. Pressures for the creation of a strong nation-state were greater in Ireland (a kind of colonial outpost) and led to the creation of the incomplete Republic of Ireland in 1922. The Scots, who had essentially joined the Union of their own will, preserved an array of separate institutions (legal and educational systems, Church, etc.); the Welsh were incorporated into the English Crown much earlier and by force, but were not 'anglicised' until well into modernity. There have been movements of national self-assertion in both Scotland and Wales since the late nineteenth century. While in the former it is based on a strong sense of history, in the latter the linguistic and cultural elements predominate.

I tend to agree with B. Crick (1991) when he says that '"British" is a political term and a legal concept best applied to the institutions of the U.K. state, to common citizenship and common political arrangements. It is not a cultural term, nor does it correspond to any real sense of a nation. And nor should it … To be British demands a kind of loyalty, but a pragmatic loyalty limited to those civil institutions we have in common' (1991: 97). For the peripheral nations of the U.K., there was a sense in which being 'British' had 'national' overtones at the height of the British Empire, but hardly today, although there is still perhaps a mystical sense of British identity via the royal family. Furthermore, at present, the U.K. consists not only of a disproportionately large dominant nation (England, with 46 million people) and three subordinated nations (Scotland, with 5 million people; Wales, 2.7 million; and Northern Ireland, 1.5 million), but also contains a number of transnational ethnic communities which create a polity which is culturally pluralistic in the extreme. A sense of British identity in such a plural society can only be understood in the sense expressed above by Crick. The nationalist demands of the Scottish, Welsh and Northern Irish peoples are of different quality and intensity, and may require specific solutions for each of them. In any case, whichever way they are satisfied, they are more likely than not to erode the idea of a British cultural nation even further. These developments, and the fear of being swallowed by Europe, are awakening the sleeping beast of English nationalism – a creature that at its worst exhibits xenophobic, chauvinistic and anti-European sentiments.

England is to the U.K. what Castile is to Spain. However, there is an initial terminological difference that should be noted. While in the British case there is only a cumbersome phrase to designate the supposed nation-state (United Kingdom of Great Britain and Northern Ireland) and no word at all to refer to their 'nationals', the very opposite occurs in the case of Spain. Although the Spanish state is very much a Castilian invention and creation, the ruling elites and their ideological spokesmen have always insisted on using the term 'Spain' to refer to an indivisible, national reality. In Spanish nationalist discourses, from the post-

French Revolutionary period to today, if there is one constant it is that Spain is always described as a single and indivisible nation. None of the constituent parts of Spain are recognised with national status (although the 1978 Constitution accepts the existence of 'nationalities') in the sense of entities endowed with contractual powers, among which figures the right to self-determination.

For 35 years the Francoist dictatorship engaged in the most active and aggressive policies of nation-building ever seen within the Spanish state. Its objective was to create a homogeneous national space of Spanishness; to that end, it was essential to erase the national identities of Catalonia and the Basque Country. If Franco failed to achieve his stated goal, it was not for lack of trying; he used all the means that a quasi-totalitarian dictatorship had in its reach – the educational system at all levels, military conscription, the media, political institutions, the fascist syndicates, the Catholic hierarchy, etc. – to project the idea of Spain as a chosen community, with a common past and a common destiny. He only underestimated one thing: the will of the people of Catalonia and the Basque Country to resist the policies of cultural extermination.

In the aftermath of Franco's death, the demands for autonomy in Catalonia and the Basque Country could only go unheeded at the cost of alienating the two most dynamic areas of the Spanish state. A democratisation of the country required as a *sine qua non* the devolution of power. The Constitution of 1978 was a compromise in that it created a moderately decentralised 'state of the autonomies', in which not only Catalonia and the Basque Country were given autonomic powers, but these were extended to all the constituent parts of the state (although the actual configuration and boundaries of the different autonomous communities were not without problems). This process of decentralisation has generated strong regionalist sentiments in most of the autonomous communities and even incipient nationalist feelings in some of them. For the majority of the population, Spain is still a 'state' and a 'nation', although this is not the case in the Basque Country and Catalonia. It is still too early to foresee the likely developments of nationalist sentiments in Spain, but it is unlikely that ethnonationalisms will subside in the near future, given the pending nationalist agenda.

Had I taken Belgium as an example of a 'nation of nations', it would have been much easier to show the clay feet of such a construct. As a recent state with eighty years of existence, it could only appear as an ideal nation-state in the musings of narrow-minded ideologists. In recent surveys 'Belgian' identity comes only in third place of choice, after ethnonational identity and a European one. In any event, I think that the cases of the U.K. and Spain show how two old European states, with similar processes of state formation, and which are often presented in the literature as successful nation-states (although, in the case of the U.K., the reference in the literature is often only to 'England'), are in fact multinational realities, even if they exist as 'nations' for a large percentage of the population of both countries; but, even for those who define themselves in ethnonational terms, the fact of the antiquity of both states and of the concomitant processes of nation-building in which both have engaged, has created an additional layer of national characteristics which live side by side with the ethnonational ones. Whether this entitles us to speak of multiple national identity is problematic, though not totally outlandish.

There is a slippery slope which leads us from the idea of a multiple identity typical of the postmodernist scenario, with a concept of culture as a global super-market in which individuals choose from a range of cultural artefacts, a combi-nation of the identity flavours of the day according to their conditioning and preferences. Whether the world in general, and Europe in particular, is heading towards such a reality is difficult to foresee, though what is worth exploring is the apparently contradictory double motion towards globalisation and fragmenta-tion.

## European History and Sociology: A Brief Encounter

When we consider the intellectual sources that have contributed to the creation of Europe a number of elements come to mind: the Judaeo-Christian tradition, Greek and Roman civilisations, the Scientific Revolution, the Enlightenment, etc. Many authors seem to maintain that Christianity was one of the key factors in the formation of Europe, although other scholars emphasise the role of reason, and particularly of scientific rationality. In the medieval period, Europe and Chris-tendom, understood as a community of peoples and a geographical area, were one and the same. In this period, Christendom was opposed to, and defined itself in opposition to, Islam. In addition, the identity of Europe was placed in a wider framework: that of the Graeco-Roman tradition.

With the advent of modernity, we have a process of secularisation in which the idea of Europe, as a unity within diversity, emerges as the central concept. Reli-gious diversification is accompanied by the increased used of the vernaculars. This does not imply that a basic, underlying cultural unity was not preserved. There is certainly no political unity, but there is a European concert in the form of a balance of power, no matter how precarious. It is not until after the French Revolution that national cultures became increasingly differentiated and antago-nistic, particularly in the context of the development of extreme nationalism.

Projects concerning European unity emerged in the eighteenth and nineteenth centuries. We can refer, for example, to Jeremy Bentham's *Project for a Lasting Peace* (1787), Immanuel Kant's *Perpetual Peace* in the late eighteenth century, Henri de Saint-Simon's *The Re-Organisation of European Society* (1814) and Vic-tor Hugo's *Discours on the United States of Europe* (1849). The Europeanist move-ment did not start in earnest until the interwar period (1919–39), in the context of the internationalist movement (League of Nations, 1919). One of the best known and most inspired animators of Europeanism was Count Coudenhove-

Kalergi, who founded the Paneuropean Union. At the political level there was the official initiative of Aristide Briand, a French politician, who in 1929 saw the need for the unification of Europe. Many well-known intellectuals of the period were also in favour of lofty Europeanist ideals. The reality of the 1930s, however, particularly with the development of fascism, of extreme nationalisms, of xenophobia and of racism, with the belief that autarchy (economic self-sufficiency) was not only possible but also desirable, contributed to the collapse of Europeanism.

In view of the differences and divergences which exist in Europe at all levels, does it make any sense 'to speak of Europe as a context which can be delineated as a unit and therefore regarded as a meaningful framework for comparative research' (Haller 1990: 186)? An answer in the affirmative has to show that it is possible to delineate the 'external boundaries of the continent' and to demonstrate that 'the internal structure does not divide up into subdivisions which are unconnected or unrelated to each other' (ibid.).

At present there are three main reasons that suggest that Europe is a unit: increased economic relations between the different European states, increased information exchange through the mass media as well as personal contact through tourism, study, work, etc. and increased political relations and integration through agreements and treaties. A number of sociological questions follow from considering Europe as a unit. For example: What are the political, cultural and economic consequences of mass immigration on Europe? What are the effects of global culture, particularly in the mass media, on European national cultures? How is increasing human contact through tourism affecting traditional stereotypes about different European national and ethnic groups? What are the effects of the process of European integration on national identity and state sovereignty? Are there any institutions or policies that are helping to generate a European consciousness?

When we consider the differences within Europe today, the generalised consensus is that with the collapse of the Soviet-type communism after 1989 market economies and liberal democracy are the dominant principles of organisation for Europe as a whole, independently of how long it might take for some of the Eastern European economies to implement these principles. However, one important element of differentiation within Europe is still the socio-economic level of development as expressed not only in the GNP per capita, but also as what is usually referred as quality of life (standard of living, level of education, state of health, access to cultural facilities, for example).

At the cultural level there are historically important differences that still persist, though there are some trends that suggest that they might be, if not fading away, at least being attenuated, that is, that they are losing force. I am referring, of course, to religion and language. In this context, it is possible to distinguish three major religious groupings: Catholics, Protestants and Orthodox; and three major linguistic groupings: Romance, Germanic and Slavonic languages. Up to a point, a correlation can be established between religion and language with the consequence that, on the whole, there is an overlapping between Catholicism and Romance languages, between Protestantism and Germanic languages and between Orthodoxy and Slavonic languages. How far can we establish other correlations, between say Protestantism, liberalism and economic development, and say Orthodoxy, authoritarianism and economic underdevelopment (with Catholicism somewhere between the two) is open for discussion (Haller 1990).

If there is something that we can call Europe, understood perhaps as an ideal-type, what characteristics does it exhibit? According to Hans Zettenberg (1991), there are a number of self-regulating and autonomous institutions, associated with specific key values and types of freedom, which can be used to describe modern Europe. These are the following:

| Institution | Key Value | Type of Freedom |
|---|---|---|
| Economy | Prosperity | Free Trade |
| Government | Order | Civic Liberties |
| Science | Knowledge | Academic Freedom |
| Religion | Sacredness | Religious Toleration |
| Arts | Beauty | Artistic Licence |
| Ethics | Virtue | Right to follow one's own conscience |

## State Sovereignty, National Identity and the European Union

'My counsel to Europe can be given in a single word: "Unite".' Thus wrote Winston Churchill in the Foreword to the Proceedings of the Congress of Europe in 1948. The message to the Europeans that emanated from the Congress of The Hague was simple: either unite or peace, economic well-being, political freedoms and independence will be at risk. The process of European union has been long, arduous and protracted. For many, in Central, Eastern and Southern Europe, the 'dream of a federation of equal nations, of a United States of Europe in which different languages and different cultures would have equal status' became, for many decades, a nightmare filled with misery and repression.

The postwar period in Europe was characterised, until 1989, by an extreme stability of political borders. A number of Western European states came to the conclusion that it was in the interest of peace and prosperity to create a united Europe. Among the essential objectives was to put an end to the state enmities which had led to two devastating conflagrations in the twentieth century. It was believed that the best course was to begin with economic integration, and later to move slowly towards the political union of the peoples of Europe. With the umbrella protection of NATO, the military threat to Western Europe by the Soviet Union could be contained, and energies concentrated on the construction of the European Economic Community. The core states that grouped together to form the future EEC – Germany, France, Italy, Holland, Belgium and Luxemburg – provided, in due course, such an attractive economic model that many other Western European countries wished to join the club; in a world constituted by economic giants, a united Europe could be an economic force to be reckoned with. Perhaps an over-economistic agenda pushed to one side the equally important task of recreating and fostering a spiritual community based on historically developed, common European values.

Many commentators have noticed that the European *fin de siècle* was characterised by two opposite tendencies: on the one hand, a concerted attempt to create a European union which would subsume a number of functions of the old national states and, on the other, a recrudescence of state nationalism, ethnonationalism and regionalism. As we shall see, the liberalisation of the Soviet system, culminating in the revolutions of 1989, triggered off a process of national affirmation in Eastern Europe and the Soviet Union, liberating forces which had been dormant for between half and three quarters of a century. Nations which were only a shadow in the collective memory shine again on the horizon; states which seemed consolidated for ever have shown their feet of clay; German unification – unthinkable only a few years ago – is now a matter of fact.

In Western Europe, a reactive, xenophobic kind of nationalism has also developed as a result of the growing presence of an immigrant population (partly economic migrants, partly political refugees) often racially, culturally, religiously and linguistically different. These transnational ethnic communities, often occupying the lower echelons of society, have come to be perceived as a potential or an actual threat to national identity by a large percentage of the autochthonous population. A number of different strategies have been developed to cope with the conflictual dimensions of such a situation. First of all, most European states have enforced stricter immigration controls. Second, an assimilation policy has been pursued. The results have been mixed, and for two reasons: the sheer number and the radical difference in cultural outlooks make it difficult for the majority of the immigrants to adapt easily; furthermore, Western societies have often rejected the assimilation of the immigrants on racial or other grounds. Third, the idea of multinationalism was floated as a possible alternative to assimilationist policies, but again this encounters noticeable resistance among the autochthonous population.

These are general trends, but there are wide variations across countries. Traditionally the French state has tended to be assimilationist, both culturally and politically, while the German state has much stricter criteria of nationality. Hence, in Germany there has been a tendency to perpetuate the existence of a community of citizens and a community of denizens. The British and particularly the Dutch governments have been more sympathetic to multiculturalism, while the southern European states have no clear policies because the phenomenon of immigration has caught them more recently, and unawares.

In the past few years the situation seems to have reached a stalemate, with no obvious solution in sight. It would appear as if the idea of Europe as a melting pot is in serious trouble, and intolerance towards 'the Other' is growing. In the medium term things are likely to deteriorate due to the increasing migratory pressures from both the South and the East on so-called 'fortress Europe' (a term that should be used with caution). All the signs seem to indicate that different types of nationalism are on the increase. Perhaps to dramatise things one could say that the spectre of nationalism is haunting Europe once again.

In the cultural arena, representations of nationalitarian values have to compete, though at times can also combine with other values, namely religious, class, racial, gender, familiar and individual representations. Europe is indeed such a value and is now an idea whose time is ripe, even if it is not clearly defined or, indeed, has a multiplicity of meanings. In any case, there are four essential problems besetting the idea of a united Europe: sovereignty of the states, nationalism of the peoples, integration of the non-European ethnic groups and enlargement of the EC, especially in the East.

Generally speaking, there is a discourse that is extremely sensitive to the effects that a centralised European Community could have on matters of identity (national and otherwise). As with the presence of aliens, the process of European union generates a real fear of losing territory, personality and the power to control one's own affairs; in a word, there arises a crisis of identity which expresses itself in a reactive nationalism, often accompanied by chauvinistic and jingoistic manifestations. It would be naive to think that the different contending actors are of equal stature. In this respect, the national state is both *de jure* and de facto the most powerful one. States may be in a position to block progress towards a more democratic and decentralised Europe. That is why J. Galtung suggested that only concerted and vigorous action of the regions could save us from an inflexible and stultified European Community. Nonetheless, the future configuration of Europe is far from having been defined.

It is not surprising that the attitude of the different European actors towards a united Europe should be fickle – at times exuding euphoria, at times manifesting anxiety. After all, what is Europe? A unique civilisational area or just a geographic denomination? An entity of the past, of the present or of the future, or maybe just a utopia? The anarchist dream of a federation of European peoples or a type of totalitarian nightmare? A federation of European peoples large and small or a centralised, bureaucratic and uniform state? A common economic market or a unified polity? A social-democratic Europe or a free-for-all 'savage' capitalist Europe?

## What Unites Europe

We know from successive Eurobarometers that in most EU countries only a very small percentage of people (around 5 per cent) declare themselves as having an exclusive European identity, while up to 50 per cent do not have any sense of European identity. Among the founding members of the community, the sentiment of Europeanness is most developed. Although it is possible, and perhaps even desirable, to criticise the methodological assumptions and categories used in most opinion surveys, including, for example, the dubious assumption that European identity and national identity are the same type of identity, nonetheless there is little doubt that the sentiment of belonging to an entity called Europe is rather limited.

What will happen in the future is not easy to ascertain. For example, the existence of an economic space is a factor that, by itself, may or may not be conducive to the development of a sentiment of European identity. The precariousness of European identity should not be surprising, even if it is accepted that all Europeans belong to the same civilisational space. The reasons for this are fairly obvious: a millennial history of conflicts and wars, the fact that identity has been traditionally expressed through the nation, and the fact that individuals are socialised within a rather restricted circle (family, town, country).

After fifty years of existence, the European Union (EU) suffers from what Marc Abeles calls a 'symbolic deficit'. The measures hitherto taken by the EU to enhance Europeanness are rather limited and fall into the following categories:

1. The suppressions of borders within the EU and the right to settle in any country of the community and enjoy the same freedoms as the nationals.
2. The creation of the following symbols: passport, flag, hymn, car registration plates, etc.
3. The idea of European citizenship (after Maastricht) (limited in scope).

Some members of the bureaucratic and governing elites of the EU have been toying with the idea of creating a superstate. Some specialists believe that this would generate a sense of belonging. There are, however, two provisos. In the first place, how long would it take: centuries? Another important question is: how successful would it be (taking into account, for example, the failure of smaller European multinational states)? There are other ways of creating unity: from bottom to top. A number of areas can be mentioned:

1. *Teaching of foreign languages.* There are 70 languages spoken in Europe, and only 15 of them are official in the EU. Although English dominates in a number of areas (popular music, science, business, tourism, etc.), multilinguistic competence will still be required. It is open to argument whether English domination will lead to Europeanisation (it is, after all, a global language).
2. *Increased exchanges at all levels* (educational, cultural, etc.).
3. *Teaching an agreed curriculum on European history.*
4. *Development of common European symbols:* community of destiny (avoiding wars, preserving environment, etc.), community of values (tolerance, freedom, human rights, solidarity, etc.) and community of life (active role of individuals in the making of Europe).

5. *Presence of Europe in the world arena* (common defence, common foreign policy, etc.).

6. *Encouraging cultural tourism.* Unlike mass tourism, which reinforces stereotypes, cultural tourism can help to dismantle prejudices and contribute to creating a genuine respect and appreciation for other cultures and languages.

7. *Europeanisation of sport.* Some authors maintain that sport can help in the process of creating unity, even if they acknowledge that it can be a way of venting national passions. It can be argued, however, that the increased Europeanisation of sport will promote a certain amount of European consciousness.

8. *Marriage and other unions across European nations.* These unions are on the increase. In these cases, the family unit becomes a microcosm of diversity, mirroring the wider European dimension and creating a space in which cultural, religious and other identities coexist and/or have to be negotiated.

9. *Europe as a cultural actor.* This is an option defended mostly by French intellectuals as a way of opposing the penetration of American culture, particularly in the audiovisual fields. In fact, this is a rather elitist position that is not shared by the majority of the people of Europe, who vote with their feet concerning cultural products. Furthermore, it is difficult to see how a continent so diverse linguistically and culturally can present a united front, unless it is to defend national cultures.

## Globalisation and Fragmentation

If prior to the collapse of the Soviet order the trends towards the internationalisation of the world economy, the progressive domination at the world level of a transnational 'culture' (initially American in origin) and the impact of the technological revolution (particularly the processing and communication of information) were already obvious, the collapse of the communist world has dispelled the few illusory hopes that existed of a possible alternative to capitalist hegemony on a world scale. Whether we believe in Fukuyama's 'End of History' ideology or not, the reality of the global village seems to be inevitable now, at least in a certain sense. We are told that we are all becoming more or less the same – or at least we tend to consume the same cultural and material products. Does that mean that we think, we feel and we behave in the same way? The answer is, of course, a resounding no, because the way in which different nations, ethnic groups and classes react to the global culture are mediated by their very different identities. Even here, however, a certain amount of uniformisation must be taking place. After all, we also have very similar educational curricula.

It is in this context of general globalisation that the phenomenon of ethnic identity has not disappeared, as modernisation theorists had predicted, but has become ever more salient. Around the world, people may watch American soap operas, have English as a lingua franca, wear jeans, drink Coke, listen to Madonna and read international pot-boilers, and yet are becoming only superficially 'Americanised'. If they live in a multinational and multiethnic state, as is likely to be the case, they may have a pragmatic allegiance to the governing institutions of the country, but they are also likely to have a strong sense of ethnic or ethnonational identity (in addition to other posssible overlapping identities such as gender and class).

For better or for worse, this is a world trend that shows no signs of abating, and which, of course, undermines the stability of unitary and centralised multinational states. I would strongly disagree with Hobsbawm's (1990) contention that these signs should be read as the swansong of nationalism. There is, of course, no way of predicting the future, but we can certainly learn from the past. The foretold death of ethnonationalism has been asserted at least since Marx and Mill in the 1840s. All those 'peoples without history' that Engels had ridiculed – the Basques, the Bretons, the Slovenians, the Welsh, etc. – have come back to haunt him; they are still all here today, with ever growing and stronger identities. I think that this should generate, at least, a cautionary attitude towards the vitality of ethnonationalism even in those who are sceptical about the long-term viability of the small, ethnonational identities in a world characterised by uniformity. I think that we still have to listen to Mazzini's idea that nationhood is the necessary intermediate identity between individualism and cosmopolitanism. Perhaps in a future 'brave new world' national identities will be totally obsolete, but this is not the case for the foreseeable future.

It may be worth exploring in some detail the recent recrudescence of ethnonationalism. First of all, I would like to insist on the obvious: that in Europe, like elsewhere, there are a good number of unsatisfied ethnonationalist demands which have manifested themselves for quite a long period of time. No doubt, this intensity has varied from period to period, and according to the structural conditions of the states and the international conjuncture. The bottom line, however, is that, unless the demands are fulfilled (through either autonomy or secession), the conflict is likely to continue. I should add immediately that in a number of cases the ethnic and national mix in a given territory is such that there are no easy solutions in sight. The collapse of rigid and authoritarian political structures has been the immediate detonator of ethnonationalism East and West; but only where there was a previous situation of supressed ethnonationalities have movements of national emancipation re-emerged (it happened in Spain, but not in Portugal, for example).

It is difficult to characterise the events that have transformed the Soviet bloc beyond recognition. Should we talk about revolution, upheaval or simply chaos? More than a decade after the beginning of the major visible changes, things are still in a state of flux, although some points can be made with some certainty. There is, first of all, the collapse of the USSR-dominated politico-military bloc. Second, the idea of a command economy has been abandoned to the gnawing rats, and substituted by more or less rapid moves towards a market economy. Third, there has been a strong assertion of ethnic and national identities and a move towards the (re)creation of nation-states.

It would theoretically be very satisfactory if we could suggest that the revival of nationalisms in the West and in the East are the result of a general movement. This, however, does not seem to be the case. Western ethnonationalism (and regionalism) is taking place in the context of waning nation-states (for the reasons mentioned above) and the appearance of the European Union as a condominium of power. The future shape of the European Union is far from decided and it matters to ethnonations and regions whether it is a centralised federalism (all powers exerted by the centre), confederalism (general goverment subordinated to constituent states) or federalism (general and regional governments to be each within a clearly defined sphere; coordinated but equal; independent; principle of subsidiarity). It is obviously the federalist option, the so-called Europe of the regions, which is favoured by ethnonations and regions. It not only responds to sound economic arguments, but is also the adequate framework in which to preserve and develop cultural authenticity and in which to exert a proper, more direct democratic control of political institutions.

As I have repeatedly indicated, in Western Europe the independentist option pure and simple is becoming unimaginable and unappealing even for radical ethnonationalist groups. For example, the slogan coined by the Scottish National Party in 1988 –'Independence in Europe' – expresses the essence of the compromise forced upon originally secessionist groups that have been induced to rethink their strategy in the light of the momentum acquired by the move towards an even closer European union. The unlikelihood of obtaining enough popular backing for a 'pure' separatist option, that is, outside the European Union, and the reluctance of the state apparatus to concede it if this were the case make such a programme unrealistic. In addition, the assumption that the newly independent country would be taken aboard the European Union is not something that can be taken for granted. However, in the eventuality of a major state crisis the independent option might prove both appealing and feasible.

The federalist perspective, by emphasising the principles of autonomy (that is, respecting the right of all the collectivities), cooperation (a union to solve common problems) and subsidiarity (the federation is organised from bottom to top; that is, the centre only takes the tasks that have been delegated to it and that it is more efficient at), offers a much better chance to achieve the major objectives of the ethnonations. However, it should be noted that, after Maastricht in 1992, the European Union is far from being or becoming a federal union. Notwithstanding the reluctance of many states to move beyond a confederalist structure (this attitude being particularly strong in the U.K.), and the dangers of a centralised federalism, the game is open to shape the European Union in many different possible ways. A growing pressure from ethnonations and regions towards having a more direct saying in the decision-making of the European Union is the precondition for achieving a federal Europe, with a strong democratic Parliament and an ever-growing role for the Committee of Regions, which in due course could constitute, along with the Council of Ministers, a 'genuine upper chamber consisting of representatives of the regions and of the existing member states' (McCready 1991: 18).

It is important to emphasise that, at least in the context of the European Union, the progressive withering away of the nation-state will not mean that ethnonations will succeed in establishing themselves as nation-states. There will certainly be a new nationalism that 'will seek to mobilise new sentiments of resistance and cultural development based on the challenges of the twenty first century' (McCrone, 1991: 8), but the old doctrine of sovereignty is in its death-throes; and boundaries of all sorts are likely to become more fluid.

In the aftermath of the collapse of the Soviet Union and Yugoslavia into internecine ethnic/national struggles, it has become *de rigueur* among 'progressive' intellectuals to revamp an old-fashioned distinction between 'good' and 'bad' nationalism under the labels 'civic' and 'ethnic' nationalism respectively (Ignatieff 1994). While the former is presented as essentially democratic in character, emphasising the loyalty to institutions and to an egalitarian political creed, the latter is depicted as denying individual freedoms and sacrificing everything to a community often understood in terms of common descent or based on blood ties. From such a definition of ethnic nationalism there is only a small step to conceptualise it as the cause of all ethnic violence and war. This seems to me a rather simplistic conception, if only because it ignores an array of other causes, among which I would point out the lack of liberal and democratic traditions in many of the countries which suffer the ravages of the so-called 'ethnic nationalism'. It also glosses over the important role of oppressive states in generating reactive nationalisms. Furthermore, the distinction between civic and ethnic nationalism seems to ignore the peaceful struggle for cultural and linguistic autonomy of stateless nations in the Western world. Last but not least, the term ethnic nationalism introduces an element of confusion in the social scientific literature, because it can be confused with the established term 'ethnonationalism', which I have used freely in this book to refer to substate nationalisms or nationalisms against the state (Connor 1994).

## Conclusion

One of the most distinctive features of the European Union, which contrasts with the way in which the national state developed, is precisely that the former is the result of a voluntary pact entered into by democratic states, while the latter was constructed on the basis of coercion and carried out by non-representative elites. In spite of the fears expressed by many, it is unlikely that Europe will ever, or at least for the foreseeable future, become a superstate or indeed a supernation, particularly if the construction of Europe is undertaken in a democratic way, respecting the rights of large, medium-sized and small states, ethnonations, regions and transnational ethnic communities. The idea that Europe will be a condominium of powers, that is a voluntary association that will share certain powers, is perhaps the closest approximation that we can offer at this stage.

The European Union will not abolish the sovereignty of the states, though undoubtedly certain aspects of the latter will be relinquished voluntarily and put into a joint pool of sovereignty. National identities, at whichever level, will continue to exist, and even flourish. Bavarian, Scottish and Catalan identities have survived for a long time, alongside German, British and Spanish identities. There is no reason to think that the situation will be different in the future. This is not to deny that there is increasing national anxiety as a result of the growing presence of culturally different aliens and of the homogenising activities of the Communitarian bureaucracy.

As I have mentioned above, the fear of losing national identity is real enough. However, it should be possible to allay many of these fears if the European Commission and the Council of Ministers operated in a more transparent and didactic way. In the medium term, one would hope to see the European Parliament and a Council of the Regions involved in decision-making. Nonetheless, the success of the European union will require the development of a European identity, with its 'common myths, values, symbols and memories drawn from the reservoir of the common heritage'. This is certainly a Herculean task for which intellectual leadership will be required.

Nearly a century ago, Emile Durkheim concluded that the only way in which humanitarian ideals could be realised in the context of Europe would be to channel the different existing patriotisms towards achieving a higher morality at all levels, towards improving society in general and towards fostering the development of artistic and scientific talents. Was this wishful thinking, or can we approach the new century approximating these European ideals?

At the beginning of this chapter I said that it is very difficult to make any kind of prediction about the future of Europe. A leading American historical sociologist, Charles Tilly (1992), ventured some prognostications concerning the future of Europe. He envisaged a number of possible scenarios. In the short term he predicted two different trends:

1.  The proliferation of states matching the more bellicose and/or diplomatically successful populations that lack states of their own (this trend applies to Eastern Europe).
2.  The continuation of the long-term trend towards consolidation into a decreasing number of more or less homogenised states; at the extreme, we are talking about a vast single European Community with increased state-like powers and a certain sense of cultural identity.

In the long run, however, Tilly saw the most important feature to be the detachment of the principle of cultural distinctness from that of statehood. The implications of such a statement are the following:

a. The creation of a strongly connected but multicultural Europe in which most individuals will function bilingually (or trilingually) and will exercise their right to territorial mobility, following job opportunities and preferences.
b. The desire of ethnonations to claim national independence within the framework of separate states will greatly diminish because the European Union will offer all the advantages of being a free nation, without the costs and inconvenience of being an independent state.
c. The existing states, in whichever form they may exist, will cease to enforce cultural homogeneity and political dominance within their domains.

Tilly was well aware that this may sound too optimistic a conjecture, given the history of mankind. That is why he allowed for two variants within the long-term trend: a benign form of the state, characterised by pluralism and diversity with an absence of squabbles and attempts at domination; and a malign form of the state, characterised by segmentation, hatred and parochialism, in the context of gross inequalities and violent ethnic conflicts.

To return to the nature of nationalism. It does not help, either cognitively or practically, to demonise nationalism; the truth is that nationalism can be put to very different uses and that the label nationalism often conceals other realities. In an article originally published in 1971, Clifford Geertz captured the ambiguous character of nationalism as a begetter of both havoc and creativity, and he added: 'It would seem, then, well to spend less time decrying it – which is a little like cursing the winds – and more in trying to figure out why it takes the forms it does and how it might be prevented from tearing apart even as it creates the societies in which it arises, and beyond that the whole fabric of modern civilisation' (Geertz 1973: 254).

To conclude on a note about the future. There is little doubt that an ethnonationalism which is too obsessed with defining itself in primordialist terms is likely to clash with other potential identities; ethnic conflict will probably follow, but there are democratic mechanisms which can help to regulate it (McGarry and O'Leary 1993). The notion of territoriality (explained in Chapter 3) is likely to become more central than the purely cultural or linguistic features. Ethnonational identity will emphasise the fact of living and working in a given territory, though no doubt there will still be a more or less important ethnic element present.

# 10
## EXPLAINING NATIONAL IDENTITY: A THEORETICAL CLOSURE

### The Resilience of Nationalism

At the beginning of *The Communist Manifesto*, Marx and Engels invoked the spectre of communism and predicted that it would haunt Europe until the final victory of the proletariat. Blinded, however, by their own discovery, they failed to see the importance of an emerging and even more threatening political force: nationalism. One hundred and fifty years later, it is not easy to decide which of the two *idées-forces* – to use Fouillée's felicitous expression – had the upper hand in European as well as world affairs. There is little doubt, though, that nationalism has been, and still is, probably the most important political force of modern times. Yet it has been poorly understood and theorised by the different social scientific traditions. A long time after Vico wrote in his *The New Science*: 'that this world of nations has certainly been made by men, and its guise must therefore be found within the modifications of our human mind. And history cannot be more certain when he who creates things also narrates them' (1975: 62–3), we do not agree as to what a nation is, or what we mean by national identity, or how we account for nationalist movements.

In the period immediately following the Second World War, it was thought, somewhat optimistically, that the end of nationalism was in sight. E.H. Carr could refer with confidence to 'the aftermath of the age of nationalism' (1968: 74), while pioneers in the study of nationalism, such as Hans Kohn and Carlton Hayes, emphasised its transient character, abhorred its effects and hoped for a more universalistic attitude. All of this was in vain, because the obscure forces of nationalism prevailed over the enlightened wishful thinking of internationalists and cosmopolitans alike. In its relentless motion, nationalism spread like wildfire into the colonial world and triggered off the struggles for national liberation in what was starting to be known as the Third World.

The process of decolonisation, with the ensuing attempts at state-building and nation-building, could only be ignored by social scientists at their own scholarly peril. And yet, although these events generated a fair amount of literature in the 1950s and 1960s, of which Balandier (1955), Kedourie (1960), Deutsch and Foltz (1963), Geertz (1963), Worsley (1964) and Wallerstein (1966) are the best known representatives, it was considered that Third World nationalisms were the last jolts of a monster that had ravaged the world for over 150 years, but was now moribund. Nationalisms were, however, part of the inevitable process of modernisation that had spread from Western Europe to other parts of the world, admittedly in an uneven way. In the final instance, these nationalisms could be dealt with within the framework of an evolutionary theory.

It is not surprising, then, that the spate of nationalisms against the state that have shattered the political fabric of the Western World in the last twenty years should have caught most social scientists theoretically unprepared. They had been working under the assumption that the modern industrialised societies of Western Europe were nationally well-integrated, that is, they were proper nation-states. Social scientists were in fact the perfect example of double false consciousness. First, they mistook what was actually state ideology for empirical reality; second, they believed, against a growing amount of evidence, that after a long process of nation-building Western European states were nationally well integrated. The existence within each European country of what were perceived at the time as regional differences and even strong identities was in no way recognised as a challenge to the basic loyalty that the citizen felt for the nation-state. Furthermore, it was believed that, with the development of the EEC, even the Europe of the *patries* would fade away in a not too distant future.

We could say, paraphrasing Durkheim, that social phenomena have a life of their own, independent of the opinions and desires of social scientists and politicians. The resilience shown by nationalism over a long historical period should have alerted social scientists to the importance of the phenomenon. It is, however, a fact that most nineteenth-century and twentieth-century social scientists not only ignored or misunderstood the nature of nationalism but also underestimated its force.

It may be argued that nationalism, as the scourge of modern times, is not there to be talked about, rather it is to be uprooted as a most dangerous evil. And yet the nation still has a role to play in the foreseeable future, because as Mazzini put it: 'the individual is too weak and mankind too vast' (1972: 59). Of course, for those who confuse Herder with Hitler, and the nation with the state, all this might be anathema. In any case, even if one were to agree that nationalism is a pathological phenomenon, it would still be the case that it is *terra incognita* for the social scientist, and hence worthy of being explained.

The wave of nationalisms against the state in Western Europe, from the 1970s to the present, has been a source of political destabilisation that has affected nearly all countries to different degrees. In recent times, following the collapse of the Soviet bloc, the political image of this area has radically changed. The radical way in which a significant percentage of the population of Northern Ireland reject British rule may only be comparable to the militant stand adopted by ETA supporters in their struggle for an independent Basque state, but the phenomenon is much more general, if not always so virulent. The Welsh and the Scots in the U.K., Catalans, Galicians and Andalusians in Spain, Friulians and other *Grenzeleute* in Italy, Walloons and Flemings in Belgium, and even the peripheral nationalities of the French state such as the Corsicans, all try to preserve a sense of national identity and rightly believe that this can only be achieved in the framework of a state that provides them with a substantial degree of political autonomy.

In West Germany the federal system had, to a great extent, pre-empted the possible emergence of peripheral nationalisms, but the *Nationalefrage* has persisted more or less consciously in the mind of most people insofar as they had not accepted the *de jure* partition of Germany into two states, which came to an end in 1991. The disintegration of the Soviet bloc opened up the opportunity for many Eastern European countries to reaffirm their 'Europeanness', as is particularly obvious in the Polish, Hungarian and Czech cases. Yugoslavia was originally a multinational state, and had achieved a delicate balance between the different nations. In 1991 there began a prolonged collapse of Yugoslavia, that is, an extremely violent separation of nationalities. As to the Soviet Union, it had partly disintegrated by 1992, but internal and external problems of a national character have survived, some of them extremely severe.

## Classical Sociology and the Nation

The reasons for the inability of social scientists to come to terms with the national question have their origins in the cosmopolitanism of the Enlightenment, but find their specific roots in the intellectual traditions of the nineteenth-century founders of the social disciplines. The underlying political philosophies of the social scientific projects of the nineteenth century were based on either liberal or socialist conceptions of the world. No matter how different these conceptions might be, liberalism and socialism are both universalistic in nature, and hence they consider nationalism as a transient phenomenon. Only conservative and romantic thinkers of the nineteenth century perceived, in all its uncontrollable turbulence, the force of nationalism in history, but they were not interested in explaining its origins, character and development, rather in asserting its eternal reality.

There is today a consensus that contemporary social theory stems from the confluence of three major streams of thought: Marx, Durkheim and Weber. This is not to deny the importance of thinkers like Comte, Spencer, Tocqueville, Tön-nies, Simmel, Freud and others whose ideas have found a way into mainstream sociology, nor is there any suggestion that a synthesis has emerged incorporating Marx, Durkheim and Weber into a single theoretical framework. Their sociolog-ical styles are irreconcilable, both at the methodological and at the theoretical level, though partial syntheses have been shown to be possible and fruitful. In fact, the greatest challenge of contemporary sociology is precisely to convince its practitioners that progress will only come as a result of abandoning their recalci-trant feudal-like positions and joining in a common enterprise. Without a com-monly agreed theoretical charter, however, all attempts to transcend the present state of affairs, no matter how well intentioned, are bound to fail. It is an idle occupation to look for a theory of nationalism among the founders of the social sciences. At best, Marx, Durkheim and Weber made occasional remarks on the nation, but on the strength of these elements it is extremely difficult, if not alto-gether impossible, to build up a theory of nationalism.

The founders of historical materialism were certainly well aware of the nation-alist phenomenon. As politically committed young intellectuals, Marx and Engels lived through the troublesome 1840s – a period in which nationalist struggles rav-aged the European arena. In their formative years, then, they had to confront the nationalist demands of a variety of European peoples. To understand their atti-tude towards nationalism, it is essential to know that they subordinated the sur-vival of nations to the progressive march of history: some peoples were fossils from a long gone past and were therefore objectively counter-revolutionary. These reactionary nations had to be sacrificed to the altar of the mightier national states. In the articles written by Marx and Engels for the *Neue Rheinische Zeitung* (1848–49), the national question was often present as part of the political sce-nario, but there was no attempt to explain the phenomenon, except perhaps in terms of crude stereotypes of national character. It is obvious that for Marx and Engels the nation was not a central category of social existence, but rather a tran-sitory institution created by the bourgeoisie. Hence the passage in *The Commu-nist Manifesto* to the effect that the 'proletariat has no fatherland'.

At the turn of the century, the vindication of the rights of nations changed the political panorama to the extent that to the Marxists of the Second International the national question was central in their political agenda. However, it was only within the Austro-Marxian tradition that a serious attempt was made to come to terms with the theoretical problems of the nation. Otto Bauer's *Die National-itätenfrage und die Socialdemocratie* (1907) presented a theory of nationalism based on the idea of national character and of national culture, though he also used the dubious idea that nations have a historical destiny to fulfil. A much bet-ter known and more influential contribution from this period is, of course, Stalin's *Marxism and the National Question* (1913). In his definition of the nation, Stalin required the simultaneous coalescence of four elements (language, territory, economic life and psychic formation) in a historically constituted community of culture. As for Lenin, he adopted a more flexible definition of the nation and, although he was in favour, like most Marxists, of the creation of large political units, he endorsed the principle of self-determination of oppressed nations, at least in theory.

As a whole, the Marxist tradition has been extremely suspicious of nationalism, though for tactical reasons they have often made use of national sentiments to achieve socialist objectives. In any case, within Marxist theory the nation is not a significant concept that can help to explain the dynamics of modern history. I would tend to agree with Tom Nairn's sweeping statement that the 'theory of nationalism represents Marxism's great historical failure' (1977: 329). The extraordinary developments of the 1960s and 1970s in which socialist countries have fought bitterly against each other along nationalist lines have opened the eyes of some Marxists (Davis 1978; Anderson 1983) to the reality that, at least at present, national interests are, in the final instance, more important than socialist internationalism.

From the 1970s a number of attempts were made to develop a theory of nationalism along a modified Marxist line. Among the most prominent approaches one should mention the following: internal colonialism (Hechter 1975), uneven development (Nairn 1977) and world systems (Wallerstein 1974; 1980; 1987). Among the most original Marxist approaches is that of Miroslav Hroch (1985). In his seminal book, *Social Precondition of National Revival in Europe*, he proposes a class analysis of the origin of the European modern nation, although he also considers the role of cultural developments. The book is based on the comparative study of the early nationalist movements of six stateless nations (Czechia, Lithuania, Estonia, Finland, Flanders and Slovakia). All these different authors, and others, are dealt with in more detail in my book (Llobera 1994).

Emile Durkheim's silence on the national question is quite intriguing considering that in his formative period, in the 1880s, he was asking the same question that Renan had formulated in 1882 – *Qu'est-ce qu'une nation?* In his early writings, mostly in the form of long book reviews, Durkheim made an inventory of a number of authors (Fouillée, Schäffle, Tönnies, Gumplowitz) who had contributed to the study of how national consciousness was created and maintained. The concepts that Durkheim evolved over this period – especially *conscience collective* and *représentation collective* – cried out to be applied to the study of national consciousness in contemporary societies. Towards the late 1890s, however, Durkheim operated a double shift, which led him to an increasing concern with primitive societies and to the *refoulément*, to use B. Lacroix's expression, of the political sphere. The result was that the two basic concepts mentioned above were never put to the test for the study of modern nations.

We have to wait until the publication of a wartime pamphlet – *L'Allemagne au desssus de tout* (1915) – to find Durkheim expressing an interest in the theory of the nation. The work was basically a tract against Treitschke and other German theorists who had deified the state and were objective accomplices of the expansionist policies of Kaiser Wilhelm. In opposition to Treitschke, Durkheim praised the German tradition of the *Volksgeist* (Savigny, Lazarus, Steinthal) because in their conception of the nation they took into account the impersonal forces of history (myths, legends, etc.). In other words, they assumed that a nation had a 'soul', a character which was independent of the will of the state. It is somewhat surprising, then, that when Durkheim proposed a definition of the nation – as a 'human group whose members, either for ethnic or simply for historical reasons, want to live under the same laws and constitute the same state' (1915: 40) – he was unable to clearly distinguish between nation and state. Could this oversight be a reflection of Durkheim's role as one of the committed ideologists of the Third Republic?

The First World War, with the collapse of socialist internationalism and the rallying of the working-class parties to the interests of their respective national states, was undoubtedly the catalyst that compelled many social scientists to think about the nation. Within the Durkheimian School, this led to a number of discontinued and failed attempts to incorporate the nation into sociological theory. In 1920–21 Marcel Mauss started to write a monograph on the nation, which he never completed. From the scattered fragments that are extant (Mauss 1969, Vol. 3), we can conclude that his standpoint was no different from that of Durkheim in that he never solved the antinomy between state and nation. The problem with Durkheim and Mauss is that they had the French historical experience of a national state too much at heart to pay enough attention to alternative conceptions. Another Durkheimian, Maurice Halbwachs, although not directly concerned with articulating a theory of the nation, was nonetheless interested in the study of one of the key elements in any definition of the nation: the idea of collective memory. His work, however, had limited diffusion, and his refined conceptual tools were applied to a variety of groups (family, class, etc.), but not to the nation (Halbwachs 1925; 1950).

Wolfgang Mommsen's *Max Weber und die deutsche Politik* (1959) empirically established for liberal and democratic ears the unpalatable truth that Weber was not only a German nationalist, but that for him the national state was the 'ultimate value'; in other words, that in the final instance, the interests of the national state should prevail over any other interests. Although in *Economy and Society* Weber defined the nation as a community of sentiment based on some objective common factor (language, traditions, customs, social structure, history, race, etc.) and the belief that this factor generated values which were worth preserving against the encroachment by other communities, he insisted on creating an indissoluble bond between nation and state. To all practical purposes the nation, that is, the cultural values of a community, could only be preserved in the framework of a purpose-built state. On the other hand, Weber knew very well that the modern state could not achieve its aims exclusively by brute force. The loyalty of the individual to the state depended on the existence of a national sentiment, and hence the centrality of the equation 'nation equals state'.

There is little doubt that Weber's understanding of the nation was far superior to that of Marx or Durkheim. For one thing, he was well aware that national sentiments were not the creation of the rising bourgeoisie, but that they were actually rooted in the population of a country as a whole. Because *Kultur* was the distinctive feature of a national community, Weber was very interested in the question of its preservation, transmission and change. In this context, he considered crucial the role played by the intellectuals in creating a literary culture. It is unfortunate that Weber did not write, as he had actually planned to do, a history of the national state (Guibernau 1996).

## Theories of Nationalism

Since the 1970s there has been an exponential growth of the literature on nationalism. Any attempt to take an inventory and systematise it is a daunting task, but already in the 1970s Anthony D. Smith's (1971; 1973) survey of the main theories and studies on nationalism included an impressive list of books and articles. A somewhat cavalier way of disposing of the problem is to assume that, as a phenomenon, nationalism is theoretically intractable due to the heterogeneity of what is supposed to be explained. How can we compare ideas, processes and groups that have appeared in different historical or social contexts (Zubaida 1978)? Whether this point of view is a remnant of the golden age of Althusserian scholasticism, with its fastidious insistence on the impossibility of constructing certain theoretical objects, or an attempt to emulate the Lévi-Straussian idea that certain theoretical realities are just the illusory products of certain ways of thinking (Lévi-Strauss 1962: 149), the question is in any case worth considering. There is always the danger, though, that if this methodological prescription is applied too rigidly we could lose sight of even the core of the nationalist phenomenon.

Most studies on nationalism, whether by historians, political scientists or sociologists, are basically descriptive and narrative in type. The enormous amount of writings on nationalism seems to dissolve into rather superficial and colourful statements. It looks as if a great number of these studies have been undertaken with a sense of expediency, as a response to urgent political needs. Not surprisingly they are theoretically jejune. Most of these studies fail the minimum standards required to fulfil the Durkheimian criterion of using well-established facts. What this amounts to is that we cannot make a scientific inventory of the social facts of nationalism, for the simple reason that we lack the basic building blocks: good monographic studies of individual nations. That most of these studies are also theoretically thin is to be expected. At best, theories of nationalism play the old labelling and typological game. Placing often ambiguous facts in differently coloured boxes is, however, no substitute for a fully-fledged theoretical pursuit.

Some social scientists have tried to construct a theory of nationalism on the basis of the comparative method *à la* Frazer, a temptation to which sociologists have been particularly vulnerable (Smith 1981). Anthropologists, having been immunised by the Malinowskian vaccine, have been less prone to forget the first functionalist commandment: ye shall not pluck out isolated facts from a variety of historical and social contexts and compare them.

Of the general theories of nationalism, that of Ernst Gellner (1983) is by far the most widely praised and accepted. Gellner's powerful argument rests on pinning down the appearance of nationalism to the transition from agrarian to industrial society. The two models of society that Gellner uses – Agraria and Industria – are extremely abstract. The facts of nationalism are, however, too complex to be accounted for by a formalistic and simplistic model of the process of modernisation that ignores history. It is precisely because Gellner's theory is ahistorical that it is so difficult to see whether it works or not. However, by pinpointing the precise role of language and culture, as well as of education, in the development of nationalism, Gellner has made what will probably be a lasting contribution to the study of state-generated nationalism; it is up to historically minded social scientists to test his provocative hypotheses.

Anthropological theories of ethnicity have suggested either that ethnic identity is the result of a primordialist affiliation (Shils 1957; Geertz 1963; Isaacs 1975; Francis 1976; Grosby 1994; Allahar 1996) or that it is highly malleable and subjective, and hence at the mercy of power games (Barth 1969). Primordialist perspectives stem from extending to a wide population the belief that they descend from a common ancestor and the idea that this generates a sense of identity and of solidarity. In the instrumentalist point of view, the emphasis is on the idea that identity is not given or fixed, but varies in time and according to circumstances. Ethnicity is the way in which human groups perceive reality. For a group to survive, what matters is not cultural or biological continuity but the maintenance of ethnic boundaries. Both approaches, primordialism and instrumentalism, have their own partisans and have proven fruitful, if only partially, in a variety of empirical studies. I can only offer, in what follows, a condensed perspective.

Primordialism assumes that group identity is a given, that there exist in all societies certain primordial, irrational attachments based on blood, race, language, religion, region, etc. They are, in the words of Clifford Geertz (1973), ineffable and yet coercive ties, which are the result of a long process of crystallisation. Modern states, particularly, but not exclusively, in the Third World, are superimposed on the primordial realities – the ethnic groups or communities. Primordialists believe that ethnic identity is deeply rooted in the historical experience of human beings to the point of practically being a given. Primordialist approaches contend that ethnic bonds are 'natural', fixed by the basic experiences that human beings undergo within their families and other primary groups. Edward Shils was the first to express this idea when he remarked that in family attachments there is a significant 'relational quality' that can only be called primordial. This is because there is an ineffable attribute to the ties of blood (Shils 1957: 142).

The primordialist position was further elaborated by Geertz (1973). It is interesting to mention the three major ideas that follow from his work: primordial identities are natural or given; primordial identities are ineffable, that is, they cannot be explained or analysed by referring to social interaction, but are coercive; and primordial identities deal essentially with sentiments or affection. Primordialism has been subjected to extensive criticism. In particular, three qualities emphasised by Geertz – apriorism, ineffability and affectivity – seem to preclude the possibility of sociological analysis. Furthermore, primordialism is unable to account for the origins, change and dissolution of ethnic groups, not to speak of the modern processes of fusion of ethnic groups through intermarriage.

It would be fair, however, to say that many of the problems with primordialism disappear if the term is understood in a more flexible, less biologically determined way. Without rejecting the idea of primordial attachments, it is possible to insist on their malleable character. These bonds are essential to human life, but the individuals of a group confer meanings on what they do in a symbolic way. For example, the passion and strong sense of loyalty that a person feels towards a socially constructed entity such as an ethnic group or nation are often as powerful as those felt for a blood-based group like the family (Connor 1994).

It is also worth mentioning another universalist theory of nationalism: the sociobiological perspective. In recent times, sociobiologists have put forward the idea that the resilience of ethnic identity is rooted in the biology of nepotism – this term is understood as the procedure used by human beings to maximise their reproductive capacity (van den Berghe 1981; Reynolds et al. 1987; Shaw and Wong 1989). This position is compatible with the idea that ethnicity may be subjected to rapid fluctuations in response to the environment. Social scientists are rightly suspicious about sociobiology, but is there biological 'reductionism' in stating that ethnicity rests in the shared belief of common ancestry?

The sociobiological approach starts with the assumption that nationalism is the result of the extension of kin selection or the tendency to nepotism by a wide sphere of individuals who are defined in terms of putative or common descent. Sociobiological explanations are not necessarily articulated in terms of genetic determinism, although it may be heuristically useful to make such an assumption. Most sociobiologists do not suggest that nationalism can be explained solely in terms of genetic mechanisms, that is, without linking them with the results of the human and the social sciences. The sociobiological approach insists that nationalism combines both rational and irrational elements, that is, a 'primitive mind' with modern techniques. The word 'nationalism' expresses different realities: a love of country, the assertion of national identity and national dignity, but also the xenophobic obsession to obtain these things through violence and sacrificing other nations. Nationalism builds on ethnocentrism towards the in-group and xenophobia towards the out-group.

For Shaw and Yuba, nationalism 'fosters pride, dignity and related sentiments among members of the in-group, thereby constituting a moral and philosophical basis on which to demand political sovereignty' (Shaw and Yuba 1989: 137). Nationalism has its roots in the past, but is a contemporary vehicle through which to vent human propensities for war. It is important in this context to emphasise the psychological dimensions of nationalism; a bond is established between the individual and the nation based on the idea that the latter is a family writ large. The individual identifies with the nation and hence tends to prefer it to other nations. The extensive use of kin terms to refer to the nation reflects this psycho-affective reality that Edgar Morin has called 'matri-patriotic', with an associated fraternal/sororal component.

As I have mentioned, Frederick Barth provides us with the best-known and most influential approach in the area of instrumentalism. His methodological steps concerning the definition of ethnicity are as follows:

1.  Ethnicity is envisaged not as an expression of vague culture, but as a form of social organisation. In any case, it refers to culture and it emphasises the cultural differences between groups.
2.  The main focus of research is the boundary that defines the group, as well as the process of recruitment of its members, and not the characteristics of the culture of the group. Boundaries have to be understood in the symbolic and social sense of the term.
3.  Boundary maintenance is thus essential for the ethnic group and is not primordial, but rather the outcome of specific ecological, economic, historical or political situations.
4.  In terms of identity, groups are characterised by both ascription and self-ascription. Constraint only follows when members agree to form part of the group.
5.  The cultural features chosen by the members of a group to differentiate themselves from other groups, that is, to establish a boundary, are to a certain extent arbitrary.
6.  Ethnic groups are mobilised, not so much by popular will but to a great extent by ethnic entrepreneurs or leaders.

Over the years, the Barthian paradigm has been subjected to a number of criticisms. It would be fair to say that not all situations permit manipulation; for example, in the situation of racial differences, absent from Barth's model, the choice may be very limited. In this respect, one should emphasise that Barth's theory of fluidity of ethnic groups applies better to the Third World than to the First World; in the latter, ethnic identities are often more fixed because of a longer period of nation-building and state formation. As an exclusively anthropological approach, Barth's theory tends to ignore the historical depth, and hence it obscures the processes of ethnic fusion and fission; equally, there is a tendency to minimise the role of the state as a result of an exclusive focus on interpersonal relationships. Finally, the transactional approach is often blind to situations of imbalance of economic or political power among ethnic groups.

## Genesis and Development of Nationalism in Western Europe

The fact that Western Europe was the birthplace and the *lieu classique* of nationalism justifies my standpoint that any theory of nationalism should start by trying to account for the emergence and development of nationalism in this area. Only when we are clear about the meaning of nationalism in Western Europe can we hope to come to terms with its 'diffusion' to other parts of the world, or test the applicability of a similar model. It is my contention that a regional (Western European) theory of nationalism should provide us with the following answers:

1. An understanding of the subjective feelings or sentiments of ethnic and national identity, along with the concomitant elements of consciousness. This is the task of an anthropological theory *sensu stricto*.
2. An account of the genesis and evolution of the idea of the nation and of national identity and consciousness in the Middle Ages and in early modern Western Europe. This is the task of a history of mentalities.
3. A spatio-temporal explanation of the varying structures (ideologies and movements) of nationalism in the modern period. This is the task of a structural history.

There are serious problems in explaining the transition from ethnic to national identity, but they are partly due to the lack of in-depth historical studies on how the transformation occurred. Attempts to correlate the appearance of national sentiments with the development of capitalism, as many social scientists do, are incompatible with the fact that nations predate capitalism. Soviet scholars have introduced an intermediary stage between tribe and nation, that of *narodnost*, but this only compounds the problem. J. Armstrong's groundbreaking *Nations before Nationalism* (1982) considers modern nationalism as part of a long cycle of ethnic consciousness. From a different standpoint, A. Smith (1981; 1986), Schulze (1996) and Hastings (1997) have also made significant contributions to the understanding of this matter. It is only the perspective of the *longue durée*, however, that will allow us to find a way out of the blind alley in which our obsession with the modernity of nationalism has placed us (Breuilly 1982). There is no miraculous appearance of the nation at the time of the French Revolution, rather a long process of evolution starting in the Middle Ages (Llobera 1994).

It has been repeated ad nauseam that nations and nationalism, as we understand them today, did not exist in the Middle Ages. This is a mere truism. To abandon for this reason any search into the processes of how nations were formed and how national sentiment developed is tantamount to sociological suicide. The history of mentalities, insofar as it combines a variety of approaches to the study of modes of thinking, perceiving and feeling, focuses on the old Durkheimian problem of how collective representations are both a social discourse and socially generated. As a phenomenon of the *longue durée*, national consciousness is well open to the kind of scrutiny operated by historians of mentalities.

There is, however, a conceptual gap between the medieval and the modern ideas of the nation, and that is why national identities had to be 're-created' or 're-invented' in modernity. However, the crucial thing is how to account for the transition from the classical *ethnies* into modern nations (Smith 1981; 1986; 1991), and why this process originally took place in Western civilisation. Only a theoretical framework that incorporates a variety of factors, not only economic (industrial capitalism), social (classes) or political (modern state), but also ideological (nationalist ideas), is likely to approximate the explanation needed, given the complexities of the phenomenon (Llobera 1994).

It should be clear by now that, within the field of comparative and historical sociology, my approach could be labelled structural history, were it not for the amphibology, that is, the ambiguous wording, of this expression. This is an area in which we truly stand on the shoulders of contemporary giants (*Annales* historians, Barrington Moore, Charles Tilly, etc.). The work of Immanuel Wallerstein (1974; 1980; 1987) on the origins, structure and evolution of the world system should receive special attention, as it is the most recent attempt to put forward a general theory in the social sciences. As such, it is a necessary starting point for any further historical and comparative endeavour. It is unfortunate, however, that Wallerstein has failed to conceptualise the nation – which he considers as part of the cultural dimension of the modern world system. Furthermore, insofar as he defines national consciousness as a cultural assertion in the political arena to defend economic interests, it is clear that Wallerstein cannot account for the phenomenon of nationalism, except in a reductionist way. These strictures notwithstanding, a non-dogmatic and cautious use of Wallerstein's world-system theory can be a valuable tool for assessing the functional and historical verisimilitude of a given hypothesis.

The fact that Western Europe is a relatively homogeneous area, where at the same time some of the key variables for the explanation of nationalism (particularly religion, level of economic development, ethnic potential, type and timing of state formation, etc.) change from country to country, permits us to use a methodology of limited and controlled comparisons, hence avoiding the pitfalls of Frazerian comparativism.

In the modern sense of the term, national consciousness has only existed since the French Revolution. The purpose of any study in this area must be to map out the different constraints that have shaped the nationalist discourse in Western Europe into what it finally came to be: the ideology of mass movements. My theoretical assumption is that nationalism is a privileged semantic field which encapsulates the structure and dynamics of modern Western Europe in general and of each specific country in particular. The problem is how to interrogate this discourse, how to uncover the rules of its formation, how to assess its effects on society. A serious epistemological obstacle to achieving these objectives is what I would call the sociological myth of the nation-state, i.e. the belief that because the nation-state happens to be the paramount ideology of the modern state it must necessarily correspond to a sociological reality.

The kind of structural history that I propose here does not seek to superimpose models on reality, rather it envisages history as a result of a complex dialectical process in which no a priori primacy is given to any factor. We attend to the unfolding of the social totality in history, and follow its meandering from one place to another, from one period to the next. However, once ideas and institutions have appeared in history they acquire a life of their own and under certain conditions, which need to be empirically investigated, have a perdurable effect on society. Structural history is not in a position to explain all that happened and why it happened. Many areas of social life, particularly in the sphere of nationalism, are the result of historical events which are difficult to predict (wars, invasions, annexations, etc.) and which, therefore, may always remain impervious to our queries. On the other hand, and as Barrington Moore put it, there is also much to be learned from trying to explain why something did not occur.

I envisage nationalism as a sort of geological formation insofar as different layers of ideological material are deposited over time, but with the difference that past ideologies set constraints on present ones and that the latter may modify the former. The end product is an apparently motionless, but in fact continuously changing discursive formation propelled by the articulation of discursive and extradiscursive practices. This conception is perfectly compatible with the Gramscian notion of cultural hegemony, with the caveat that it is the very idea of nation as a *Gemeinschaft* that is the stake of the ideological struggles (Bourdieu 1982: 16). Finally, and paraphrasing Marx, one could say that nations make history but not in circumstances of their own choice, because the past lingers on in the present. In other words, the way in which the past is perceived by a community plays a key role in determining the formation of a nationalist ideology and in developing a national consciousness. As I have briefly shown, there are certain structural constraints that shape the ways in which people look at the past.

There can never be a totally satisfactory answer to the question of why modernity values national identity so highly. At best, we can map out the different elements or forces that have produced this state of affairs. In the context of modernity the problem is not so much to explain the salience of cultural nationalism across the board as a solid refuge for the individual at a time of accelerated secularisation and of the disintegration of the traditional, but rather why the modern state did not tolerate polyethnic structures in its midst and aim at creating, with varied success, a homogeneous space within which to project a single culture, an official language and a uniform conception of history both by persuasion and by coercion. My answer is that part of the explanation lies in the force of ideology, and particularly the deification of the unitary state that was characteristic of the French Revolution. Once the idea that national cultures were worth identifying, preserving and fighting for had gathered momentum, as it did in the first half of the nineteenth century, it then followed that any *ethnie* that could make a bid for nationhood-cum-statehood tried its luck, and multinational states tried to homogenise their territory.

On the whole, neither classic nor contemporary social science has considered nationalism a central phenomenon of modern societies, but rather a passing ideology; only recently some authors seem to have realised its endemic character. Not surprisingly, the scientific efforts to account for nationalism have been rather limited. Today there appears to be an array of people writing on nationalism; unfortunately, they do it mostly from a normative or moralistic perspective. Generally speaking, most studies of nationalism are more or less superficial historical or ethnographic descriptions of concrete cases; comparisons tend to be scarce, limited to two or three cases, and generally methodologically flawed. Nationalism is, and will continue to be for the time being, a theoretical challenge; whether the present generation of social scientists can do better than the previous one remains to be seen.

# BIBLIOGRAPHY

Akomolafe, O. (1995) 'Nationalism', *International Encyclopaedia of Ethics*. London: FD, pp. 592–96.

Albareda, J. (1991) 'L'Onze de Setembre: realitat i "mite"', *L'Avenç*, 15: 62–5.

Albareda, J. (1992) 'L'Onze de Setembre', *Diccionari d'Història de Catalunya*. Barcelona: Edicions 62, pp. 757–58.

Albertoni, E. (1987) *Mosca and the Theory of Elitism*. Oxford: Basil Blackwell.

Allahar, A. (1996) 'Primordialism and Ethnic Political Mobilisation in Modern Society', *New Community*, 22(1): 5–21.

Almirall, V. (1972) *España tal como es*. Madrid: Seminarios y Ediciones.

Almirall, V. (1886) *Lo Catalanisme*. Barcelona: Estudis.

Altamira, R. (1902) *Psicología del pueblo español*. Madrid: Biblioteca Moderna de Ciencias Sociales.

Anderson, B. (1983) *Imagined Communities*. London: Verso.

Anderson, B. (1991) *Imagined Communities*, 2nd ed. London: Verso.

Anderson, B. (1993) 'Nationalism', *The Oxford Companion of Politics of the World*. New York: Oxford University Press, pp. 614–19.

Appadurai, A. (1990) 'Disjuncture and Difference in the Global Cultural Economy' in Featherstone, M. ed. *Global Culture*. London: Sage.

Arbós, X. and Puigsec, A. (1980) *Franco i l'espanyolisme*. Barcelona: Curial.

Argelaguet, J. (1998) *El procés d'elaboració de la llei de política lingüistica*. Barcelona: Editorial Mediterrànea.

Argente, J.A. (1981) 'Stateless Nation, Tongueless People?' *The Bulletin of Scottish Politics* 2: 162–81.

Armstrong, J. (1982) *Nations before Nationalism*. Chapel Hill: The University of North Carolina Press.

Arnulf, S. (1939) 'Scholarly Forerunners of Fascism', *Ethics*, 50: 16–34.

Aron, R. (1969) *Les Désillusions du progrès*. Paris: Calman-Levy.

Aun, K. (1980) 'A Critique of the Nation-State', in Nyri, N.A. and Miljan, T. (eds) *Unity and Diversity*. Waterloo, Ontario: W. Laurier University Press.

Bada, J. (1987) *Guerra civil i eglesia catalana*. Montserrat: Abadia.

Baggioni, D. (1997) *Langues et nations en Europe*. Paris: Payot.

Balaguer, V. (1888) *Obras*. Madrid: Tello.

Balandier, G. (1955) *La Sociologie de l'Afrique noire*. Paris: PUF.

Balcells, A. (1994) *La Història de Catalunya a debat*. Barcelona: Curial.

Balcells, A. (1996) *Catalan Nationalism*. London: MacMillan.

Balcells, A. et al. (1980) *Història dels Països Catalans*, 3 Vols. Barcelona: Edhasa.

Balcells, A. et al. (1985) 'História nacional i història social', *L'Avenç*, 87: 66–77.

Barceló, M. et al. (1982) 'Sobre l'historiografia catalana', *L'Avenç*, 50: 456–73.

Barrera, C. (1990) *Casa, herencia y familia en la Cataluña rural*. Madrid: Alianza Editorial.

Barrera, C. (1996) *La dialéctica de la identidad*. Madrid: Centro de Investigaciones Sociológicas.

Barth, F. (ed.) (1969) *Ethnic Groups and Boundaries*. Bergen: Universitets Forlaget.

Batista, A. and Playà, J. (1991) *La gran conspiració. Crònica de l'Assemblea de Catalunya*. Barcelona: Empúries.

Batista i Roca, J.N. (1959) 'Martí d'Eixalá i la introducció de la filosofia escocesa a Catalunya' in *Hispanic Studies in the Honour of I. Gónzalez Llubera*. Oxford: The Dolphin Book.

Bennassar, B. (1979) *The Spanish Character*. Los Angeles: University of California Press.

Benet, J. (1973) *Catalunya sota el règim franquista*. Paris: Edicions Catalanes de Paris.

Ben-Israel, H. (1986) 'The Role of Religious Nationalism' in *Religion, Ideology and Nationalism*. Jerusalem: Historical Society of Israel, pp. 331–40.

Ben-Yehuda, N. (1995) *The Masada Myth. Colloective Memory and Mythmaking in Israel*. Madison, Wisconsin: The University of Wisconsin Press.

Berkowitz, L. (1993) *Aggression*. New York: McGraw Hill.

Berrio, J. (1966) *El pensament filosòfic català*. Barcelona: Edicions 62.

Bestard, J. (1995) 'Law, Tradition and the Making of the Catalan Family', *Critique of Anthropology*, 15(3): 249–63.

Bilbeny, N. and Pes, A. (eds.) (2001) *El Nou Catalanisme*. Barcelona: Ariel.

Billig, M. (1995) *Banal Nationalism*. London: Sage.

Bisbes de Catalunya, Els (1986) *Arrels cristianes de Catalunya*. Barcelona: Bisbes.

Bisson, T.N. (1986) *The Medieval Crown of Aragon*. Oxford: Clarendon Press.

Bonet, J. (1984) *L'església catalana, de l'illustració a la Renaixença*. Montserrat: Publicacions de l'Abadia de Montserrat.

Botella, J. (1995) 'L'élite gouvernemental espagnole' in Suleiman, E. and Mandras, H. (eds.) *Le Recrutement des élites en Europe*. Paris: La Découverte, pp. 181–91.

Bourdieu, P. (1982) *Leçon sur la leçon*. Paris: Minuit.

Branchadell, A. (1997) *Liberalisme i normalització lingüística*. Barcelona: Empúries.

Braudel, F. (1985–86) *L'identité de la France*, 3 Vols. Paris: Arthaud-Flammarion.

Breton, A. et al. (1996) *Nationalism and Rationality*. Cambridge: Cambridge University Press.

Breuilly, J. (1982) *Nationalism and the State*. Manchester: Manchester University Press.

Brown, M. (1997) *Nationalism and Ethnic Conflict*. Cambridge, Mass.: Massachusetts Institute of Technology.

Brubaker, R. and Laitin, D. (1998) 'Ethnic and Nationalist Violence', *Annual Review of Sociology*, 24: 423–52.

Bruno, G. (1905)(1983) *Le Tour de la France par deux enfants*. Paris: Belin.

Cahner, M. et al. (1977) *Debat sobre els Països Catalans*. Barcelona: Curial.

Camps i Arboix, J. (1963) *La Mancomunitat de Catalunya*. Barcelona: Bruguera.

Camps i Giró, J. (1978) *La Guerra dels Matiners i el catalanisme politic (1846–49)*. Barcelona: Curial.

Candel, F. (1964) *Els altres catalans*. Barcelona: Edicions 62.

Carbonell, J. (1979) 'Elements d'història social i politica de la llengua catalana', *Treballs de sociolingüistica* 2: 87–102.

Caro-Baroja, J. (1970) *El mito del carácter nacional*. Madrid: Seminarios y Ediciones.

Carr, E.H. (1968) *Nationalism and After*. London: Macmillan.

Carr, R. (1966) *Spain, 1808–1939*. Oxford: Clarendon Press.

Casanova, E. et al. (1993) Introducció a la Història de Catalunya. Barcelona: La Magrana.

Castellet, J.M. (1983) *Per un debat sobre la cultura catalana*. Barcelona: Edicions 62.

Castells, M. (1997) *The Power of Identity*. Oxford: Blackwell Publishing.

Certeau, M. et al. (1975) *Une politique de la langue*. Paris: Gallimard.

Citron, S. (1987) (1991) *Le Mythe national. L'histoire de la France en question*. Paris: Les éditions ouvrières.

Cohen, A. (1985) *The Symbolic Construction of Reality*. London: Routledge.

Cohen, S.B. and Maier, E. (1983) 'Partitioning and the Search for Core–Boundary Equilibrium: The Case Study of Israel' in Maier, J.B. and Waxman, C.I. (eds). *Ethnicity, Identity and History*. New Brunswick: Transaction, pp. 291–320.

Colomer, J. (1984) *Espanyolisme i catalanisme*. Barcelona: L'Avenç.

Colomer, J. et al. (1976) *Els grups politics a Catalunya*, 2 Vols. Barcelona: L'Avenç.

Comas, D. (1993) 'L'arbre et la maison. Métaphores de l'appartenance' in Fabre, D. (ed.) *L'Europe entre cultures et nations*. Paris: Maison des sciences de l'homme, pp. 199–212.

Connerton, P. (1989) *How Societies Remember*. Cambridge: Cambridge University Press.

Connor, W. (1994) *Ethnonationalism. The Quest for Understanding*. Princeton: Princeton University Press.

Conversi, D. (1997) *The Basques, the Catalan and Spain*. London: Hurst.

Cortada, J. (1965) *Catalunya i els catalans*. Barcelona: Edicions 62.

Crick, B. (1991) 'The English and the British' in Crick, B. (ed.) *National Identities*. Oxford: Blackwell Publishing, pp. 90–104.

Crowley, T. (1996) *Language in History*. London: Routledge.

Cruells, M. (1978) *La societat catalana durant la guerra civil*. Barcelona: Edhasa.

Davies, N. (1981) *God's Playground: A History of Poland*, 2 Vols. Oxford: Oxford University Press.

Davies, N. (1984) *Heart of Europe*. A Short History of Poland. Oxford: Oxford University Press.

Davis, H. (1978) *Towards a Marxist Theory of Nationalism*. New York: Monthly Review Press.

De Miguel, A. (1980) *Los intelectuales bonitos*. Barcelona: Planeta.

Descartes, R. (1649) (1953) *Oeuvres et Lettres*. Paris: Gallimard (Bibliothèque de la Pléiade).

Descartes, R. (1649) (1968) *The Philosophical Works*, Vol. I. Cambridge: Cambridge University Press.

Deutsch, K. (1953) *Nation and Social Communication*. Cambridge, Mass.: Massachusetts Institute of Technology.

Deutsch, K. and Foltz, W. (eds.) (1963) *Nation-Building*. New York: Atherton Press.

Diccionari d'Història de Catalunya (1992) 'Pairalisme'. Barcelona: Edicions 62.

Diez-Medrano, J. (1995) *Divided Nations. Class, Politics, and Nationalism in the Basque Country and Catalonia*. Ithaca: Cornell University Press.

Durkacz, V.G. (1983) *The Decline of the Celtic Languages*. Edinburgh: John Donald.

Durkheim, E. (1912) (1960) *Les Formes élémentaires de la vie religieuse*. Paris: PUF.

Durkheim, E. (1912) (1995) *The Elementary Forms of Religious Life*. New York: Free Press.

Durkheim, E. (1915) *L'Allemagne au dessus de tout*. Paris: Colin.

Durkheim, E. and Mauss, M. (1913) 'Sur la notion de civilisation', *L'Année Sociologique*, XII: 46–50.

Durkheim, E. (1975) *Durkheim on Religion*. Ed. by W.S.F. Pickering. London: RKP.

Elliot, J.H. (1963) *The Revolt of the Catalans*. Cambridge: Cambridge University Press.

Englund, S. (1992) 'The Ghost of Nations Past', *Journal of Modern History*, 64: 299–320.

Espriu, S. (1975) *The Lord of the Shadow*. Oxford: The Dolphin Book.

Esteva, C. (1984) *Estado, etnicidad y biculturalismo*. Barcelona: Ediciones Península.

Estivill, J. and Giner, S. (1985) 'La identitat social de Catalunya' in *Actes de les primeres jornades catalanes de sociologia*. Barcelona: Institut d'Estudis Catalans.

Fabre, J. et al. (1978) *Vint anys de resistència catalana*. Barcelona: Edicions de la Magrana.

Featherstone, M. (ed.) (1990) *Global Culture*. London: Sage.

Featherstone, M. (1996) 'The Formation of an European Culture' in Dukes, P. (ed.) *Frontiers of European Culture*. Lampeter: Mellen Press.

Fentress, J. and Wickham, C. (1992) *Social Memory*. Oxford: Blackwell Publishing.

Ferrater-Mora, J. (1944) (1955) *Les formes de vida catalana*. Barcelona: Editorial Selecta.

Ferrer, F. (1985) *La persecució política de la llengua catalana*. Barcelona: Edicions 62.

Ferrer, J. (ed.) (1993) *Les Bases de Manresa 1892–1992. Cent anys de Catalanisme*. Barcelona: Generalitat de Catalunya.

Figueres, J.M. (ed.) (1992) *Les Bases de Manresa i el futur de Catalunya*. Barcelona: La Llar del Llibre.

Firth, R. (1973) *Symbols. Public and Private*. London: Allen and Unwin.

Fishman, J. (1972) *Language and Nationalism*. Rowley, Mass.: Newbury House.

Fishman, J. (1991) *Reversing Language Shift: Theory and Practice of Assistance to Threatened Languages*. Clevedon: Multilingual Matters.

Flaquer, L. (1996) *El català, llengua pública o privada?* Barcelona: Empúries.

Font, J. et al. (1998) *L'abstenció en les eleccions al Parlament de Catalunya*. Barcelona: Editorial Mediterrània.

Fontana, J. et al. (1980) *La invasió napoleònica*. Bellaterra: Publicacions de la UAB.

Fouillée, A. (1903) *Esquisse psychologique des peuples européens.* Paris: Alcan.

Fradera, J.M. (1992) *Cultura nacional en una societat dividida.* Barcelona: Curial.

Francis, E.K. (1976) *Interethnic Relations.* New York: Elsevier.

François, E. et al. (eds.) (1992) *Nation und Emotion.* Götingen: Vandenhopek & Ruprecht.

Friedmann, J. (1997) 'Global Crises, the Struggle for Cultural Identity and Intellectual Porkbarrelling' in Werbner, P. and Modood, T. (eds.) *Debating Cultural Hybridity.* London: Zed Books.

Frigolé, J. (1980) 'Inversió simbòlica i identitat ètnica: una aproximació al cas de Catalunya', *Quaderns* de l'ICA, 1: 3–27.

Fuster, J. (1962) *Nosaltres el valencians.* Barcelona: Edicions 62.

Gali, A. (1978) *Història de les institucions i del moviment cultural de Catalunya,* Vols. I–III. Barcelona: Fundació A. Galí.

Gane, M. (1992) *The Radical Sociology of Durkheim and Mauss.* London: Routledge.

García-Cárcel, R. (1985) *Historia de Cataluña. Siglos XVI–XVII,* 2 Vols. Barcelona: Ariel.

García-Ramón, M. and Nogué, J. (1994) 'Nationalism and Geography in Catalonia' in Hooson, D. (ed.) *Geography and National Identity.* Oxford: Blackwell Publishing, pp. 197–211.

Geertz, C. (1963) 'The Integrative Revolution, Primordial Sentiments in the New States' in Geertz, C. (ed.) *Old Societies and New States.* New York: Free Press.

Geertz, C. (1973) *The Interpretations of Cultures.* New York: Free Press.

Gellner, E. (1983). *Nations and Nationalism.* Oxford: Basil Blackwell.

Gellner, E. (1993) 'Nationalism' in *Blackwell Dictionary of Twentieth Century Social Thought.* Oxford: Blackwell Publishing, pp. 409–11.

Gellner, E. (1997) *Nationalism.* London: Weidenfeld and Nicolson.

Gener, P. (1888) *Heregias.* Barcelona: Estudios.

Genieys, W. (1997) *Les Elites espagnoles face à l'état.* Paris: L'Harmattan.

Gerpe, M. (1977) *L'Estatut d'Autonomia de Catalunya i l'estat integral.* Barcelona: Edicions 62.

Giddens, A. (1985) *The Nation-State and Violence.* Cambridge: Polity Press.

Gifreu, J. et al. (1987) *Segones reflexions critiques sobre la cultura catalana.* Barcelona: Department de Cultura de la Generalitat.

Gillis, J.R. (ed.) (1994) *Commemorations. The Politics of National Identity.* Princeton: Princeton University Press.

Giner, S. (1980) 1984 *The Social Structure of Catalonia.* Sheffield: The Anglo-Catalan Society Occasional Publications.

Giner, S. (ed.) (1998) *La societat catalana.* Barcelona: Institut d'Estadística de Catalunya.

Giner, S. et al. (1996) *La cultura catalana: el sagrat i el profà.* Barcelona: Edicions 62.

Goddard, V., Llobera, J.R. and Shore, C. (1994) 'Introduction: The Anthropology of Europe' in Goddard, V. et al. (eds.) *The Anthropology of Europe.* Oxford: Berg, pp. 1–40.

Gomis, J. (1995) *La conferència episcopal catalana.* Barcelona: Tassàlia.

Gonzalez-Casanova, J.A. (1974) *Federalismo y autonomia.* Barcelona: Grijalbo.

Gordon, D. (1978) *The French Language and National Identity.* The Hague: Mouton.

Greenfeld, L. (1992) *Nationalism.* Cambridge, Mass.: Harvard University Press.

Grillo, R. (1989) *Dominant Languages.* Cambridge: Cambridge University Press.

Grosby, S. (1994) 'The Veredict of History: The Inexpugnable Tie of Primordiality', *Ethnic and Racial Studies,* 17(2): 164–71.

Guibernau, M. (1996) *Nationalisms. The Nation-State and Nationalism in the Twentieth Century.* Oxford: Polity Press.

Guibernau, M. (1999) *Nations without States.* Oxford: Polity Press.

Gunther, R. (1992) 'Spain: The Very Model of Elite Settlement' in Higley, J. and Gunther, R. (eds.) *Elites and Democratic Consolidation in Latin America and Southern Europe.* Cambridge: Cambridge University Press, pp. 38–80.

Hagège, C. (1992) *Le Souffle de la langue.* Paris: Odile Jacob.

Halbwachs, M. (1925) (1975) *Les Cadres sociaux de la mémoire.* Paris: PUF.

Halbwachs, M. (1941) (1971) *La Topographie légendaire des évangiles en Terre Sainte.* Paris: PUF.

Halbwachs, M. (1950) (1968) *La Mémoire collective.* Paris: PUF.

Halbwachs, M. (1992) *On Collective Memory.* Chicago: Chicago University Press (Introduction by Lewis Coser).

Haller, M. (1990) 'The Challenge for Contemporary Sociology in the Transformation of Europe', *International Sociology,* 5: 183–204.

Hannerz, U. (1992) *Cultural Complexity.* New York: Columbia University Press.

Hannerz, U. (1996) *Transnational Connections.* London: Routledge.

Hansen, E.C. (1977) *Rural Catalonia under Franco.* Cambridge: Cambridge University Press.

Hansen, E and Parrish, T. (1983) 'Elite versus State' in Marcus, G. (ed.) *Elites. Ethnographic Issues.* Albuqerque: University of New Mexico Press.

Harris, M. (1999) *Theories of Culture in Postmodern Times.* London: Sage

Hastings, A. (1997) *The Construction of Nationhood. Ethnicity, Religion and Nationalism.* Cambridge: Cambridge University Press.

Hayes, C. (1960) *Nationalism. A Religion.* New York: Macmillan.

Hechter, M. (1975) *Internal Colonialism.* London: RKP.

Hechter, M. (1995) 'Explaining Nationalist Violence', *Nations and Nationalism,* 1: 53–68.

Heller, A. and Feher, F. (1988) *The Postmodern Political Condition.* Oxford: Polity Press.

Herder, J. (1772) (1966) *Essay on the Origin of Language.* Chicago: University of Chicago Press.

Hertz, F. (1944) *Nationality in History and Politics.* London: Kegan Paul.

Hillgarth, J.N. (1976) *The Spanish Kingdoms.* Oxford: Clarendon Press.

Hobsbawm, E. and Ranger, T. (eds.) (1983) *The Invention of Tradition.* Cambridge: Cambridge University Press.

Hroch, M. (1985) *Social Preconditions of National Revival in Europe.* Cambridge: Cambridge University Press.

Hobsbawm, E. (1990) *Nations and Nationalism since 1780.* Cambridge: Cambridge University Press.

Hutchinson, J. (1987) *The Dynamics of Cultural Nationalism. The Gaelic Revival and the Creation of the Irish Nation State.* London: Allen and Unwin.

Hutton, P. (1993) *History as an Art of Memory.* Hanover: University of Vermont.

Ignatieff, M. (1994) *Blood and Belonging.* London: Vintage.

Isaacs, H. (1975) *Idols of the Tribe.* Cambridge, Mass.: Harvard University Press.

Izard, M. (1978) *El segle XIX. Burgesos i proletaris.* Barcelona: Dopesa.

Jerez-Mir, M. (1982) *Elites políticas y centros de extracción en España.* Madrid: CIS.

Johnston, H. (1991) *Tales of Nationalism: Catalonia, 1939–1979.* New Brunswick: Rutgers University Press.

Johnston, R.J. et al. (eds.) (1988) *Nationalism Self-determination and Political Geography.* London: Croom Helm.

Kantorowicz, E. (1957) (1981) *The King's Two Bodies. A Study in Medieval Political Theology.* Princeton: Princeton University Press.

Keating, M. (2001) *Nations against the State,* 2nd ed. London: Palgrave.

Kedourie, E. (1960) *Nationalism.* London: Hutchinson.

Khleif, B. (1979) 'Language as Identity: Toward an Ethnography of Welsh Nationalism', *Ethnicity,* 6: 346–57.

Khleif, B. (1980) *Language, Ethnicity and Education in Wales.* The Hague: Mouton.

Kibre, P. (1948) *The Nations in the Medieval Universities.* Cambridge: Medieval Academy of America.

Kohn, H. (1944) *The Idea of Nationalism.* New York: Macmillan.

Kosik, K. (1976) *Dialectics of the Concrete.* Dordrecht: Reidel.

Kroeber, A. and Kluckholn, C. (1952) *Culture.* New York: Knopf.

Kundera, M. (1988) *The Art of the Novel.* London: Faber and Faber.

Laitin, D. (1995) 'National Revivals and Violence', *European Archives of Sociology,* 36(1): 3–43.

Laponce, J.A. (1985) 'Protecting the French Language in Canada', *Journal of Commonwealth and Comparative Politics,* XXIII(2): 157–70.

Laponce, J.A. (1987) *Languages and Their Territories.* Toronto: University of Toronto Press.

Lévi-Strauss, C. (1962) *La Pensée sauvage.* Paris: Plon.

Lewis, B. (1975) *History. Remembered, Recovered, Invented.* New York: Simon and Schuster.

Linz, J. (1973) 'Early State-Building and Late Peripheral Nationalisms against the State', in Eisendstadt, S.N. and Rokkan, S. (eds.) *Building States and Nations.* Beverly Hill: Sage, Vol. 2, pp. 32–116.

Llobera, J.R. (1987) 'Nationalism: Some Methodological Issues', *JASO* XVIII(1): 13–25.

Llobera, J.R. (1993) 'The Role of the State and the Nation in Europe' in García, M. (ed.) *European Identity and the Search for Legitimacy.* London: Pinter, pp. 64–80.

Llobera, J.R. (1994) *The God of Modernity. The Development of Nationalism in Western Europe.* Oxford: Berg.

Lluch, E. (1973) *El pensament econòmic a Catalunya (1760–1840).* Barcelona: Edicions 62.

Loewenberg, P. (1992) 'The Psycho-Dynamics of Nationalism', *Journal of the History of European Ideas,* 15: 94.

Lorés, J. (1985) *La transició a Catalunya (1977–1984).* Barcelona: Editorial Empúries.

Lowental, D. (1985) *The Past as Another Country*. Cambridge: Cambridge University Press.

Mach, Z. (1994) 'National Anthems: The Case of Chopin as a National Composer' in Stokes, M. (ed.) *Ethnicity, Identity and Music*. Oxford: Berg.

Mackenzie A. (1964) 'Introduction' in Mickiewicz, A. *Pan Tadeusz*. London: Polish Cultural Foundation.

Marcet, J. (1984) *Convergència Democràtica de Catalunya*. Barcelona: Edicions 62.

Marger, M. (1981) *Elites and Masses*. New York: Van Nostrand.

Martinez-Fiol, L. (1993) 'Commemoracions, catalanisme i historiografia', *L'Avenç*, 175: 42–7.

Masnou, R. (1986) *El problema català*. Barcelona: Publicacions de l'Abadia de Montserrat.

Massot, J. (1987) *La persecució religiosa de 1936 a Catalunya*. Montserrat: Abadia.

Mauss, M. (1901) (1968) *Essais de sociologie*. Paris: Minuit.

Mauss, M. (1969) *Oeuvres*. Paris: Minuit.

Mazzini, G. (1972) *Dei doveri dell'uomo*. Milano: Murcia.

McCarthy, M.J. (1975) 'Catalan, Modernisme, Messianism and Nationalist Myths', *Bulletin of Hispanic Studies*, LII: 379–95.

McCready, B. (1991) 'Scotland's Ace', *Radical Scotland*, 5: 17–18.

McCrone, D. (1991) 'Post-Nationalism and the Nation-State', *Radical Scotland*, 49: 6–8.

McDonogh, G. (1986) *Good Families of Barcelona*. Princeton: Princeton University Press.

McGarry, J. and O'Leary, B. (eds.) (1993) *The Politics of Ethnic Conflict*. London: Routledge.

Mestre, J. (ed.) (1992) *Diccionari d'Història de Catalunya*. Barcelona: Edicions 62.

Middleton, D. and Edwards, D. (eds.) (1990) *Collecting Remembering*. London: Sage.

Miller, D. (1995) *On Nationality*. Oxford: Clarendon Press.

Milo, D. (1986) 'Le nom des rues' in Nora, P. (ed.) *Les Lieux de mémoire. La nation*. Vol. III. Paris: Gallimard, pp. 283–315.

Montero, J.R. and Font, J. (1991) 'El voto dual en Catalunya', *Revista de Estudios Políticos*. 73: 7–34.

Moore, B. (1967) *The Social Origins of Dictatorship and Democracy*. London: Allen Lane.

Moreu-Rey, E. (1966) *El pensament il. lustrat a Catalunya*. Barcelona: Edicions 62.

Morin, E. (1987) 'Il problema dell'identitá europea' in Krali, A. (ed.) *Identitá culturale europeatra Germanismo et Latinitá*. Milano: Jaca Book, pp. 33–39.

Morin, E. (1990) *Penser l'Europe*. Paris: Gallimard.

Morin, E. (1994) 'Pour une théorie de la nation' in *Sociologie*. Paris: Fayard, pp. 165–73.

Mosca, G. (1939) *The Ruling Class*. New York: McGraw Hill.

Nadal, J.M. and Prats, M. (1982) *Història de la llengua catalana*, 3 Vols. Barcelona: Edicions 62.

Nairn, T. (1977) *The Break Up of Great Britain*. London: New Left Books.

Nairn, T. (1988) *The Enchanted Glass. Britain and Its Monarchy*. London: Radius.

Namer, G. (1987) *Mémoire et société*. Paris: Klimcksieck.

Nogué, J. (1991) *Els nacionalismes i el territori*. Barcelona: El Llamp.

Nora, P. (1978) 'Mémoire collective', in le Goff, J. et al (eds.) *La Nouvelle Histoire*. Paris: CEPL.

Nora, P. (ed.) (1986–1992) *Les Lieux de la mémoire*, 7 Vols. Paris: Gallimard.

Nutall, S. and Coetzee, C. (eds.) (1999) *Negotiating the Past. The Making of Memory in South Africa*. Oxford: Oxford University Press.

Ortner, S. (ed.) (1999) *The Fate of Culture. Geertz and Beyond*. Berkeley: University of California Press.

Pallarés, F. (2000) 'The Elections of 17 October 1999 in Catalonia', *Regional and Federal Studies*, 10(3): 149–56.

Permanyer, L. (1990) *Història del Eixample*. Barcelona: Plaza y Janés.

Pessoa, F. (1979) *Sobre Portugal*. Lisboa: Atica.

Pi de Cabanyes, O. (1979) *La Renaixença*. Barcelona: Dopesa.

Pi-Sunyer, O. (1971) 'The Maintenance of Ethnic Identity in Catalonia' in Pi-Sunyer, O. (ed.) *The Limits of Integration; Ethnicity and Nationalism in Modern Europe*. Amherst: University of Massachusetts; Research Report No 9.

Poblet, J.M. (1975) *Història de l'ERC (1931–1939)*. Barcelona: Editorial Pòrtic.

Poulantzas, N. (1978) *State, Power and Socialism*. London: New Left Books.

Prat de la Riba, E. (1906) (1977) *La nationalitat catalana*. Barcelona: Editorial Barcino.

Prats, M et al. (1990) *El futur de la llengua catalana*. Barcelona: Empúries.

Prazauskas, A. (1994) 'The Influence of Ethnicity on Foreign Policies of the Western Littoral States', in Szporluk, R. (ed.) *National Identity and Ethnicity in Russia and the New States of Eurasia*. Armonk, N.Y.: Sharpe, pp. 150–84.

Price, G. (1984) *The Languages of Britain*. London: Edward Arnold.

Puig-Salellas, J.M. (ed.) (1988) *Encontre*. Barcelona: Generalitat de Catalunya.

Pujol, J. (1976) *L'immigració, problema i esperança de Catalunya*. Barcelona: Nova Terra.

Pujol, J. (1993) *La diada de Catalunya*. Barcelona: Generalitat de Catalunya.

Ramirez, M. (1978) *España 1939–1975. Régimen político e ideologia*. Barcelona: Guadarrama.

Ramisa, M. (1985) *Els origens del catalanisme conservador*. Vic: Eumo.

Reglá, J. (1973) *Introducció a la història de la Corona d'Aragó*. Palma de Mallorca: Editorial Moll.

Renan, E. (1977) *Oeuvres complètes*, Vol. I. Paris: Calman Levy. (Original 1882).

Reynolds, V. et al. (eds.) (1987) *The Sociobiology of Ethnocentrism*. London: Croom Helm.

Riquer, B. (1977) *Lliga Regionalista*. Barcelona: Edicions 62.

Riquer, B. (1994) 'La faiblesse du processus de construction nationale en Espagne au XIXe siècle', *Revue d'histoire moderne et contemporaine*, 41–2: 353–66.

Riquer, B. (2000) *Identitats contemporànies: Catalunya i Espanya*. Vic: Eumo.

Roca, F. (2000) *Teories de Catalunya. Guia de la societat catalana contemporània*. Barcelona: Pòrtic.

Rossinyol, J. (1974) *Le Problème national catalan*. Paris: Mouton.

Rougemont, D. de (1970) *Lettre ouverte aux Européens*. Paris: Albin Michel.

Roura, J. (1980) *Ramon Marti d'Eixelà i la filosofia catalana del segle XIX*. Monserrat: Publicacions de l'Abadia.

Sahlins, M. (1999) 'Two or three things that I know about culture', *JRAI*, 5: 399–421.

Salles, A. (1986) *Quan Catalunya era d'esquerra*. Barcelona: Edicions 62.

Santayana, G. (1905) (1980) *Reason and Society*. New York: Dover.

Schnapper, D. (1991) *La France de l'intégration*. Paris: Gallimard.

Schnapper, D. (1994) *La Communauté des citoyens*. Paris: Gallimard.

Schneider, D. (1977) 'Kinship, Nationality and Religion in American Culture' in Dolgin et al. (eds.) *Symbolic Anthropology*. New York: Columbia University Press, pp. 63–71.

Schulze, H. (1996) *States, Nations and Nationalism*. Oxford: Blackwell Publishing.

Schumpeter, J. (1950) *Capitalism, Socialism and Democracy*. New York: Harper and Row.

Seton-Watson, H. (1981) 'Language and National Consciousness', *Proceedings of the British Academy*, LXVII: 83–100.

Shaw, R.P. and Wong, Y. (1989) *Genetic Seeds of Warfare*. London: Unwin Hyman.

Shils, E. (1957) 'Primordial, Personal and Civil Ties', *British Journal of Sociology*, 8: 130–45.

Shils, E. (1995) 'Nation, Nationality, Nationalism and Civil Society', *Nations and Nationalism*, 1: 93–118.

Shore, C. (1993) 'Inventing the People's Europe', *Man*, 28(4): 779–200.

Shore, C. (1996) 'Transcending the Nation-State? The European Commission and the Rediscovery of Europe', *Journal of the History of Sociology*, 9: 474–96.

Shore, C. (1997) 'The Myth of a Euro-identity', *Demos*, 13: 48–50.

Smart, N. (1995) *Sacred Nationalism*. Leeds: Occasional Papers of the British Association for the Study of Religion.

Smart, N. (1996) *Sacred Nationalism*. Leeds: British Association for the Study of Religion.

Smith, A.D. (1971) *Theories of Nationalism*. London: Duckworth.

Smith, A.D. (1973) *Nationalism. A Trend Report*. The Hague: Mouton.

Smith, A.D. (1981) *The Ethnic Revival in the Modern World*. Cambridge: Cambridge University Press.

Smith, A.D. (1986) *The Ethnic Origins of Nations*. Oxford: Blackwell Publishing.

Smith, A.D. (1990) 'Towards a Global Culture?' in Featherstone, M. (ed.) *Global Culture*. London: Sage.

Smith, A.D. (1991) *National Identity*. London: Penguin.

Smith, A.D. (1998) *Nationalism and Modernism*. London: Routledge.

Smith, G. (ed.) (1994) *The Baltic States*. London: Macmillan.

Sobrequés, J. (1982) *El pactisme a Catalunya*. Barcelona: Edicions 62.

Soldevila, F. (1961) *Un segle de vida catalana*. Barcelona: Alcides.

Solé, J. and Villaroya, J. (1993) *Cronologia de la repressió de la llengua i la cultura catalanes*. Barcelona: Curial.

Solé-Tura, J. (1966) *Catalanisme i revolució burgesa*. Barcelona: Edicions 62.

Solé-Tura, J. (1974) *Catalanismo y revolución burguesa*. Madrid: Cuadernos para el Diálogo.

Solé-Tura, J. (1985) *Nacionalidades y nacionalismos en España*. Madrid: Alianza Editorial.

Stalin, J. (1913) (1975) *Marxism and the National Question*. San Francisco: Proletarian Publishers.

Steiner, G. (1997) *Errata: An Examined Life*. London: Weidenfeld and Nicholson.

Strauss, C. (1992) 'Introduction' in D'Andrade and Strauss (eds) *Human Motives and Cultural Models*. Cambridge: Cambridge University Press.

Strubell, M. (1981) *Lhengua i població a Catalunya*. Barcelona: Edicions de la Magrana.

Termes, J. (1976) *Federalismo, anarcosindicalismo y catalanismo*. Barcelona: Anagrama.

Termes, J. (1984) *La immigració a Catalunya*. Barcelona: Editorial Empúries.

Termes, J. and Colomines, A. (1992) *Les bases de Manresa de 1892 i els orígens del Catalanisme*. Barcelona: Generalitat de Catalunya.

Terradas, I. (1984) *El mon històric de les masies*. Barcelona: Curial.

Terry, A. (1972) *Catalan Literature*. London: E. Benn.

Tilly, C. (ed.) (1975) *The Formation of National States in Western Europe*. Princeton: Princeton University Press.

Tilly, C. (1992) 'The Future of European States', *Social Research*, 59: 705–18.

Tomlinson, J. (1999) *Globalization and Culture*. Cambridge: Polity Press.

Tonkin, E. (1992) *Narrating Our Pasts*. Cambridge: Cambridge University Press.

Torras i Bages, J. (1892) (1966) *La tradició catalana*. Barcelona: Editorial Selecta.

Trias-Vejarano, J. (1975) *Almirall y los orígenes del catalanismo*. Madrid: Siglo XXI.

Trudgill, P. (1987) (ed.) *Language in the British Isles*. Cambridge: Cambridge University Press.

Valls, R. (1984) *La interpretación de la historia de España y sus orígenes ideológicos en el bachillerato franquista*. Valencia: ICE.

Vallverdú, F. (1980) *Aproximació critica a la sociolingüistica catalana*. Barcelona: Edicions 62.

Vallverdú, F. (1990) *L'ús del català: un futur controvertit*. Barcelona: Edicions 62.

Van Den Berghe, P. (1981) *The Ethnic Phenomenon*. New York: Elsevier.

Van Den Berghe, P. (ed.) (1990) *State Violence and Ethnicity*. Newot, Colo.: University Press of Colorado.

Van Der Dennen, J. and Falger, V. (eds.) 1990 *Sociology and Conflict*. London: Chapman and Hall.

Varela, A. et al. (1989) *Història de Cataluña*. Barcelona: Columna.

Vicens-Vives, J. (1954) *Noticia de Cataluña*. Barcelona: Destino.

Vicens-Vives, J. and Llorens, M. (1958) *Industrials i politics* segle XIX. Barcelona: Teide.

Vico, G. (1975) *The New Science*. Ithaca: Cornell University Press.

Vila, M.A.(1980) *Compendi de Geografia de Catalunya*. Barcelona: Curial.

Vilar, P. (1962) *La Catalogne dans l'Espagne moderne*, 3 Vols. Paris: Sevpen.

Vilar, P. (1973) *Assaigs sobre la Catalunya del segle XVIII*. Barcelona: Curial.

Vilar, P. (1980) 'Catalonia', *Review*, 3: 554–72.

Vilar, P. et al. (1983) *Reflexions sobre la cultura catalana*. Barcelona: Departament de Cultura de la Generalitat.

Viroli, M. (1995) *For Love of Country. An Essay on Patriotism and Nationalism*. Oxford: Clarendon Press.

Wachtel, N. (1986) 'Introduction', *History and Anthropology*, 2: 207–24.

Walker, D. (1991) 'Convergencia Democràtica de Catalunya. Its Successes and Its Problems', *Regional Politics and Policy*, 1: 284–302.

Wallerstein, I. (ed.) (1966) *Social Change*. New York: Wiley.

Wallerstein, I. (1974–1987) *The Modern World System I, II & III*. New York: Academic Press.

Wallerstein, I. (1987) 'The Construction of Peoplehood', *Sociological Forum*, 2: 373–88.

Wallerstein, I. (1990) 'Culture as the Ideological Battleground of the Modern World System', in Featherstone, M. (ed.) *Global Culture*. London: Sage.

Wardhaugh, R. (1987) *Languages in Competition*. Oxford: Blackwell Publishing.

Weber, E. (1979) *Peasants into Frenchmen*. London: Chatto and Windus.

Weber, M. 1978. *Economy and Society*, 2 Vols. Berkeley: University of California.

Wood, N. (1994) '"Memory" Remains: Lieux de mémoire', *History and Memory*, 6: 123–49.

Woolard, K. (1989) *Double Talk. Bilingualism and the Politics of Ethnicity in Catalonia*. Stanford, Cal.: Stanford University Press.

Worsley, P. (1964) *The Third World*. London: Weidenfeld and Nicholson.

Zettenberg, H. (1991) 'The Structuration of Europe', *Journal of Public Opinion Research*, 3: 309–12.

Zubaida, S. (1978) 'Theories of Nationalism' in Littlejohn, G. et al. (eds) *Power and the State*. London: Croom Helm.

# INDEX